SCHOOL DEVELOPMENT SERIES
General Editors: David Hopkins and David Reynolds

EFFECTIVE SCHOOLING

OTHER TITLES IN THE SCHOOL DEVELOPMENT SERIES

R. Bollington, D. Hopkins and M. West:
An Introduction to Teacher Appraisal

M. Fullan:
The New Meaning of Educational Change

D. H. Hargreaves and D. Hopkins:
The Empowered School

K. S. Louis and M. B. Miles:
Improving the Urban High School

D. Reynolds and P. Cuttance:
School Effectiveness

EFFECTIVE SCHOOLING
Research, Theory and Practice

Jaap Scheerens

CASSELL

Cassell

Villiers House
41/47 Strand
London WC2N 5JE, England

387 Park Avenue South
New York
NY 10016-8810, USA

© Jaap Scheerens 1992. Original Dutch edition © het Instituut voor
Onderzoek van het Onderwijs (SVO) 1989

First published 1992. Parts of this book have previously appeared in
Dutch, published in 1989 by the Institute for Educational Research in
the Netherlands (SVO) under the title *Wat maakt scholen effectief?
Samenvatting en analyse van onderzoeksresultaten.*

British Library Cataloguing-in-Publication Data
A catalogue record for this book is available from the British Library.
ISBN 0-304-32509-0 (hardback)
     0-304-32506-6 (paperback)

Typeset by Litho Link Ltd, Welshpool, Powys, Wales
Printed and bound in Great Britain by Dotesios Ltd, Trowbridge, Wilts.

Contents

Series Editors' Foreword

The last decade has seen a veritable explosion of interest in the field of school effectiveness in many countries of the world. The amount of research, writing and creative thinking about school effects, their measurement and their improvement has consequently increased very greatly.

Jaap Scheerens's book performs a very valuable function in attempting to organize, systematize and explain the large body of knowledge that now exists. It is truly international in its scope, with material utilized from the United States, the Netherlands, the United Kingdom, Canada and many other societies. It is comprehensive in its scope, looking at the classroom or instructional level, at the school level, and at the educational policies at national and local level that are related to the generation of effective organizational structures. It also crosses the all too familiar disciplinary boundaries that exist between school 'effectiveness' and school 'improvement' by looking both at our knowledge concerning 'what works' at school and classroom level, and at the issues concerned with how we improve schools by making a higher proportion of them 'work'. It is also, as a look at the references at the end will indicate, thoroughly up to date in its literature citations.

Effective Schooling, though, does more than simply lay out the existing knowledge for us. It represents also an original and creative addition to that knowledge, particularly in its use of 'public choice theory' and other theoretical positions to relate together the disparate and varied sets of empirical studies. Its chapters 'What makes schooling effective?' and 'School improvement' must rate as some of the most creative, yet authoritative, work published on these themes.

It is fitting that the book comes from the Netherlands, given that country's recent dramatic contributions to the study of school effectiveness and the practice of school improvement, and in fact the book is in part based upon a highly successful Dutch-language publication. We are confident that Jaap Scheerens's volume is an original, yet comprehensive, analysis that deserves the widest possible audience internationally.

David Hopkins
David Reynolds

July 1992

Acknowledgements

This book is in part a re-edited and updated version of a Dutch book, the publication of which was made possible by a grant from the Institute for Educational Research. This institute and the Committee for Programme Evaluation funded the translation of the part of the book that originally appeared in Dutch.

I am indebted to my secretary, Mrs Carola Groeneweg, for typing the manuscript.

Introduction

In an earlier review of school effectiveness research findings, Reynolds (1985, p. 6) called school differences research 'a sort of fledgling, still seeking the intellectual status that has been associated with the dominant individualizing paradigm and still not completely convincing the wider educational research community that it has the potential to make a major contribution to knowledge'. Seven years after this statement was made, and after a considerable number of studies in various countries have been completed, it may be worthwhile to examine the theoretical, methodological and practical status of school effectiveness research once again. This book explores the issue of school effectiveness from three major perspectives: (a) conceptualization and theory, (b) research and (c) the use of school effectiveness research findings to improve educational practice. These three perspectives serve as the foundation for the structure of the book.

In Part One the – often implicit – model of school effectiveness research is confronted with other views on organizational effectiveness. Although the usual way of defining school effectiveness, as the presumed causal influence of school characteristics on educational performance to put it simply, is quite defensible from the viewpoint of economic rationality or an educational process–product outlook, other organizational effect criteria, such as survival, adaptability to the environment and internal cohesion, are also worth considering. The existence of models and theories in various disciplines that are explicitly concerned with organizational process–output relationships demonstrates that school effectiveness models can – and should – be related to fundamental studies that may originate from each of these disciplines (economics, instructional psychology, sociology of education and organization theory). The major challenge in the area of model-building and theory-formation lies in the theoretical foundation of comprehensive school effectiveness models. By these are meant models that include contextual, organizational and instructional conditions presumed to enhance educational performance. Approaches to the development of school effectiveness theory are syntheses of existing models and theories, formal analysis and a constant exchange between analytic models and 'grounded theory', based upon qualitative work that closely coincides with educational practice.

In Part Two the available research evidence with respect to school effectiveness is reviewed. Again, a broader outlook than is usual in this type of review has been selected. Various research traditions with different disciplinary origins are shown to have a direct bearing on school effectiveness issues. The findings of a set of representative research projects are described in considerable detail; case studies of major British and American, and Dutch studies are included in Appendices 1 and 2.

Specific attention is given to research-technical issues and problems of interpreting the results of school effectiveness studies. It is established that school effectiveness research by means of multi-level analysis techniques has reached a considerable level of sophistication, allowing for a closer correspondence between the complexity of the available conceptual models and empirical research. The agenda for future school effectiveness research includes investigations into differential and contextual effectiveness that examine the robustness of available models for different sub-groups of pupils and within different environmental settings. International comparative school effectiveness studies are particularly interesting in this respect.

From these first two parts of the book it is quite clear that the intellectual status of school effectiveness research has risen considerably during the past decade. However, this does not mean that all the problems have been solved. One of the major difficulties in advancing school effectiveness research is the complexity – in a practical, organizational sense – of fully fledged school effectiveness studies, like those by Rutter *et al.* (1979) and Mortimore *et al.* (1988). Unfortunately, the budget requirements accompanying these complexities can only rarely be met in most countries. Because of practical limitations and research-technical problems, the available knowledge-base on school effectiveness issues still contains quite a few uncertainties and 'blank areas', about which we have some good ideas but insufficient hard evidence. Nevertheless, an attempt is made to summarize and integrate the major research results in what is called a 'practical theory' of school effectiveness. This exercise comprises the first chapter of Part Three, which is the part of the book dedicated to educational practice. Research results are translated into a related set of principles offering general suggestions – by no means a blueprint of recommendations – for improving educational practice.

In Chapter 7 a more dynamic use of the research results is presented in a discussion of levers for enhancing school effectiveness. After a consideration of case descriptions of recent school improvement programmes, it is recommended that comprehensive strategies for school improvement be used in two ways: by focusing on multiple levels of educational functioning (school context, school organization and management, and instruction at classroom level), and by using several levers for school improvement (such as reshaping incentive structures, technological innovations and enhancing the evaluative and self-renewing capacity of schools). An attractive way of enhancing both future school improvement programmes and school effectiveness inquiry is systematic evaluation of carefully designed and theoretically inspired innovatory programmes.

PART ONE

THEORY

Chapter 1

Perceptions of School Effectiveness

What do we mean by the statement that a school is 'effective'? In educational discussion the term 'effective' is often associated with the quality of education. Some authors (e.g. Corcoran, 1985) give an even broader meaning to the word by speaking of the general 'goodness' of a school. Other concepts that, rightly, or wrongly, are used as synonyms for effectiveness include efficiency, productivity and the survival power of an organization.

It is clear that a more precise definition is required. Moreover, we also run up against the problem that effectiveness is defined differently according to various disciplines. In this chapter, economic, organization-theoretical and pedagogical definitions will be considered.

ECONOMIC DEFINITIONS OF EFFECTIVENESS

In economics, concepts like effectiveness and efficiency are related to the production process of an organization. A production process can be summed up in a rather stylized form as a turnover or transformation of inputs to outputs. Inputs of a school or school system include pupils with certain given characteristics and financial and material aids. Outputs include pupil attainment at the end of schooling. The transformation process or throughput within a school can be understood to be all the instruction methods, curriculum choices and organizational preconditions that make it possible for pupils to acquire knowledge. Longer-term outputs are called 'outcomes' (see Table 1.1).

Table 1.1 *Examples of factors in the education production process*

Input	Process	Output	Outcome
Funding	Instruction methods	Final primary school test scores	Dispersal on the labour market

Effectiveness can be described as the extent to which the desired output is achieved. Efficiency can then be defined as the maximum output for the lowest possible cost. In other words, efficiency is effectiveness with the additional requirement that this is achieved in the cheapest possible manner (for variations on the meaning of efficiency see Boorsma and Nijzink, 1984, pp. 17–21; Windham, 1988).

Naturally enough, it is vitally important for the economic analysis of efficiency and effectiveness that the value of inputs and outputs can be expressed in terms of money. For determining efficiency it is necessary that at least input costs like teaching materials and teachers' salaries are known. When the outputs can also be expressed in financial terms efficiency determination is more like a cost–benefit analysis (Lockheed, 1988, p. 4). It has to be noted, however, that an extreme implementation of the above-mentioned economic characterization of school effectiveness runs up against many problems.

These start with the question of how one should define the 'desired output' of a school. For instance, the 'production' or return of a secondary school can be measured by the number of pupils who successfully pass their school-leaving diploma. The unit in which production is measured in this way is thus the 'final examination pupil'. Often, however, one will want to establish the units of production in a finer way and will want to look, for instance, at the grades achieved by pupils in various examination subjects. In addition, there are all kinds of choices to be made with regard to the scope of effectiveness measures. Should only performance in basic skills be studied? Is the concern also perhaps with higher cognitive processes, and should not social and/or affective returns on education be established? Other problems related to the economic analysis of schools are the difficulty in determining monetary value on inputs and processes, and the prevailing lack of clarity on how the production process operates (precisely what procedural and technical measures are necessary to achieve maximum output). Relevant to the question of how useful one regards the characterization of effectiveness in economic terms is the acceptability of the school being seen as a production unit.

ORGANIZATION-THEORETICAL VIEWS ON EFFECTIVENESS

Organizational theorists often adhere to the thesis that the effectiveness of organizations cannot be described in a straightforward manner. Instead, a pluralistic attitude is taken with respect to the interpretation of the concept in question. It is assumed that the chosen interpretation depends on the organization theory and the specific interests of the group posing the question of effectiveness (Cameron and Whetten, 1983, 1985; Faerman and Quinn, 1985). The main views on organization, which are used as background for a wide range of definitions of effectiveness, will be briefly reviewed.

Economic Rationality

The already mentioned economic description of effectiveness is seen by organizational experts as deriving from the idea that organizations function rationally – that is to say, purposefully. Goals that can be operationalized as pursued outputs are the basis for choosing effect criteria (effect criteria are the variables by which effects are measured, i.e. study achievement, well-being of the pupils, etc.). There is evidence of economic rationality whenever goals are formulated as outputs of the primary production process of the school. In the entire functioning of a school other goals can also play a part, such as having a clear-cut policy with regard to increasing pupil intake. With regard to this type of objective a school can also operate rationally, but this falls outside the specific interpretation given to economic rationality. Effectiveness as defined in terms of economic rationality can also be identified as the productivity of an organization. In education the rational or goal-oriented model is mainly propagated via Tyler's (1950) model, which can be used for both curriculum development and educational evaluation. The remaining views on organization, to be discussed shortly, dismiss the economic rationality model as both simplistic and out of reach. It is well known in the teaching field how difficult it is to reach a consensus on goals and to operationalize and quantify these. From the position that values other than productivity are just as important for organizations, the rational model is regarded as simplistic.

The Organic System Model

According to the organic system model, organizations can be compared to biological systems that adapt to their environments. The main characteristic of this approach is that organizations openly interact with their surroundings. Thus, they need not be passive objects of environmental manipulation but can actively exert influence on the environment themselves. Nevertheless, this viewpoint is mainly preoccupied with an organization's 'survival' in a sometimes hostile environment. For this reason, organizations must be flexible, to assure themselves of essential resources and other inputs. According to this idea flexibility and adaptability are the most important conditions for effectiveness, in the sense of survival. A result of this could be that the effectiveness of a school is measured according to its yearly intake, which could partly be attributed to intensive canvassing or school marketing.

No matter how remarkable this view of effectiveness may seem at first glance, it is supported by an entirely different scientific area: microeconomics of the public sector. Niskanen (1971) demonstrated that public sector organizations are primarily targeted at maximizing budgets and that there are insufficient external incentives for these organizations – schools included – to encourage effectiveness and efficiency. In this context I think it would be interesting to examine whether the canvassing activities of schools mainly comprise the display of acquired facilities (inputs) or the presentation of output data, such as previous years' examination results. Finally, it should be mentioned that it is conceivable that the inclination towards inputs of the organic system model coincides with a concern for satisfying outputs, namely in those situations where the environment makes the availability of inputs dependent on the quantity and/or quality of realized achievements (output). This principle is presently applied in the so-called output financing of universities and vocational colleges in the Netherlands.

The Human Relations Approach to Organizations

If in the open-system view of organizations there is an inclination towards the environment, with the so-called human relations approach the eye of the organization analyst is explicitly focused inward. This fairly classical school of organizational thought has partly remained intact in more recent organizational characterizations. In Mintzberg's (1979) concept of the professional bureaucracy, aspects of the human relations approach re-occur, in its emphasis on the importance of the well-being of the individuals in an organization, of consensus and collegial relationships, and of motivation and human resource development. From this viewpoint, the job satisfaction of workers and their involvement with the organization are likely criteria for measuring the most desired characteristics of the organization. The organizational theorists who share this view regard these criteria as effectiveness criteria.

The Bureaucracy

The essential problem with regard to the administration and structure of organizations, in particular those like schools that have many relatively autonomous sub-units, is how to create a harmonious whole. For this, appropriate social interaction and opportunities for personal and professional development – see the human relations approach – provide a means. A second means is provided by organizing, clearly defining and formalizing these social relations. The prototype of an organization in which positions and duties are formally organized is the 'bureaucracy'. It is well known that bureaucratic organizations tend to produce more bureaucracy. The underlying motive behind this is to ensure the continuation, or better still the growth, of one's own department. This continuation can start operating as an effect criterion in itself.

The Political Model of Organizations

Certain organizational theorists see organizations as political battlefields (Pfeffer and Salancik, 1978). Departments, individual workers and management staff use the official duties and goals in order to achieve their own hidden – or less hidden – agendas. Good contacts with powerful outside bodies are regarded as very important for the standing of their department or of themselves. From a political model perspective the question of the effectiveness of the organization as a whole is difficult to answer. The interest is more in the extent to which internal groups succeed in complying with the demands of certain external interested parties, in order to bolster their own positions. In the case of schools these bodies could be school governing bodies, parents of pupils and the local business community. From studies carried out by Van der Krogt and Oosting (1988) it appears that the external orientation of intermediate vocational secondary schools in the Netherlands is by no means highly developed.

It has already been mentioned that organizational concepts of effectiveness depend not only on theoretical answers to the question of how organizations are pieced together but also on the position of the factions posing the effectiveness question. On this point there are differences between these five views of organizational effectiveness. In the economic rationality and the organic system models, the management of the organization is the main 'actor' posing the effectiveness question. For the other models, department heads and individual workers are the actors that want to achieve certain effects.

In Table 1.2 the chief characteristics of the organization-theoretical perceptions on effectiveness are summarized. The diversity of views on effectiveness within organizational theory leads to the question of which position should be taken. Should we operate from a position of there being several forms of effectiveness, should a certain choice be made, or is it possible to develop, from several views, one all-embracing concept of effectiveness?

Table 1.2 *Organizational effectiveness models*

Theoretical background	Effectiveness criterion	Level at which the effectiveness question is asked	Main areas of attention
Economic rationality (business)	Productivity	Organization	Output and its determinants
Organic system theory	Adaptability	Organization	Acquiring essential inputs
Human relations approach	Involvement	Individual members of the organization	Motivation
Bureaucratic theory; system members theory; social and psychological homeostatic theories	Continuity	Organization and individuals	Formal structure
Political theory of organizations	Responsiveness to external stakeholders	Sub-groups and individuals	Interdependence and power

A BROAD OUTLINE OF THE UNDERLYING MODEL OF SCHOOL EFFECTIVENESS RESEARCH

School effectiveness research has various disciplinary backgrounds and has acquired a certain life history of its own. Here only a broad outline of school effectiveness research is given.

In school effectiveness research school characteristics are linked to output data. The most widely employed output data are test results in basic skills, such as language and arithmetic, in elementary schools, and in the mother tongue, mathematics and foreign languages in secondary schools. The school characteristics chosen vary according to the different areas of educational effectiveness research. Sometimes the emphasis is on financial inputs and organizational characteristics like a school's size, at other times process characteristics are studied, such as school leadership, aspects of the curriculum and teaching methods.

Associating these latter characteristics and output data is largely done by means of calculating correlations. Put simply, correlations are totals that indicate how much high or low scores of a group of schools or pupils on one variable converge with similar high or low scores on another variable. Correlational relationships can be distinguished from associations between variables that can be established in experimental research. The main difference is that, strictly speaking, with correlations it is impossible to obtain an unequivocal insight into the question of whether one variable can be seen as the cause of the other, even though a certain impression can be gained. Experimental research gives more certainty on this point. The fact that most school effectiveness research is correlational creates problems for interpreting results. While it is largely assumed that school characteristics are the causes, and levels of achievement the results (outputs), in some cases the reverse is true. Several studies have established that in schools where teachers have high expectations of pupils, the level of achievement is higher. One interpretation here could be that pupils are motivated by the positive attitude of the teachers. Another interpretation, just as plausible, is that the teachers, on the basis of knowing the levels of achievement of their pupils, have realistic expectations, so that high expectations go hand-in-hand with high levels of achievement. In short, the high expectations characteristic can be both a cause and an effect of high levels of achievement.

THE POSITION WITH REGARD TO ECONOMIC AND ORGANIZATION-THEORETICAL DEFINITIONS OF EFFECTIVENESS

The above general outline of school effectiveness research will be compared to the economic and organization-theoretical definitions of effectiveness discussed in previous sections. Cameron and Whetten (1983) have developed a checklist to determine organization-effectiveness models. This will be applied to the general outline of school effectiveness research.

Question 1: From Whose Perspective Is Effectiveness Judged?

This question draws attention to the practical implications of school effectiveness research, which are not always self-evident. In fact, this research can also be seen as an area of scientific research in which theory development is uppermost and the practical application of results takes second place. Notwithstanding this, most areas of school effectiveness research are narrowly linked to specific application. Political questions on education regarding unequal opportunity, developing compensatory education and encouraging school improvement programmes are probably more important sources of inspiration for school effectiveness research than pure scientific questions. According to Ralph and Fennessey (1983) school effectiveness research is dominated by the school improvement perspective and by educational support institutions. They mention the effective schools movement and imply that in the adoption of results of school effectiveness research there is a discernible 'ideology of reform'. According to them this ideological movement explains the important practical significance given to the results of school effectiveness research. They believe that the impact of the fairly limited number of empirical school effectiveness studies does not justify this degree of practical influence.

It is still difficult to answer the question of which area of the education service should make most use of school effectiveness research. There are examples of applications both within local school guidance services and for education department initiatives in studies attached to national assessment programmes and evaluation studies. A third category of potential users is the consumers of education, parents and pupils. And, last but not least, schools could be inspired to use these results to improve their own practices. So the conclusion is that school effectiveness may be judged from multiple perspectives.

Question 2: Which Area of Activity within an Organization Determines Effectiveness?

In some of the models of organizational effectiveness looked at in the preceding section the emphasis was on the activities of management to acquire, for instance, essential resources or on activities directed at increasing staff motivation. In school effectiveness research the results of the primary production process – pupils' attainment levels – are mainly studied. In addition, one looks for 'predictors' or 'determinants' of these results (outputs). In effective schools research these determinants are defined as characteristics of the school. Sometimes characteristics like management, organization and curriculum can be defined purely at the school level. There are also characteristics that are the sum total of education in the various classes: classroom characteristics aggregated to school characteristics, in fact. Figure 1.1 shows the main focus of effective schools research.

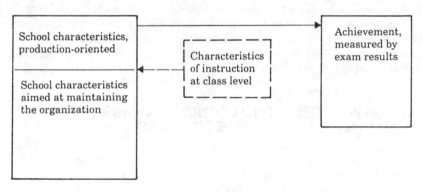

Figure 1.1 The area of activity (in terms of effectiveness determinants and criteria) of school effectiveness research: the variables in the dashed box are classroom characteristics aggregated to school level; the broken arrow indicates the aggregation to school level of instruction characteristics measured at class level

Question 3: At Which Level of the Organization Is Effectiveness Analysed?

This question has in fact been answered above. As a rule, school effectiveness is analysed at school level. However, more can be said on this question because of research technicality. The output variables in school effectiveness research – for instance, the scores in final primary school year tests – are determined for each individual pupil. School characteristics are only defined on a school level. Thus the concern here is to relate variables defined at school level to those defined at pupil level. Especially when we are establishing these sorts of links and wish to correct for background characteristics of pupils, there are advantages in keeping the information at the lowest aggregate level (the pupil) in the analysis. There are specific technical problems linked to relating data measured at different levels to one another, but multi-level analysis techniques provide a solution.

Question 4: How Is Effectiveness Defined in Terms of Time?

Subsidiary questions that play a role here are (a) the frequency with which effectiveness is determined and (b) the specific times of measurement of management and/or production processes by which effectiveness is gauged.

With regard to the first question it is conceivable that there are instruments to keep a more or less permanent check on whether an organization functions well and produces sufficiently. At national level, monitoring by means of so-called educational indicators makes such permanent quality control possible. At the individual school level a school management information system fulfils this role (Essink and Visscher, 1987). In most school effectiveness research the effectiveness is determined once only. Examples of research in which the output of schools is determined at several times (longitudinal study) are rather scarce. Studies where this is the case are those of Rutter *et al.* (1979), Mortimore *et al.* (1988) and Brandsma and Knuver (1988).

With regard to the second question, concerning the point at which effectiveness is gauged, this generally occurs at the end of education. According to some critics of school effectiveness research it is unreasonable to call a school effective just because at the end of the last school year it appears that the average level of achievement is relatively high. Ralph and Fennessey (1983) state, for instance, that an effective school should be able to demonstrate relatively high levels of attainment in every school year. Moreover, they feel that schools only deserve the label 'effective' when they have performed well over several years; in other words, when school effectiveness appears as a stable factor.

Question 5: What Data Are Used to Form an Opinion on Effectiveness?

Cameron and Whetten (1983) mentioned using objective data as opposed to subjective data. In effective schools research objective data are mainly used to measure effect criteria, whereas in establishing determinants of effectiveness subjective opinions from those directly involved can often be decisive. In some studies use is made of expert assessments (essentially subjective data); Hoy and Ferguson (1985) is an example.

Question 6: What Standards or Measures Are Used in Order to Make Effectiveness Judgements?

Organizational effectiveness assessments can be made by comparing similar sorts of organizations, like schools, to one another (cross-sectional comparative measurement), by assessing the same organization at various times (longitudinal comparative) or by comparing the output achieved to an absolute standard, such as a prefixed target figure.

In school effectiveness research the cross-sectional comparative measurement is most used. More specifically, comparisons between schools can be in the nature of (a) placing 'extremely good' schools against 'extremely bad' schools; (b) comparing a particular school with standard data, which could be established per country or province; (c) comparing schools that have taken part in an improvement programme with schools that have not. An important question when using comparative measurements is to decide what size of difference between schools is to be considered as meaningful.

To sum up, it can be established that the underlying model for school effectiveness research compared to other models for organization effectiveness can be described as a multi-level, process–product model of learning achievement propelled by the quest for knowledge of school reformers and national policy-makers, in which as much use as possible is made of objective data, a short-term perspective is discernible and assessment standards are largely comparative.

The problem of defining school effectiveness could have been approached more directly by simply pointing out the obvious common ground it shares with the economic typification of effectiveness (within the broader perspective of efficiency and productivity) and with the related organizational model of economic rationality. However, a conscious choice has been made to discuss alternative effectiveness views within the field of organization theory. This broader conceptual framework is regarded as necessary in order to reach a more balanced position. It is important to have in mind that various points of view exist when considering effectiveness. Even when one rejects this plurality in the long run, as will be the case here, confusion of ideas can be avoided by comparing the final choice of typification with alternative concepts.

More important is that this excursion within the area of organizational theory demonstrates that for organizations to function properly more is needed than a smooth-running production process. Back-up functions, often identified as buffers, are necessary in order that the primary production process can run undisturbed. Moreover, it is important to be aware that organizations can lose out with these back-up functions, by, for instance, acquiring far too many resources than are strictly needed for an efficient production, or allowing 'conviviality' to be such an aim in itself that it is at the expense of productive working hours.

Means–Goal Ordering of Criteria

The above formulation conveys that productivity, that is to say an effective output of the primary process, should be seen as the actual dimension of effectiveness. Alternative effectiveness criteria, such as adaptability towards the environment, job satisfaction, consensus and continuity guaranteed by a formalized structure, can be seen as 'means' or intermediary goals. Figure 1.2 illustrates the means–goal character of the various effectiveness perceptions. In Figure 1.2 the arrows pointing in both directions express the fact that satisfaction, solidarity and the oneness of structures can be seen as both the cause *and* the effect of high productivity. It is not implausible that staff of a productive organization are more satisfied than the personnel of one that is hardly productive.

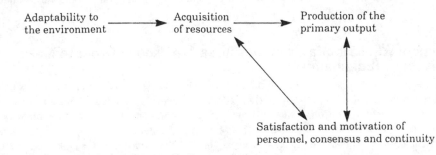

Figure 1.2 Means–goal relationship between effectiveness criteria

Putting the relationship pattern of Figure 1.2 within an educational context, one can see as an example of the criterion 'adaptability', specific measures, instruments and organizational forms to make the school curriculum more relevant to the needs of the labour market. Another example is to have an organizational structure that can withstand drastic changes in the direct environment, such as externally imposed increases in scale (Gooren, 1989). As an example of acquiring vital resources one can think of machines that are needed for technical education and that can sometimes be obtained through contacts with local industry. Examples of process-support criteria like solidarity, motivation and continuity are: working on a shared vision of education within a teaching team; working with specialist departments and their accompanying consultative bodies; and a certain amount of decision-making delegated from the school management to the teaching staff.

The Criteria as Competing Values

An integral 'harmonious model' of alternative effectiveness criteria was discussed above. It has already been stated that the whole thing gets unstuck when the means become goals in themselves. For further information on this phenomenon of 'goal displacement' see Etzioni (1964, pp. 10–12). Particularly when one does not want to choose between effectiveness criteria and support conditions, one can also see the various alternative criteria in competition with one another. This viewpoint has been elaborated upon by Faerman and Quinn (1985). They emphasize the fact that organizations vary between one another in the extent to which they focus on productivity, adaptability to the environment, continuity and solidarity. The first two categories of criteria express an external orientation, while the second two have an internal inclination. The more energy spent on one or two of these criteria, the less time can automatically be spent on the others. An interesting elaboration of this competing values framework is the assumption that the pattern of priorities among these criteria changes during the course of an organization's development. Young organizations will be largely externally oriented, to obtain vital resources, while more established organizations will be more concerned with consensus and internal stability. Ultimately, more of a balance could exist, in which productivity and acquiring input again receive slightly more emphasis than the internal support values. The competing values perspective can be linked with the means–goal perspective by the assumption that the support conditions (see Table 1.1) could reach certain optimum values, whereby 'too much' emphasis on consensus, for instance, would be literally counterproductive.

In this book the term 'effectiveness' has been reserved for the quantity and quality of the outputs of the primary production process. Within this viewpoint, school effectiveness studies always employ output data (or possibly outcome data) as criteria. Of course, effectiveness research is not only concerned with the measuring of these outputs, but also strives to ascribe differences in outputs to certain school characteristics. Alternative effectiveness criteria, such as adaptability and cohesion, are seen as conditions that are supportive of productivity. This choice in no way implies that these support conditions are unimportant. On the contrary, they are seen as essential points for attention in order to understand the effective functioning of schools. When translating the results of school effectiveness research to specific practical situations, one should take into account such accompanying organizational conditions. A final observation is that the question of what priority a school gives to increasing effectiveness or productivity amid other competing value positions is seldom gone into in empirical studies.

SUMMARY AND CONCLUSIONS

The concept of effectiveness is clearly related to means–end relationships. When applied to educational phenomena, effectiveness refers to the degree to which educational means or processes result in the attainment of educational goals. In the language of a simple input–process–output systems model of education, effectiveness could be referred to as the transition of inputs by means of processes into desired outputs and outcomes.

This abstract definition, however, does not resolve all debate on the delineation of the concept of educational effectiveness. Although it is easily aligned with *economic* constructs like productivity (i.e. the delivery of outputs in a sufficient quantity and quality) and efficiency (sufficient productivity at the lowest possible cost), contributions from organization theory paint a more divergent picture of the construct. Productivity in the economic sense is judged as just one of several definitions of effectiveness. Alternative criteria are the flexibility or adaptability of the organization to external circumstances, its responsiveness to external shareholders, the involvement and satisfaction of personnel and continuity in the internal functioning of the organization.

Various positions with respect to these alternative effectiveness criteria are possible:

1 A pluralistic and relativistic attitude, where the adherence to any one of the criteria is thought to be dependent on the actor's position regarding the organization or one's organization-theoretical preference.

2 A 'contingency' perspective, where the predominance of a particular effectiveness criterion is thought to be dependent on the stage in the life-history of organizations or other contingencies.

3 A view, which is the one preferred by this author, according to which the available effectiveness criteria are ordered as means to an end and productivity is seen as the ultimate effectiveness criterion. The dominant underlying model in school effectiveness research more or less coincides with this latter notion, although the idea of using alternative effectiveness criteria as antecedent conditions to productivity is hardly represented in the available research literature. Questions about the perspective of actors concerned with effectiveness issues, the scope and temporal context of these issues and the dominant methods in assessing achievement serve to make the underlying conception of the dominant model employed in school effectiveness research more explicit. It is concluded that this model can be described as a multi-level, process–product model of learning achievement, propelled by the quest for knowledge of school reformers and national policy-makers, in which as much use as possible is made of objective data, a short-term perspective is discernible and assessment standards are largely comparative.

This chapter has sought to convey a taste of the complexity of the effectiveness issue. Apart from the various perspectives from which effectiveness has been approached, it should be emphasized that, so far, it has been treated in a formal, relatively 'empty' way. In practice, substantive differences will occur in answer to the question of which educational goals (cognitive or affective, academic or more directly functional in everyday practice, etc.) are more important than others. As will become clear when I discuss the actual practice of school effectiveness research in Part Two, there has been a strong emphasis on basic skills in the traditional school subjects of reading, language and arithmetic. In the next chapter the available 'substantive' social-scientific theories and models that bear upon the issue of school effectiveness will be examined. Substantive theories and models produce general principles that could explain why certain methods and organizational arrangements work better than others.

Chapter 2

School Effectiveness Theory Development

INTRODUCTION

One of the most serious criticisms confronting the enquiry into school effectiveness is its alleged atheoretical nature. Although we now have quite a few ideas about *what* works in education, there is as yet little consistency in the ideas about *why* certain approaches appear to be effective. The overall message of this chapter is that, as far as the development of school effectiveness theory is concerned, matters are not as bleak as they are sometimes made to appear. Nevertheless, it is felt that explicit efforts to elaborate school effectiveness models and connect these models to more general explanatory structures (theories) deserve more attention than they have been given. Theory development is important not only for stimulating further research; the well-known cliché 'nothing is more practical than a good theory' definitely also applies to the field of school effectiveness. Before these evaluative comments are explained in more detail, the terms 'theory', 'model' and 'theory development' will be clearly defined, since they are often confused and used with various connotations.

Generally stated, a *theory* is an explanation of an observed relationship between phenomena (Odi, 1982, p. 55). It consists of (a) a set of units (facts, concepts, variables), (b) a system of relationships among units and (c) interpretations about (b) that are comprehensible and predict empirical events (Snow, 1973, p. 78). A (somewhat) hypothetical example concerning educational effectiveness would be the explanation of an established positive causal link between structured teaching and cognitive educational achievement by means of the principles of classical learning theory. Another example could be the interpretation of teachers' feelings of their own efficacy as a specific instance of expectancy theory.

A *model* can be seen as a prerequisite for a theory in the sense that it specifies or 'visualizes' in a simplified or reduced way phenomena that cannot be easily or directly observed (Snow, 1973, p. 78; De Groot, 1986). A model contains the (a) and (b) elements of the definition of theory above, but does not necessarily contain element (c).

Theory development can be either deductive (specific empirical hypotheses are deduced from general theoretical principles) or inductive (general constructs are developed as 'common denominators' of more specific observed relationships). Glaser and Strauss (1967) use the term 'grounded theory' for inductive theory development. A specific characteristic of their construct of grounded theory that is worth noting is that it can result from both quantitative and qualitative (or naturalistic) data. The world of school effectiveness described in this book largely depends on formal, quantitative educational research data. It is absolutely necessary – and this occurs in many current school improvement projects inspired by the school effectiveness research results – that this stylized and somewhat abstract realm is confronted with the everyday reality of schools. This approach is important, not only to provide researchers with a 'firm foothold', but also to generate new insights and ideas that could inspire further theory development and formal research.

A sensible method for treating the process of theory development is Snow's conceptualization of 'grades of theory' (Snow, 1973, p. 82). In this method, theory development in a particular field can be seen as a sequence of levels of sophistication of theory, ranging from 'formative hypotheses' to axiomatic theory. Intermediate stations relevant to the field of school effectiveness are 'relatively simple summarization of empirical relationships without substantial inferences or deductive logic' (p. 87), conceptual theories and eclecticism (i.e. using 'bits and pieces' of theories and models developed in education and other disciplines).

The current state of development of school effectiveness theory is aptly described by Snow as being a 'relatively simple summarization of empirical relationships'. At the same time, quite a few causal models of school effectiveness exist that are really causal models of educational achievement (see Clauset and Gaynor, 1982; Parkerson *et al.*, 1984; Oakes, 1989; Bossert, 1988; Scheerens, 1989). The model developed by Scheerens is included in this book as an example. In the present chapter a modest attempt is made to examine how eclecticism can affect the development of school effectiveness theory.

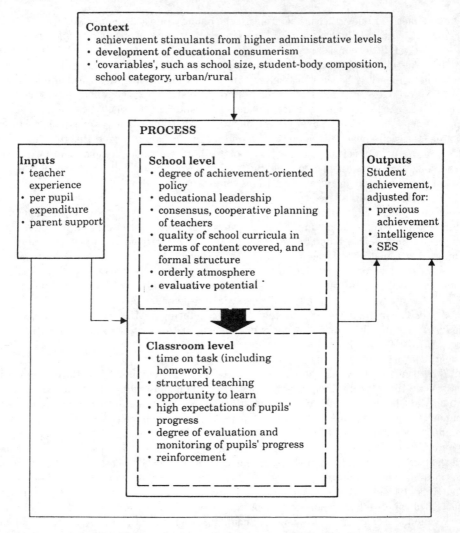

Figure 2.1 An integrated model of school effectiveness (from Scheerens, 1990)

Considering the complexity of the phenomenon of school effectiveness, it is not surprising that an eclectic approach has been chosen. In this way partial theories or formalized models can be used to highlight certain parts of the general model depicted in Figure 2.1.

The complexity of school effectiveness does not just mean taking many variables into account. The formal characteristics of many conceptual models of school effectiveness reveal that we have to deal with:

- multi-level relationships (e.g. the degree to which characteristics of the school context influence school policies, or the way in which school characteristics can be seen as facilitators of conditions for effective instruction at the classroom level);
- intermediate causal effects (e.g. an indirect effect of 'instructional leadership' on pupil achievement via certain didactive arrangements made by teachers);
- reciprocal relationships (e.g. teachers have high expectations of pupils' achievement, enhancing achievement; high achievement levels raise teacher expectations).

The partial theories that will be discussed in the subsequent sections of this chapter are public choice theory, models of coordination in educational organizations, and what is called the 'nested layers metaphor of school organizations'. The disciplinary background of the public choice theory is economics and political science. Coordination models have been developed by organizational analysts. The third approach is an effort to integrate instructional and organizational models, with the Carroll model as its instructional core.

PUBLIC CHOICE THEORY

The economic theory of the political process, more often labelled 'public choice theory', was developed in the United States in the 1950s. Economists such as Downs (1957) and Buchanan and Tullock (1965) applied economic constructs to political processes and the functioning of public sector organizations (bureaucracies), a field of investigation that traditionally had been the territory of sociologists and experts on constitutional law.

Political processes in the welfare state, with respect to the division of tasks, rights and the products of public services between actors such as voters, politicians and government officers (defined as bureaucrats), are represented in terms of imperfect exchange mechanisms. In this respect the basic question is: do citizens obtain from the government what they want? Van Mierlo (1984, p. 65) mentions four problems in this area:

1. There is insufficient responsiveness between politicians and voters, i.e. voters are not clear on what they want and politicians take many liberties in honouring the wishes of their constituencies.
2. Politicians are inept at making government officers implement the policies resulting from their decisions.
3. The central bureaucracy is insufficiently successful in 'selling' its policy measures to citizens as the consumers of these products.
4. There are severe delays between elections – when voters are allowed to express their preferences – and the actual provision of policy products to the policy consumers (i.e. the former voters).

These imperfect exchange mechanisms set the stage for the analysis of the functioning of public sector organizations (bureaucracies, or 'bureaus' as the public choice theorists refer to them). In particular, the leeway that government officials within sections of the governmental apparatus have implies that tendencies towards inefficiency cannot be properly controlled. One reason is that bureaucracies are not controlled by the market mechanism, since 'the owners and employees of these organizations do not appropriate any part of the differences between revenues and costs as personal income [and] some part of the recurring revenues of the

15

organization derive from other than the sale of output as a per-unit rate' (Niskanen, 1971, p. 15). A second reason for lack of control – as authors such as Niskanen point out – is that evaluation and review of public sector organizations by higher-level agencies (for example, committees) is usually ineffective owing to lack of time and expertise, and because of successful attempts by bureaus to mask the true input–output characteristics of their primary production process.

Public choice theory explains the inherent tendencies towards inefficiency of bureaus by means of the principle of 'methodological individualism' (Van Mierlo, 1984, p. 59) as opposed to the holistic treatment of organizations. Methodological individualism recognizes that individuals or sub-groups within larger organizations have their own preferences and goals, which do not necessarily coincide with the overall organizational aims.

Niskanen (1971, p. 38) mentions the following variables that might affect the bureaucrat's utility function: 'salary, perquisites of the office, public reputation, power, patronage, output of the bureau, ease of making changes and ease of managing the bureau'. He goes on to state that he considers 'budget maximization' as an adequate proxy for all these variables. The operation of these kinds of incentives for managers of public sector organizations gives rise to the general phenomenon of 'goal displacement', particularly when the means of the organization (higher budgets, more staff, more activities, more management) become ends in themselves.

Other authors have offered somewhat different analyses of what makes bureaucrats tick. Liebenstein (1978) has introduced the concept of X-inefficiency, i.e. organizational inefficiency resulting from factors such as 'selective rationality' (individuals decide the extent to which they deviate from maximizing behaviour), 'inert areas' (individuals are seen to experience inertial costs of moving to a superior position) and 'incomplete contracts' (the existence of effort discretion). In addition to the incentives inherent in budget maximization, Liebenstein's factors refer to leisure and 'shirking' one's duties as additional incentives in the functioning of public sector organizations. Breton and Wintrobe (1982) shift the emphasis from the motivational structure of bureaucrats as superiors (Niskanen) to that of bureaucrats as subordinates, and the interaction between superiors and subordinates. The essence of their theory is that bureaucrats choose whether to be efficient or inefficient, i.e. they behave selectively. This type of selective behaviour is perceived as the outcome of a trading process conducted within the informal structure of bureaus. Implicit in this notion is the possibility that subordinates purposefully behave counter-productively, for instance as a signal of discontent to their superiors.

Other instances of 'poorly' functioning organizations, particularly bureaucracies, are treated by Masuch and Verhorst (1987) and Masuch et al. (1989). In one investigation they found evidence of Parkinson's concept of 'make-work', the phenomenon that officials make work for each other. In their interpretation of make-work they depart from the notion implied in public choice theory that bureaucrats are cleverly maximizing their personal utility functions. Instead, bureaucrats are viewed as being caught in vicious circles created by uncertain tasks, growing complexity and fallible feedback.

As far as formal characteristics are concerned, public choice theory is an axiomatic deductive theory, while behavioural postulates are based on the rational choice paradigm. From this, specific hypotheses concerning the (in)efficient functioning of organizations are generated. Niskanen (1971, p. 64) predicts, for instance, that 'a bureau will supply an output up to twice that of a competitive industry faced by the same demand and cost conditions'. The explicit postulates about the inefficiency of bureaucracies also point to ways of making them more efficient. Niskanen (1971, p. 228) mentions the following changes that are necessary to make public services efficient:

1   Increase the competition among bureaus for the supply of the same or similar public services.
2   Change the incentives in the bureaucracy to induce more efficient behaviour by the senior bureaucrats.

3 Increase the competition of the bureaucracy by greater use of private sources of supply of public services.
4 Reassert control of the review process by the president and the legislative representatives of the voters.

The relevance of public choice theory has only slowly been recognized by authors in the field of educational administration. Boyd and Crowson (1985) underline the merit of the public choice theory for the field of educational administration. First, they point out that public choice theory stands in sharp contrast to many organizational 'theories' in that it provides a deductive approach yielding empirically testable propositions. These former organizational theories, Boyd and Crowson state, are no more than an '*ad hoc* melange of related insights' (p. 322).

Second, Boyd and Crowson give evidence that schools are like bureaus, as they are described by public choice theory. Thus, for instance, they cite Michaelsen (1977) in stating that 'The needs of teachers and principals for control over their jobs most often take precedence over the needs of individual children and their families,' and Mann (1981): 'The current procedures for resource allocation at the building level have more to do with the equitability of adult working conditions than with the production of responsive learning environments for children.'

Third, Boyd and Crowson point to the frequently established fact that public school principals spend considerably more time on maintenance tasks than on the instructional programme and entrepreneurship. They relate this finding to predictions that can be derived from public choice theory, since there is little in the relevant environment of public schools that stimulates principals to be instructionally directed and active in external public liaison activity.

In answering the question of what public choice theory means for understanding school effectiveness it might be instructive to examine which results of empirical school effectiveness studies fit its hypotheses. Particularly interesting are the results from those studies that were developed from a completely different conceptual context, since they demonstrate the robustness of the theory. As mentioned above, in reference to the review by Boyd and Crowson, the predictions generated from public choice theory are in line with the results of descriptive studies in educational administration directed to the question of what school principals do. The strong emphasis on internal maintenance functions and administrative leadership, as opposed to entrepreneurship and instructional leadership, could be interpreted as an example of goal displacement. In most educational systems the incentives for 'running a smooth ship', perhaps as an instrumental goal in safeguarding student enrolment, are much more in evidence than rewards and 'punishments' with respect to pupils' educational achievement. US and British school effectiveness studies have shown that differences in instructional leadership matter with respect to output.

Second, the construct of 'opportunity costs', which draws attention to the phenomenon that functionaires in public sector organizations have opportunities to be active in non-task-related activities, can be seen as indicative of the general finding that more 'time on task', and thus less 'forgone teaching and learning', leads to better educational achievement (phenomena such as lessons not taught, truancy, time required to maintain discipline).

Third, public choice theory offers a general explanation for the results of comparisons between private and public schools. Generally, in developed countries, private schools appear to be more effective, even in countries where both private and public schools are financed by the state (Scheerens, 1989). One explanation for the alleged superiority of private schools is that parents who send their children to these schools are more active educational consumers and make specific demands on the educational philosophy of schools.

In the fourth place, the analysis of the functioning of bureaus within the framework of public choice theory is concerned with generally inefficient review processes by higher administrative levels. Results from empirical school effectiveness studies (e.g. Kyle, 1985) have indicated that school districts that exercise more explicit demands (in terms of goals and standards to be achieved) enhance school effectiveness.

A fifth and final point connected to evaluation and review is the general assumption in public choice theory that administrative evaluation cannot replace the market as a control mechanism. A modified interpretation of this postulate could be the recognition of differences in the fallibility of evaluations. In this respect, empirical studies have shown that effective schools evaluate progress in educational achievement more frequently than less effective schools.

Apart from the explanation of some findings from school effectiveness studies, public choice theory describes certain measures for making public schools more like private companies, such as:

- differentiating the reward structure for teachers by means of perquisites and more opportunities for promotions;
- making schools more financially autonomous;
- voucher systems;
- strengthening consumer influence over schools by making schools publish achievement records;
- stimulating competition between schools.

In stressing the importance of factors such as instructional leadership, effective learning time and output-oriented evaluations, public choice theory makes great strides in providing the explanatory background of major results from school effectiveness studies. Again it should be emphasized that empirical studies in educational administration and school effectiveness have largely developed outside the sphere of influence of public choice theory. It therefore seems fair to say that the usefulness of public choice theory for understanding school effectiveness has not yet been fully understood. A valuable analytical exercise would be to deduct hypotheses from the postulates of public choice theory that take specific instances of the functioning of schools into consideration. These hypotheses might then be employed, for instance, in comparing private and public schools, perhaps leading to more definite results regarding the reasons why private schools are generally more effective.

Despite the great potential of public choice theory there are also some limitations. Public choice theory departs from a strongly pessimistic assumption about the knowledge of educational production functions, yet another aspect of school functioning that has been studied by economists. Educational effectiveness studies – particularly instructional effectiveness studies at the micro level – have made important progress in delineating productive instructional processes. When educational technology becomes less fuzzy, certain central parameters in hypotheses drawn from public choice theory might change, specifically those connected with transaction costs.

A more fundamental issue, perhaps, is the degree to which the analysis of bureaus from the perspective of public choice theory is fully equatable to the reality of public schools. Examples of this reality that should be scrutinized before reward structures, competition, etc. are tinkered with are the efficiency-enhancing characteristics of professional autonomy and 'loose coupling' (see the next section), and the importance of an open exchange of ideas among professionals (see also Boyd and Crowson, 1985, p. 360).

In subsequent sections, the 'gaps' that remain in the application of public choice theory to educational organizations will be filled by examination of conceptual approaches that focus on the internal structure of schools and educational technology respectively.

MODELS OF COORDINATION IN EDUCATIONAL ORGANIZATIONS

The two basic parameters of organizational analysis are the division of tasks and authority on the one hand and measures to interrelate these part-systems on the other. Mintzberg (1979, p. 2) describes these two processes, division and coordination, as 'two fundamental and opposing requirements' of every human activity.

Coordination within organizations can be achieved in two ways. First, the design of the organizational structure in terms of hierarchy, and lateral relationships between organizational sub-units, can be seen as the basis for coordination. Kickert (1979) calls this 'structural' coordination as opposed to 'procedural' coordination. The essential idea of structural coordination is that by means of changes in the structure of units and sub-units and the more permanent relationships between them, the pattern of adjustments and unifications is also changed. In this way, the classical organizational forms, such as the functional hierarchy, the product hierarchy or the matrix organization, are considered alternative ways of structural coordination.

Procedural coordination, the second way to achieve unity and integration within an organization, accepts the organizational structure as a given fact, and deals with purposeful adjustment between the sub-units of the organization. Mintzberg (1979, p. 3) mentions five 'coordinating mechanisms': mutual adjustment, direct supervision, standardization of work processes, standardization of work outputs and standardization of worker skills. He speaks of these coordinating measures as 'the glue that holds organizations together'. In mutual adjustment, coordination is achieved simply by means of informal communication. Direct supervision presupposes a hierarchical structure of authority; in its simplest form one individual takes responsibility for the work of others. The three types of standardization rely on the ability to preplan and specify processes and outputs. For instance, in standardization of worker skills, the kind of training required to perform the work is specified (Mintzberg, 1979, p. 6).

The shape that coordination (structural and procedural) generally takes in educational organizations is important for two reasons. First, specifying the coordination structure and dominant coordination mechanisms exposes the essential features of a specific type of organization. Exposing these essential features of schools is the best method for describing the organizational context of specific effectiveness models. For instance, when one is attempting to apply some of the insights from public choice theory to enhance school effectiveness, it is quite important to consider to what extent such measures might upset traditional ways of coordination.

Second, there is a general belief that 'improving' coordination structures and mechanisms within schools is one of the keys to effectiveness. The general hypothesis is that more integrated rather than more segmented school organizations are more effective. This hypothesis has received some support in school effectiveness research literature: several authors report a positive association between factors such as collegiality, consensus and cooperation among staff and educational achievement (see Part Two of this book).

Three models of cooperation within educational organization will be briefly discussed, the concept of 'organized anarchies', the notion of 'loose coupling' and the general typology of the school as a 'professional bureaucracy'. Attention will be placed on the potential each model has for understanding school effectiveness, i.e. in the sharpening and specification of hypotheses, in offering explanations for available research results and in generating further research.

Organized Anarchies

Cohen *et al.* (1972) describe organized anarchies as characterized by 'problematic preferences', 'unclear technology' and 'fluid participation'. With respect to problematic preferences, they state that the organization can 'better be described as a loose collection of ideas than as a coherent structure; it discovers preferences through action more than it acts on the basis of preferences'. Unclear technology means that the organization members do not understand the organization's production processes and that the organization operates on the basis of trial and error, 'the residue of learning from the accidents of the past' and 'pragmatic inventions of necessity'. When there is fluid participation, participants vary in the amount of time and effort they devote to different domains of decision-making (Cohen *et al.*, 1972, p. 1).

According to Cohen *et al.*, decision-making in organized anarchies is more like rationalizing after the fact than rational, goal-oriented planning. 'From this point of view, an organization is a collection of choices looking for problems, issues and feelings looking for decision situations in which they might be aired, solutions looking for issues to which they might be the answer, and decision-makers looking for work' (Cohen *et al.*, 1972, p. 2). They see educational organizations as likely candidates for this type of decision-making. In terms of coordination, organized anarchies have a fuzzy structure of authority and little capacity for standardization mechanisms.

Cohen *et al.* (1972) developed a computer simulation of garbage can decision-making. Generally speaking this model simulates the ways in which problems, decision-makers and solutions 'meet' as a function of the time of occurrence of choices, problems and solutions, as well as the energy participants can spend on a particular choice at a particular point in time and the energy that is required for a particular solution. The number of problems solved, and the total energy and time it takes to solve them, are then examined by comparing different structural arrangements. These are:

- The *decision structure*, the relationship between decision-makers and choices; e.g. there are hierarchical decisions when 'important', i.e low numbered, choices must be made by important decision-makers, and specialized decisions when each decision-maker is associated with a single choice and each choice has a single decision-maker.
- Three arrangements with respect to *energy distribution:* one in which important people spend less energy, another in which unimportant people spend less energy, and a third in which all decision-makers spend equal energy.
- *Net energy load*, defined as the difference between the total energy required to solve all problems and the total effective energy available to the organization over all time periods.
- The *access* structure, or the relation between problems and choices. Three types are distinguished: unsegmented access (any active problem has access to any active choice), specialized access (each problem has access to only one choice) and hierarchical access (important problems are accessible only to important choices, and vice versa).

Some illustrative findings of this computer simulation are that 'decision-making by flight and oversight is a major feature of the process in general'. When the net energy load increases, 'problems are less likely to be solved and choices are likely to take longer.' Access hierarchy (important problems meet important decision-makers) leads to the resolution of important problems more than unimportant ones. Choice failures that occur (i.e. decisions that are not made) 'are concentrated among the most important and less important choices'. The authors interpret this last outcome as illustrating the fate of organizations that 'do not know what they are doing', that proceed by undertaking trivial activities to keep up appearances and avoiding 'extraordinary violence to the domains of participants or to their model of what an organization should be' (Cohen *et al.*, 1972, p. 11).

Cohen *et al.*'s garbage can model is often treated as a provocative description of extremely poor decision-making. It should also be recognized, however, as an important methodological exercise in showing the merits of computer simulation of organizational problems, and as a substantive contribution to organizational theory. The garbage can model generates a lot of specific hypotheses amenable to empirical tests. The implicit message of the garbage can model with regard to the issue of school effectiveness is that schools could be run more efficiently if structural and procedural coordination were improved. The garbage can simulation model might be used further as an exploratory device; for instance, by introducing modifications that would allow more *a priori* knowledge and control over problems (e.g. by assigning higher probabilities of problem solution for certain decision-maker/problem/choice combinations).

Loosely Coupled Systems

The notion that organizational structures vary in the degree to which they need coordination is central in classical texts on organization theory. Thompson's (1967) distinction between 'pooled', 'serial' and 'reciprocal interdependence' of the elements of an organization's core technology is a case in point. Simon's (1964) concept of 'near decomposability' is another. The latter conveys the principle that complex systems will tend to decompose into sub-systems in such a way that interrelationships between sub-systems become minimized. In schools there are many instances of the least demanding form of interdependence, i.e. pooled coupling, when interdependence is limited to the sharing of common facilities. Although 'serial' interdependence is implied in the longitudinal planning of subject matter (for example, when pupils move from one grade to the next), the tightness of coupling varies according to the course subject and teacher habits.

Weick (1976) has used loosely coupled systems as a central construct to determine the specific nature of educational organizations. Weick uses loose coupling as a critique and a strong modification of the rational image of organizations (all-encompassing organizational goals, clear technology and a clearly formalized structure). Loose coupling expresses the notion that events or elements are somehow related, but at the same time separate or autonomous. Two broad classes of coupling mechanisms are those related to the functioning of the technical core of the organization on the one hand and those related to the authority of office on the other. In the latter case, the amount of discretionary power of teachers with respect to principals could be questioned. In the former case, a central question is whether the educational production function is explicitly determined; that is, whether or not established means–end relationships exist in the production of educational outcomes. Weick mentions the following elements of educational organizations, of which the tightness or looseness might be examined: intentions and actions, top and bottom, yesterday and tomorrow, administrators and teachers, means and ends ('frequently several different means lead to the same outcome'), teachers and materials, voters and school board, administrators and classroom, process and outcome, teacher–teacher, parent–teacher and teacher–pupil.

Weick is emphatic in stating that loose coupling has advantages and disadvantages and that it can be functional and dysfunctional, depending upon the particular context of specific organizations. Advantages of loose coupling are:

- flexibility of response, in the sense that some portions of the organization can adapt to environmental changes, while others persist as they are (this feature becomes dysfunctional when archaic traditions are perpetuated);
- the provision of a sensitive sensing mechanism, in that loosely coupled systems contain many semi-independent elements that can be externally constrained (a negative interpretation of this characteristic being a certain vulnerability to producing faddish responses);
- the possibility of localized adaptation, which, in principle, affords a loosely coupled system a strong potential for change and innovation;
- a breakdown in one portion of a loosely coupled system need not affect other parts of the organization (the negative aspect of this feature is that it is probably difficult to repair the defective element);
- there is room for self-determination by the actors, which might have a favourable effect on their sense of efficacy (of course, self-determination could also have negative effects, for instance where individual teachers remain unaffected by a sensible initiative for innovation at the school level);
- reduction of coordination costs in terms of money (overhead) and a reduction of conflicts; at the same time fund allocation (investment in coordination) will not be of much use as a means of change.

Weick's tentative answer to the question of what, given the loosely coupled character of educational organizations, keeps them together is that certification of teachers, a strict delineation of the recipients of education (i.e. the pupils) and inspection imply tighter coupling, while loose coupling is concentrated in the work processes. He further indicates that external conditions, such as competition for scarce resources, conflict and centralization in the national educational system, might force educational organization in the direction of tighter coupling.

An interesting implication of Weick's conception of loose coupling with respect to school effectiveness seems to be the realization that loose coupling has quite a few advantages for educational organizations. This means that the road to increased effectiveness does not simply run via more integrated educational organizations. Instead, more differentiated answers are needed to decide how much and in which part-systems of educational organization coordination is required. This point will be taken up further on, after discussion of a third organizational image relevant to the issue of coordination.

Schools as Professional Bureaucracies

Certain aspects of loose coupling as described by Weick, particularly the alleged adaptability and flexibility of sub-systems, do not seem to coincide with experiences in the field of educational innovation. In this respect Weick presents a differentiated picture, arguing that schools (or rather individuals within schools) might be open to adapting innovative ideas but that the actual implementation could be blocked by the features of loose coupling. The general experience is that it is difficult to change schools. The nature of the primary process in educational organizations as a conservative factor is somewhat underplayed in Weick's analysis. This aspect, the 'professional' nature of teachers' work, is the focus of another organizational image that sheds light upon the issue of coordination, namely, Mintzberg's (1979, p. 372) characterization of the school as a 'professional bureaucracy'.

The professional bureaucracy is depicted as a 'flat' structure, in which most of the power resides with the professionals in the operating core. Leadership in the professional bureaucracy is mostly to do with handling disturbance and performing maintenance and boundary-spanning tasks in order to 'buffer' the professional work. These buffering tasks are not supposed to be very spectacular since the environment is considered to be complex but stable. The major coordination mechanism within the professional bureaucracy is the standardization of skills acquired during a lengthy training period. Mintzberg (1979, p. 373) calls standardization of skills 'a loose coordinating mechanism at best, failing to cope with many of the needs that arise in the professional bureaucracy'. There is little room for interference of the leadership with the work of the professionals, nor is work-related interaction among the professionals common; they operate autonomously and resist rationalization of their skills. Consequently it is hard for educational administrators to control the work of the professionals even when cases of dysfunction are clear. Professionals oppose strict planning and external evaluation of their work.

The image of schools as professional bureaucracies explains the general resistance to change on the part of these organizations. Leadership, technological innovation and adaptation to environmental changes are not likely channels to make professionals alter their routines. The best approach to change, according to this organizational image, would be long-term alteration of the training programmes of teachers, with respect to teaching technologies and educational ideologies (for instance, when changing an orientation towards personal development into a more achievement-oriented attitude).

The professional bureaucracy explains why schools tend to be segmented organizations. When we are looking for organizational conditions that could help schooling to be more effective, the image of the professional bureaucracy can be seen as the null hypothesis. The message is that effective schools are those with a large percentage of effective teachers. Levers to enhance effectiveness should be sought by appealing to professional values and the mission of teaching, rather than through rationalization, technology or monetary incentives.

The descriptive 'entrance situation' of the organizational reality of schools has yielded some warnings with regard to the applicability of economical and technological approaches to enhancing effectiveness. This message should be borne in mind, but it should be realized that the models discussed, particularly the image of the professional bureaucracy, are ideal-type descriptions and thus prone to exaggeration.

With regard to coordination as a specific effectiveness-enhancing condition, a differentiated picture emerges. First and foremost, a simple answer, such as 'more integrated school organizations are better', must be rejected. Generally speaking an inverted U-shape relationship between coordination and achievement is more realistic, particularly when coordination costs are also considered, which they should be. Second, the advantage of loose coupling and the nature of professional work should provide some answers to the question of which type of coordination measures are expected to be more fruitful than others. In my opinion it follows that coordination of goals to arrive at an overall achievement-oriented school mission is of central importance, although difficult to achieve. Coordination via selective recruitment of teaching personnel is feasible. Coordination of work-related issues within sub-systems, such as departments, is likely to be more effective than overall coordination of work in larger secondary schools. At the school level, summative output control is more feasible and effective than process control, and environmental conditions leading to greater school autonomy and less environmental stability will enhance the possibility of instructional leadership – the same applies to major changes in educational technology (e.g. the intensive use of computers in schools). The null hypothesis with regard to the importance of organizational conditions for school effectiveness – namely that effective schools are no more (and no less) than aggregates of effective teachers – remains a very real challenge, since the image of the school as a professional bureaucracy underlines the disjointed nature of the production process in educational organizations.

THE NESTED LAYERS METAPHOR AND THE CARROLL MODEL

As Berliner (1985, p. 127) says: 'It is a reasonable belief to hold that effective teachers can exist outside exemplary schools but an exemplary school cannot exist without a large number of effective teachers.' In organizational models of the functioning of schools it was more or less understood that the technology of the primary production process was unclear. However, this view denies the existence of a large body of empirical evidence directed to the questions of instructional effectiveness: which approaches to teaching, classroom management and which characteristics of curricula and instructional media are generally effective? (See Part Two.) Although the fact that this knowledge base exists does not make the actual work processes in schools completely predictable (the idea of teacher-proof curricula is not viable), this base cannot be neglected when model-building and school effectiveness theory development are our concerns. On the contrary, models of effective instruction (including characteristics of curricula and teaching approaches) should be seen as the core of more encompassing models of school effectiveness. In this way educational organizations are seen as 'nested layers', a metaphor used by Purkey and Smith (1983) in their review article. The basic idea is that conditions of effective instruction (micro level) are constrained or facilitated by organizational conditions (meso level), which, in turn, could be constrained or facilitated by environmental conditions (macro level) (see also Bossert, 1988; Scheerens and Creemers, 1989).

Relationships between conditions at higher and lower levels can be interpreted in various ways:

1 As *contextual effects*, when the aggregates of certain favourable (or unfavourable) characteristics at the micro level are seen as having an additional causal

influence on achievement. For instance, Erbring and Young's (1979) model of endogenous feedback predicts that should a school have a majority of effective teachers and sufficient feedback among the staff, the minority of less effective teachers will be stimulated to become more effective.

2   Conditions at higher levels as *mirrors* of conditions at lower levels. As Berliner (1985, p. 143) notes: 'The evidence on effective classrooms and effective schools is amazingly congruent.' Features such as achievement pressure, high expectations, monitoring and an orderly atmosphere are found in studies of effective classrooms as well as in school effectiveness studies. Congruence between levels could create a consistent school culture.

3   Conditions at higher levels as *incentives* to provoke efficiency-enhancing conditions at lower levels. Teachers rewarded for effective teaching by their heads, and schools that receive monetary grants from their district if they reach certain achievement standards, are examples of this kind of incentive (see Purkey and Smith, 1985). Educational consumers demanding effective schooling is another type of external incentive.

4   Conditions at higher levels as *material facilities* for conditions at lower levels. An example is a computerized monitoring system implemented at the school level to provide teachers with more sophisticated means of monitoring student progress.

5   Conditions at higher levels as *overt measures* to create effectiveness-enhancing conditions at lower levels. Examples are increasing the allocated learning time, the recruitment of 'effective' teachers, the selection of teaching materials that have efficiency-enhancing characteristics, stimulating evaluations at classroom level, keeping records of pupils' progress, etc.

6   Conditions at higher levels as *buffers* against disturbances of efficiency-enhancing conditions at lower levels. Examples are 'maintenance' functions of school leaders like safeguarding sufficient student enrolments, providing occasions for informal contacts between teachers, making efficient use of governmental regulations, representational activities, etc.

The nested layers metaphor of school effectiveness should be given substance by using empirically tested models at the various aggregation levels. Ultimately, after formulating cross-level hypotheses, these various models or partial theories might be integrated to yield the basic structure of an overall causal model of school effectiveness (which then would probably need to be adapted to modifications with respect to context and population characteristics; see Chapter 5). In developing such a theory a 'bottom up' and 'inside out' perspective seems the best strategy. This would mean that the core of the theory should be a model of instructional conditions that stimulate student learning. The next basic question would be directed to the way organizational conditions at school level facilitate effectiveness-enhancing instructional conditions. The third elementary question would examine external incentives that could stimulate schools to acquire the characteristics that the second step would have revealed.

In the remaining part of this section the Carroll model will be discussed as a basic model of instructional effectiveness. Elaborations of the original model, particularly with respect to the factor 'quality of instruction', will also be referred to. Finally, some other pieces of theorizing with relevance for cross-level relationships within the framework of a nested layers structure will be examined.

The Carroll Model

The Carroll model consists of five classes of variables that are expected to explain variations in educational achievement. All classes of variables are related to the time required to achieve a particular learning task. The first three factors are directly expressed in terms of amounts of time. The two remaining factors are expected to have direct consequences for the amount of time that a student actually needs to achieve a certain learning task. The five classes of variables are:

- aptitude: variables that determine the amount of time a student needs to learn a given task under optimal conditions of instruction and student motivation;
- opportunity to learn: the amount of time allowed for learning;
- perseverance: the amount of time a student is willing to spend on learning the task or unit of instruction (the actual learning time is the smallest of these three time variables);
- quality of instruction: when the quality of instruction is sub-optimal, the time needed for learning is increased;
- ability to understand instruction: for example, language comprehension, the learners' ability to figure out independently what the learning task is and how to go about learning it (Carroll, 1963, 1989).

The model can be seen as a general, encompassing causal model of educational achievement. In a more recent attempt to formulate an encompassing model of educational productivity (Walberg, 1984) the basic factors of the Carroll model remained intact, while an additional category of environmental variables was included. Numerous research studies and meta-analyses have confirmed the validity of the Carroll model (see Chapter 5). The Carroll model has also been the basis for Bloom's concept of mastery learning (Bloom, 1968) and is related to 'direct instruction', as described by Rosenshine (1983). Characteristics of mastery learning are:

1 Clearly defined educational objectives.
2 Small discrete units of study.
3 Demonstration of competence before progress to later, hierarchically related units.
4 Remedial activities keyed to student deficiencies.
5 Criterion-referenced rather than norm-referenced tests (Block and Burns, 1970).

Direct instruction also emphasizes structuring the learning task, frequent monitoring and feedback and high levels of mastery (success rates of 90–100 per cent for initial tasks) in order to boost the self-confidence of the students.

The one factor in the original Carroll model that needed further elaboration was 'quality of instruction'. As Carroll pointed out himself in a 25-year retrospective of his model, the original formulation was not very specific about the characteristic of high-quality instruction, 'but it mentions that learners must be clearly told what they are to learn, that they must be put into adequate contact with learning materials, and that steps in learning must be carefully planned and ordered' (Carroll, 1989, p. 26).

The cited characteristics are to be seen as a further operationalization of this particular factor, which is of course one of the key factors (along with provision of optimal learning time) for a prescriptive use of the model. Incidentally, it should be noted that Carroll's reference to students who must be put into adequate contact with learning materials developed into a concept of 'opportunity to learn' different from his own. In Carroll's original formulation, opportunity to learn is identical to allocated learning time, while now opportunity to learn is mostly defined in terms of the correspondence between learning tasks and the desired outcomes. Synonyms for this more common interpretation of opportunity to learn are 'content covered' or 'curriculum alignment' (Berliner, 1985, p. 128). In more formal mathematical elaborations the variable 'prior learning' has an important place (Aldridge, 1983; Johnston and Aldridge, 1985).

Allocated learning time has been further specified in later conceptual and empirical work. Karweit and Slavin (1982), for instance, divide allocated learning time (the clock time scheduled for a particular class) into *procedural time* (time spent on keeping order, for instance), *instructional time* (subject matter related instruction) and *time on task* (the proportion of instructional time during which behaviour appropriate to the task at hand took place). Ability to understand instruction can be seen as the basis for further elaboration in the direction of learning to learn, meta-cognition, etc. The comprehensiveness of the Carroll model is shown by this potential to unite two schools of instructional psychology, the behaviouristically inclined structured teaching approaches and the cognitivist school (see Bruner, 1966; De Corte and Lowyck, 1983).

When the Carroll model is taken as the core of a larger, multi-level, theory of school effectiveness it is necessary to determine what conditions could be seen as antecedents of the five central factors of the model. A general answer might be the following. To avoid discussion of the degree to which intelligence is seen as amenable to schooling – in a way that is not absorbed in measuring progress in educational achievement – aptitude is taken as a genuine exogenous background variable. Allocated learning time (Carroll's opportunity to learn) and time on task are malleable characteristics that could be influenced by school policies for allocating time, the design of the school curriculum, characteristics of the school building (more or less distractions), homework policies and an orderly atmosphere. Perseverance could be stimulated by means of adaptive instruction, proper feedback, reinforcement, high expectations for achievement, exemplary behaviour of enthusiastic and motivated teachers, and attitudes in the peer group (endogenous feedback). Quality of instruction could be stimulated by reinforcing structured teaching by the school leadership (by means of recruitment policy, in-service training or professional supervision), the selection of adequate learning material, and the implementation of school-based evaluation and monitoring procedures. Ability to understand instruction could be enhanced by learning to learn programmes and by the development of meta-cognitive skills.

Expectations, Efficacy and Evaluative Potential

Several factors that have been proven to be significant in empirical school effectiveness studies – and that can be applied to the nested layers metaphor – are not directly implied in the Carroll model. These factors partly have to do with the 'soft' material of attitudes, values and school climate (expectations for student achievement, 'academic pressure', and teachers' sense of efficacy or academic futility). Evaluation can be seen as an essential prerequisite to effectiveness-enhancing measures at all levels. Contributions analysing these factors will be touched upon briefly.

The 'high expectations' variable that emerged from empirical studies has often evoked suspicion. As pointed out before, it was readily recognized that this variable was as much a cause as an effect of comparatively high achievement. Clauset and Gaynor (1982) and De Vos (1989) state that the perceived learning gap between student aptitude and achievement is the key factor in determining whether teachers' expectations are high or low. The former authors recognize the reciprocity of expectations and achievement. In their 'dynamic theory of schooling' the discrepancy between expected achievement and actual achievement is the vital factor in bringing about a positive chain of events leading to greater effectiveness.

The experience of an achievement gap by teachers can be activated directly, through efforts to raise teacher expectations, or indirectly, by interventions designed to raise achievement, thus causing teachers to adjust their expectations (Clauset and Gaynor, 1982, p. 57). To trigger these events, interventions at the level of school policy, the principal or the community are required. Examples of such measures are staff development to raise teacher expectations and improve teaching practices, policies to maximize the available time for instruction, and the setting and monitoring of explicit achievement standards.

De Vos (1989) uses the phenomenon of an achievement gap to explain the operation of established compositional or contextual effects (for instance, the finding that low-aptitude pupils achieve more when the average achievement in their learning group is higher). One of De Vos's central hypotheses is that an increase in the average achievement raises achievement expectations for all pupils, including those with less favourable entrance characteristics.

It is important to recognize that both approaches demonstrate that the soft world of expectations and the complexity of reciprocal relationships within educational organizations are amenable to formalized methods, from which specific empirical hypotheses can be generated.

The construct of efficacy, 'the individual's perceived expectancy of obtaining valued outcomes through personal effort' (Fuller *et al.*, 1982), is related to the personality trait of inner and outer directedness. The common element is the perceived (in)ability to change the relevant environment in a way that one values. However, efficacy is seen as a more situation-specific characteristic of individual functioning. Fuller *et al.* (1982) cite research results supporting the hypothesis that a teacher's sense of efficacy enhances student achievement. They also generate specific hypotheses about the way organizational efficacy conditions affect the performance of teachers, for instance in the relationship between superiors and subordinates:

> High differentiation between the role and tasks performed by the superordinate compared to the role and tasks performed by the subordinate is positively associated with the subordinate's performance efficacy ... Higher levels of convergence between subordinate and superordinate actors' beliefs in and commitment to priority goals and implementation means (tasks), are associated with high levels of performance efficacy ... of both actors ... When the subordinate actor perceives that evaluation of his/her program is soundly-based, the subordinate will hold a higher level of performance efficacy.
>
> (Fuller *et al.*, 1982, pp. 22–5)

The first hypothesis points at some of the subtleties that surround the operation of 'instructional leadership' in school organizations. The implication is that instructional leadership might only be effective if it is experienced as 'government at arm's length' and does not explicitly interfere with the domain of professional autonomy of teachers. The second hypothesis is in line with the frequently reported research result about the importance of a shared mission of the school. The third hypothesis raises some questions about the way teachers should judge whether or not evaluations are 'soundly based'. The literature on the use of evaluation results by decision-makers strongly suggests that interpretations of results are often biased to the extent that results are favourable or unfavourable (Weiss and Bucuvalas, 1980). The merit of the construct of teacher efficacy and the way it is linked to organizational conditions, as in the cited hypotheses, is again the fact that it is a helpful explanatory tool in making 'container constructs' such as the school climate more amenable to analysis, practice and further research.

The place of evaluation mechanisms within school effectiveness models is intriguing. It is no exaggeration to conclude that in all the theories and models discussed in this chapter proper evaluation emerges as an essential prerequisite to effectiveness, whereas unsound evaluation or no evaluation at all is associated with bad or even perverted organizational functioning. From the perspective of public choice theory a pessimistic view on evaluation mechanisms in public sector organizations emerges: at best evaluation could be a weak surrogate for control induced by the market mechanism. It is 'weak' because the way public choice theory describes these kinds of organizations lays bare all kinds of motives for 'political bias' in evaluation (like goal displacement among managers, self-protection of officers against accountability requirements and inabilities of governing bodies).

Unclear technology, i.e. insufficient information on the essential means–end relationships of an organization's primary process, is one of the basic postulates of the garbage can model of organizational choice. Feeding back information on successful problem–choice–solution combinations and allowing for conditions to 'use' this information in bringing about later combinations would alter the model in a fundamental way.

One of the most important phenomena of loose coupling is the 'zoning' (see Hanson, 1981) of administration and teaching. Output control by means of evaluation has been described as a more acceptable way of achieving tight coupling in schools than process control. The image of the professional bureaucracy explains teachers' resistance to evaluations as a conflict between professional autonomy on the one hand and formal authority and technocratic tendencies on the other. Evaluation and monitoring of student progress is one of the fundamental aspects of structured teaching or direct instruction, and thus one of the vital levers for improving the core technology of educational organizations. Finally, the presence or absence of proper evaluation appears to be central to constructs that have been introduced to make broad concepts like 'achievement-oriented culture' more amenable to analysis (e.g. the perceived gap between aptitude and actual achievement and the organizational context of individual efficacy).

On the basis of the centrality of evaluation to these various models of school effectiveness one might venture a central hypothesis with respect to enhancing organizational effectiveness: *organizations become more effective to the extent that evaluation mechanisms are improved and the coupling of evaluation results and incentives is enhanced.* Improving the quality of evaluation would help in improving the technology of educational organizations, stimulate the preservation of positive feedback loops that keep teachers' expectations high and provide a basis for adequate outside control (for instance, by providing educational consumers with more appropriate information).

The theories supporting this notion of the centrality of evaluation mechanisms in enhancing organizational effectiveness are also quite explicit about the sources of corruption of these mechanisms. Within the context of public policy-making, evaluations have been described as the ball that is being kicked between the various interested parties (Hofstee, 1982). Scheerens (1987) introduced the concepts of evaluability and evaluative potential. Evaluability refers to properties of the evaluation object. The degree to which outputs can be measured, *a priori* knowledge of the system's technology and the attitudes of people in the object situation are aspects of evaluability. Evaluative potential is a characteristic of the evaluator (or team of evaluators). Evaluation methodology, independence and evaluation management skills are basic aspects of this construct. When the evaluability is low, high investments should be made to ensure sufficient evaluative potential, making allowances for circumstances where any investment evaluation would be simply inefficient. The concept of evaluative potential could be used within the perspective of a nested layers image of schools, as a more encompassing way to describe evaluation as an effectiveness-enhancing condition.

SUMMARY AND CONCLUSIONS

As will become apparent from the summary of school effectiveness research findings in Part Two of this book the question of what 'works' in education has repeatedly been addressed in all types of educational research. A more fundamental explanation of the research findings by means of more general principles, models and theories is somewhat lacking in the disciplined enquiry into school effectiveness phenomena. Models and theories not only list certain educational 'treatments' that correlate positively with educational achievement but in addition are more explicit on the precise nature of the relationships between antecedent conditions and achievement. Ideally, these relationships should also be explained by more general principles. General principles that could explain the superiority of certain educational procedures and organizational arrangements as compared to others can be deduced from various theories and models in education and related disciplines. Public choice theory, originally developed in the field of political economy, deals with the alleged inefficiency of public sector organizations in a way that appears to be helpful in explaining some recurring findings in school effectiveness research, for instance the finding that private schools tend to outperform otherwise comparable public schools. Public choice theory also draws attention to the importance of review and evaluation procedures in enhancing organizational effectiveness.

Models of cooperation within organizations provide a lot of insight into the special way educational organizations function. Effective coordination of educational institutes requires a rather subtle treatment of the professional autonomy of individual teachers and a delicate balance between 'top-down' initiatives and the participation of all teachers in a shared 'mission' of the school.

A more research-based and 'inductive' approach to modelling school effectiveness uses the metaphor of school organizations as a set of nested layers: pupils within classrooms, teachers within schools, school managers acting in the larger context of local and national authorities and other relevant external parties, such as the consumers of education, teachers' unions etc. According to this perspective conditions for effective instruction, as have been summarized in models such as Carroll's, are the kernel of comprehensive school effectiveness models. Organizational arrangements are seen as both direct and indirect 'causes' of the performance of pupils. In the latter case it becomes paramount to determine how conditions for effective instruction at classroom level can be facilitated by organizational and curricular arrangements at school level. At the next level up the external incentives that may stimulate schools to be more achievement-oriented and effective are to be examined; for instance, achievement standards formulated at a higher administrative level or consumer demands.

Within the perspective of the nested layers metaphor patterns of standard setting and teachers' sense of efficacy may be examined. Evaluation mechanisms, finally, are seen as basic preconditions for organizational effectiveness; their relevance is apparent from all the theories and conceptual models that have been discussed in this chapter. From this observation a central hypothesis on enhancing organizational effectiveness may be formulated, which states that organizations become more effective to the extent that evaluation mechanisms are improved and the coupling of evaluation results and reformative action is made stronger.

After this review of the various partial theories and models that could explain aspects of school effectiveness, the conclusion that we are still in the 'bits and pieces' stage as far as a more integrated theory of school effectiveness is concerned is inescapable. Nevertheless, the models discussed have revealed fruitful areas for further conceptual elaboration and empirical research (with computer simulations and expert systems as useful mediators between conceptualization and 'new' data collection).

The main areas for further investigation are:

- the way incentives work in educational organizations;
- further refinement of already existing models of coordination in schools;
- organizational facilitators of conditions for effective instruction;
- optimization of the evaluative potential of educational organizations.

The elaboration of school effectiveness models and hypothetical explanations of the way they work also provides 'levers' for practical school improvement. Some of these levers were indicated in the discussion of the models in this chapter: changing the structure of incentives; introducing a well thought out balance between loose and tight coupling; creating school-wide conditions for effective instruction with supportive organizational measures; improving mechanisms of evaluation and feedback. These means of enhancing school effectiveness will be discussed further in the third part of this book, which deals with practical implications of school effectiveness research and theoretical conceptualization. But first, in Part Two, the actual research evidence on school effectiveness will be discussed.

PART TWO

RESEARCH

Chapter 3

Types of School Effectiveness Research

INTRODUCTION

When we interpret education as a goal-oriented process and school as an institution with a specific social purpose, it is no wonder that in nearly all areas of educational research, questions of effectiveness play a rather important role. One obvious question to be asked from a socially relevant as well as a scientifically interesting viewpoint is: what 'works' in education, whether this be concerned with developing national school curricula or with new methods for computer-assisted learning?

The various types of effectiveness studies that will be reviewed in this chapter thus reveal the entire gamut of educational approaches from sociological, economic, general pedagogic and psychological viewpoints. In view of the fact that this book is to do with *school* effectiveness, studies in which school characteristics are seen as having a possible influence on effectiveness are cited in particular. For reasons that will become clearer in the following chapters, due consideration will also be given to studies of factors influencing effectiveness within the school, such as characteristics of teachers, classrooms and teaching methods.

Five effectiveness-related areas of research will be examined:

1 Research on equality of opportunities in education and the significance of the school in this.
2 Economic studies of education production functions.
3 The evaluation of compensatory programmes.
4 Studies of effective schools and the evaluation of school improvement programmes.
5 Studies of the effectiveness of teachers, classes and instructional procedures.

In Table 3.1 certain general characteristics of these areas of research are reproduced. In the discussion of these five areas of research a general summary is given of the way in which the research was carried out and the most important study findings are broadly indicated.

SCHOOL EFFECTIVENESS IN EQUAL EDUCATIONAL OPPORTUNITY RESEARCH

Coleman's research into equal educational opportunity, about which a final report known as the Coleman Report was published in 1966, forms the cornerstone for school effectiveness studies (Coleman *et al.*, 1966). His Equal Educational Opportunity survey took place in no fewer than 4000 primary and secondary schools with data collected among 60,000 teachers and 600,000 pupils. While this study was intended to give a picture of the extent to which school achievement is related to pupils' ethnic and social background, the possible influence of the 'school' factor on learning attainment was also examined.

In the survey three clusters of school characteristics were measured: (a) teacher characteristics; (b) material facilities and curriculum; and (c) characteristics of the groups or classes in which the pupils were placed. Achievement was measured in the following areas: verbal skills, mathematical skills and, in higher grades, tests in practical knowledge, natural

Table 3.1 *General characteristics of types of school effectiveness research*

	Independent variable type	*Dependent variable type*	*Discipline*	*Main study type*
1 (Un)equal opportunities	Socio-economic status and IQ of pupil, material school characteristics	Attainment	Sociology	Survey
2 Production functions	Material school characteristics	Achievement level	Economics	Survey
3 Evaluation of compensatory programmes	Specific curricula	Achievement level	Interdisciplinary pedagogy	Quasi-experiment
4 Effective schools	'Process' characteristics of schools	Achievement level	Interdisciplinary pedagogy	Case study
5 Effective instruction	Characteristics of teachers, instruction, class organization	Achievement level	Educational psychology	Experiment, observation

sciences, social sciences and humanities. After the influence of ethnic origin and socio-economic status of the pupils had been statistically eliminated, it appeared that these three clusters of school characteristics together accounted for 10 per cent of the variance in pupil performance.[1] Moreover, the greater part of this 10 per cent variance was due to the third cluster, which was operationalized as the average background characteristics of pupils, meaning that again the socio-economic and ethnic origin – now defined at the level of the school – played a central role. In reactions to the Coleman Report there was general criticism of the limited interpretation of school characteristics. Usually, only the material characteristics were referred to, such as the number of books in the school library, the age of the building, the training of the teachers, their salaries and expenditure per pupil. Nevertheless, there were other characteristics included in Coleman's survey, such as the attitude of school heads and teachers to pupils and the attitude of teachers to integrated education, i.e. multi-racial and classless teaching. In Chapter 5 special consideration will be given to the question of how one should actually interpret school outcomes, such as the 10 per cent explained variance. In any case, at the time of the Coleman Report the relative unimportance of school characteristics compared to pupil background characteristics was strongly emphasized.

A study just as large was carried out after the publication of Coleman's report by Jencks *et al.* (1972). They re-analysed statistical data at national level (USA): the Coleman findings;

---

[1] The variance is a measure that indicates how far measurement scores of a test deviate from the mean. By studying how much deviations from the mean in one variable 'covary' with deviations in another variable, one comes to the statement that one variable explains variance of the other variable.

findings from a longitudinal study of more than 100 high schools; and data from numerous smaller studies. The conclusions read as follows:

1 Schools contribute little towards bridging the gap between rich and poor, able and less able pupils.
2 The quality of education received hardly affects the post-school careers of pupils, especially their future incomes.
3 School achievement is largely determined by one particular input factor and that is the family circumstances of a pupil. All other factors are of secondary importance and even irrelevant.
4 There are few indications that educational reforms like compensatory programmes can greatly redress cognitive inequality.
5 Taking the above into account, total economic equality, irrespective of intellectual capacity, can only be realized by means of a redistribution of incomes.

After re-analysing another 11 important studies, which included data on the relationship between schooling and career, seven years later Jencks *et al.* (1979) came to a similar conclusion.

In addition to Coleman's and Jencks's surveys into unequal opportunity, there are two other important American school career studies that should be mentioned, in which attention was given, indirectly, to school characteristics. While these were commonly billed as educational attainment studies, here too the influence of social class and ethnic origin on school career was closely looked at. The surveys were centred around two longitudinal data files: the Explorations in Equality of Opportunity Survey and the Wisconsin Longitudinal Study of Social and Psychological Factors. The first-mentioned file included school characteristics related to differentiation and internal selection procedures (track placement). According to the authors, these internal selection policies were important for pupils' careers (Alexander and Eckland, 1980). Analysis of the second file focused on the influence of school characteristics in the sense of contextual factors, such as the average socio-economic status of pupils. Hauser *et al.* (1976) concluded that the influence of these contextual effects – after individual pupils' background characteristics, such as socio-economic status and intelligence, had been taken into account – was slight.

In conclusion, there is one other survey that falls into this category of large-scale studies of school careers and the environmental background of pupils (Thorndike, 1973). This was an international comparative study (15 countries) in which reading comprehension was the main achievement variable. The survey was conducted as one of the projects of the International Association for the Evaluation of Educational Achievement. The school and class characteristics in this study included not only the more material factors of the Coleman survey that had aroused criticism, but also variables like individualized instruction and the use of reading tests. The results of this survey were, however, to a great extent in keeping with the previously mentioned findings: a relatively high correlation between socio-economic family characteristics and learning attainment, and an insignificant influence from school and instruction characteristics.

In summary, the following points may be raised about this research tradition:

1 Unequal opportunity, that is to say the limitations imposed by environment on learning attainment, was central, and this explanation for differences in achievement between pupils and schools was strongly borne out by the findings.
2 The school characteristics chosen were usually – though not in all cases – limited to material input factors, and appeared to account for little variance in individual pupil attainment.

3 Questions that should be asked about this study area, especially when one is particularly interested in school characteristics, are:

- how one should interpret the range of school effects found;
- whether or not the inclusion of school characteristics that would have been more like throughputs would have led to different results;
- critical questions regarding the analysis techniques employed (see, for example, Aitkin and Longford, 1986).

These questions will be addressed in this and other chapters. Incidentally, studies on inequality of opportunity largely similar to the Wisconsin longitudinal survey have been carried out in the Netherlands (Dronkers, 1978, for example). Another Dutch longitudinal study, that from Meijnen (1984), will be discussed in a later chapter.

ECONOMIC RESEARCH INTO EDUCATION PRODUCTION FUNCTIONS

The focus of economic approaches to school effectiveness is on the manipulative inputs that can increase outputs. If there was stable knowledge available on the extent to which variety of inputs is related to variety of outputs it would also be possible to specify a function that is characteristic of the production process in schools – in other words, a function that could accurately indicate how a change in the inputs would affect the outputs.

This leads to a research tradition that is identified as 'input–output studies' or as 'research into education production functions'. In theory the research model for economic production studies hardly differs from that for other types of effectiveness research: the relationship between manipulative school characteristics and attainment is studied, while the influence of background conditions like social class and pupils' intelligence is eliminated as far as possible. The specific nature of economic production research is a concentration on what can be interpreted in a more literal sense as input characteristics: the teacher–pupil ratio, teacher training, teacher experience, teachers' salaries and expenditure per pupil. In more recent research of this type it is suggested that effectiveness predictors used in educational psychology research be taken into account (Hanushek, 1986). It should be noted that the Coleman Report is often also included in the category of input–output studies. In view of its emphasis on the more material school characteristics, the association is an obvious one.

The findings of this type of research may be called disappointing. Review studies like those of Mosteller and Moynihan (1972), Averch *et al.* (1974), Glasman and Biniaminov (1981) and Hanushek (1979, 1986) always produce the same conclusions: inconsistent findings throughout the entire available research and, at most, little effect from the relevant input variables. To illustrate, Table 3.2 is reproduced here from Hanushek's review study (1986) summarizing the findings of 147 studies on education production functions.

From Table 3.2 it appears that only 'teacher experience' shows some consistency across studies – 30 per cent of the estimated coefficients are statistically significant. Hanushek's general conclusion is, however, that there is currently no correlation between educational expenditure and attainment. According to Hanushek, only if the differences between schools in these sorts of inputs were considerably greater than they are at present could a clear effect of these factors be expected. Thus class size now varies from about 15 to 40 pupils; an effect of the class size factor would only appear if the range varied from, say, 10 to 300 pupils. Teachers' salaries is another example. In most countries these are linked to strict regulations governing training and years of experience. Implementing a system of 'merit pay' would no doubt create a wider discrepancy, and thus a significant correlation with attainment might appear.

Table 3.2   *A review of 147 input–output studies*
A + indicates a positive correlation while a − indicates a negative correlation between input and output variables. Based on Hanushek (1986, p. 1161)

Input	Statistically significant			Statistically insignificant		
	Number of studies	+	−	*Total insignificant*	+	−
Teacher–pupil ratio	112	9	14	89	25	43
Teacher training	106	6	5	95	26	32
Teacher experience	109	33	7	69	32	22
Teachers' salaries	60	9	1	50	15	11
Expenditure per pupil	65	13	3	49	25	13

THE EVALUATION OF COMPENSATORY PROGRAMMES

Compensatory programmes may be seen as the active branch in the field of equal educational opportunity. In the United States, compensatory programmes like Head Start were part of President Johnson's 'war on poverty'. Other large-scale American programmes were Follow Through – the sequel to Head Start – and special national development programmes that resulted from Title 1 of the Elementary and Secondary Education Act, enacted in 1965. Compensatory programmes were intended to improve the levels of performance of the educationally disadvantaged. In the late 1960s and early 1970s there were also similar programmes in the Netherlands, including the Amsterdam Innovation project, the Playgroup Experiment project, Rotterdam's Education and Social Environment (OSM) project and the Differentiated Education project (GEON) of the city of Utrecht.

Compensatory programmes manipulate school conditions in order to raise achievement levels of disadvantaged groups of pupils. The level to which this is achieved demonstrates the importance of the school factor – and in particular the conditions and educational provisions within it. However, it proved to be not that simple to redress the balance with effective compensatory programmes. In fact no overwhelming successes could be established. There was heated debate on the way available evaluation studies should be interpreted.

The key question is: what results can be realistically expected from compensatory education given the dominant influence in the long run of family background and cognitive aptitudes on pupils' attainment level? Scheerens (1987, p. 95) concluded that the general image provided by the evaluation of compensatory programmes reveals that relatively little progress in performance and cognitive development can be established immediately after a programme finishes. ('Relatively little progress' means an average progress of one-quarter to one-half of a standard deviation on the effect variable.) Long-term effects of compensatory programmes cannot usually be established although studies and meta-analyses give a somewhat divided picture in this respect.[2] Moreover, it has been occasionally demonstrated that it was the 'moderately' disadvantaged in particular that benefited from the programmes, while the most educationally disadvantaged made the least progress, relatively speaking. In view of the variety of compensatory programmes the evaluation studies gave some insight into the best type of educational provision. When the various components of Follow Through were compared, programmes aimed at developing elementary skills, like language and mathematics, using highly structured methods turned out to be winners (Stebbins *et al.*, 1977; Bereiter and Kurland, 1982; Haywood, 1982).

As will be seen later, there is a remarkable similarity between these findings and the findings of other types of effectiveness research. In any case, when interpreting the results of evaluations of compensatory programmes one should be aware that the findings have been established among a specific pupil population: very young children (infants or first years of junior school) from predominantly working-class families.

EFFECTIVE SCHOOLS RESEARCH AND THE EVALUATION OF SCHOOL IMPROVEMENT PROGRAMMES

Research labelled as 'identifying unusually effective schools' or the 'effective schools movement' can be regarded as the type of research that most touches the core of school effectiveness research. All other research areas that are mentioned here essentially have a focus of interest other than the effectiveness of school as a whole, that is to say the effectiveness of characteristics that can be defined at school level. In Coleman's and Jencks's surveys the inequality of educational opportunity was the central problem. In economic input–output studies the school was even conceived as a 'black box'. During the evaluation of compensatory programmes the concern was for the effect of these particular programmes. In research on the effectiveness of classes, teachers and instruction methods, education characteristics on a lower aggregation level than the school are the primary research object. Effective schools research is only lightly covered in this chapter because it is dealt with at some length in the next two chapters.

Effective schools research is generally regarded as a response to the results of studies like Coleman's and Jencks's from which it was concluded that schools did not matter very much when it came to differences in levels of achievement. From titles such as *Schools Can Make a Difference* (Brookover *et al.*, 1979) and *School Matters* (Mortimore *et al.*, 1988) it appears that refuting this message was an important source of inspiration for this type of research. The most important distinguishing feature of effective schools research was its attempt to break open the 'black box' of the school by studying characteristics related to the organization, form and content of schools. As far as practical research goes, a few main types of effective school studies may be distinguished.

First, there are studies that identify schools that, despite the starting characteristics of the pupil population, display an exceptionally favourable output. These schools are then examined to see what distinguishes them from schools with an unfavourable output. A second category of effective schools research was made possible by the influence the first sort had on education practice: the findings of studies of exceptionally effective schools were adopted with great dispatch for school improvement programmes. Against this background, evaluating the programmes naturally produces extremely useful data on the question of which school

---

[2] For instance, researchers belonging to the Consortium for Longitudinal Studies report sustained effects of early intervention programmes like Project Head Start (Lazar *et al.*, 1982), while Mullin and Summers (1983) conclude from a meta-analysis of 47 studies that the evidence is fairly strong that early gains are not sustained.

characteristics are important for improving performance level. A third, fairly recent, research category can be distinguished, in which on a somewhat larger scale a study is made of the school characteristics related to achievement level. This last category integrates the models of the various research areas discussed in this chapter. Examples are Mortimore *et al.* (1988) and Brandsma and Knuver (1988).

Effective schools research findings appear to converge on five factors:

- strong educational leadership;
- emphasis on acquiring basic skills;
- an orderly and secure environment;
- high expectations of pupil attainment;
- frequent assessment of pupil progress.

In the literature this summary is sometimes identified as the 'five-factor model of school effectiveness'. It should be mentioned that effective schools research has been largely carried out in primary schools, in inner cities and in predominantly working-class neighbourhoods.

STUDIES OF THE EFFECTIVENESS OF TEACHERS AND TEACHING METHODS

The topic of this book is school effectiveness. The teaching techniques that occur within a school can best be studied at the teacher and individual classroom level. Study of the effectiveness of teaching techniques thus takes place on a different level from study of school effectiveness. Nevertheless, attention is given here to studies of effective instruction because the impact of effectiveness-promoting school characteristics on pupil performance largely happens via class teaching techniques. This is indicated as a step-by-step, causal process in Figure 3.1.

In Figure 3.1, C expresses the fact that school characteristics can also directly influence performance. The thinking behind this approach to school and teaching effectiveness is elaborated upon in Chapters 5 and 6. As an illustration, the often-found research result establishing the favourable effect of frequent assessment of pupils' progress can be referred to. In the first instance this is a matter that takes place at class level (the influencing connection is arrow B in Figure 3.1). Evaluation at class level can also be highly stimulated when importance is ascribed to assessment at school level – in other words when a certain policy priority is adhered to. Another evaluation-promoting condition at school level could be a pupil monitoring system or a so-called 'test–service system' for the entire school (represented by arrow A in Figure 3.1). Finally, it is conceivable that, as part of his or her management duties in running a school, the school head – with or without the help of a testing system – checks on the progress of pupils in various classes from time to time (this is an example of relation C in Figure 3.1).

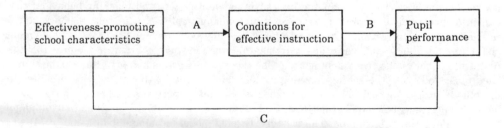

Figure 3.1 A step-by-step casual process with school and instruction conditions as manipulable factors

A review of study findings within the field of effective teaching could easily fill a separate book. Here, only a short review of various approaches to research on teaching and a review of meta-analyses findings will be given.

A Review of Approaches to Research on Teaching

In the 1960s and 1970s the effectiveness of certain personal characteristics of teachers was studied. Medley and Mitzel (1963), Rosenshine and Furst (1973) and Gage (1965) are among those who reviewed the research findings. From these it emerged that there was hardly any consistency between personal characteristics of the teacher, such as warm-heartedness or inflexibility, and pupil achievement. In studies of teaching styles (Davies, 1972), the behavioural repertoire of teachers was generally looked at more than the deeply rooted aspects of their personality. Within the framework of 'research on teaching' there followed a period in which much attention was given to observation of teacher behaviour during lessons. The results of these observations, however, in so far as they were related to pupil achievement, seldom revealed a link with pupil performance (see Lortie, 1973, for instance). In a following phase more explicit attention was given to the relation between observed teacher behaviour and pupil achievement. This research is identified in the literature as 'process–product studies'. Lowyck, quoted by Weeda (1986, p. 68), summarizes variables that emerged 'strongly' in the various studies:

1 Clarity: clear presentation adapted to suit the cognitive level of pupils.
2 Flexibility: varying teaching behaviour and teaching aids, organizing different activities, etc.
3 Enthusiasm: expressed in verbal and non-verbal behaviour of the teacher.
4 Task-related and/or businesslike behaviour: directing the pupils to complete tasks, duties, exercises, etc. in a businesslike manner.
5 Criticism: much negative criticism has a negative effect on pupil achievement.
6 Indirect activity: taking up ideas, accepting pupils' feelings and stimulating self-activity.
7 Providing the pupils with an opportunity to learn criterion material: that is, a clear correspondence between what is taught in class and what is tested in examinations and assessments.
8 Making use of stimulating comments: directing the thinking of pupils to the question, summarizing a discussion, indicating the beginning or end of a lesson, emphasizing certain features of the course material.
9 Varying the level of both cognitive questions and cognitive interaction.

Weeda (1986, p. 69) observes that in the study from which these nine teaching characteristics were drawn there was much criticism regarding methodology/technique. He divides the later research studies focused on instructional effectiveness into two areas: (a) pedagogic studies aimed at tracing certain environmental factors and teaching behaviour that can influence levels of performance of certain groups of pupils; (b) instructional psychology research aimed at establishing the interaction between teaching variables and pupil characteristics; the so-called aptitude–treatment interaction studies. A central factor within the first area is that of effective teaching time. The theoretical starting points of this can be traced back to Carroll's (1963) teaching–learning model. Chief aspects of this model, as were cited in Chapter 2, are: (a) actual net learning time, as a result of perseverance and opportunity to learn; (b) necessary net learning time, as a result of pupil aptitude, quality of education and pupil ability to understand instruction. The mastery learning model formulated by Bloom (1976) was largely inspired from Carroll's model.

The findings of the aptitude–treatment interaction (ATI) studies were generally judged to be disappointing. There were scarcely any interactions discovered, which was later confirmed by a replication study. De Klerk (1985) regarded the fact that the ATI had failed to reveal any simple interaction between pupil characteristics and instruction methods as a challenge to carry out more refined empirical research on more complex interaction patterns.

The Findings of Reviews and Meta-analysis

Stallings (1985) summarized research literature on effective instruction – in so far as it was concerned with primary education – under the headings effective net learning time, class organization and management, instruction, assessment and teacher expectations. In studies of net learning time it emerged that simply making the school day longer did not necessarily lead to better levels of performance. More important, ultimately, is how effectively time is spent. Stallings and Mohlman (1981) established that effective teachers spent 15 per cent of the school day on organization and management, 50 per cent on interactive teaching and 35 per cent on monitoring pupils' work. Aids to effective use of instruction time include all types of lesson planning. Under the classification *class organization and management*, Stallings discusses streaming and maintaining order. Studies on streaming or working with ability groups indicate that this type of teaching works more positively with the more gifted pupils, and that with less able groups – taking the average result of the large numbers of surveys – hardly any effect was found (see also Kulik and Kulik, 1982; Van Laarhoven and De Vries, 1987). Moreover, from various types of studies it emerges that in classes where there is disruptive behaviour, pupil performance is lower; disruption, naturally enough, is at the cost of effective learning time.

The question of what makes good teaching should be looked at on different levels. Direct question-and-answer type knowledge requires different teaching strategies from problem-solving and insight. For learning tasks that greatly depend on memory, a highly ordered and consistent approach is the most effective. For acquiring insight a clear presentation of the information offered is important, as are questions to check whether pupils have actually absorbed a specific insight. With regard to problem-solving, some empirical evidence shows that it is desirable for pupils to take a lot of initiative themselves. Collins and Stevens (1982) mention five teaching strategies to support the learning of problem-solving: (a) a systematic variation of examples; (b) counter-examples; (c) entrapment strategies; (d) hypothesis identification strategies; (e) hypothesis evaluation strategies.

From studies of *teacher assessments and expectations* of pupils it seems that self-fulfilling prophecies can occur. If a teacher has formed negative expectations of certain pupils he or she is likely to give them less attention and expose them less to more difficult and challenging tasks. Obviously this is even more of a disadvantage if the initial assessment was a wrong one. Thus it is imperative that teachers should try to avoid negative stereotyping of pupils.

In a review of the literature on effective teaching at *secondary school level*, Doyle (1985) deals broadly with the same category as Stallings's, namely 'time on task' and 'quality of instruction'. Because in secondary education the total teaching spectrum from which a choice must be made is far greater than in primary education, the variable 'opportunity to learn' is associated here with the concept of effective net learning time. 'Opportunity to learn' is generally understood to mean that pupils are offered a range of subjects and tasks that cover educational goals. In educational research, opportunity to learn concentrates on the extent to which classroom exercises correspond with the content of the tests for monitoring performance.

As far as the quality of instruction is concerned, there is a stronger emphasis in secondary education on learning higher cognitive processes, such as insight, flexible adoption of knowledge and problem-solving. Doyle considers the effectiveness of direct teaching, which he defines as follows:

1   Teaching goals are clearly formulated.
2   The course material to be followed is carefully split into learning tasks and placed in sequence.
3   The teacher explains clearly what the pupils must learn.
4   The teacher regularly asks questions to gauge what progress pupils are making and whether they have understood.
5   Pupils have ample time to practise what has been taught, with much use being made of 'prompts' and feedback.
6   Skills are taught until mastery of them is automatic.
7   The teacher regularly tests the pupils and calls on the pupils to be accountable for their work.

The question of whether this type of highly structured teaching works equally well for the acquisition of complicated cognitive processes in secondary education can be answered in the affirmative (according to Brophy and Good, 1986, p. 367). However, progress through the subject matter can be taken with larger steps, testing need not be so frequent and there should be space left for applying problem-solving strategies flexibly. Doyle also emphasizes the importance of varying the learning tasks and creating intellectually challenging learning situations. For the latter an evaluative climate in the classroom, where daring to take risks even with a complicated task is encouraged, is a good means. In addition, Doyle deals with the effect of certain ways of working and grouping, including individual teaching and working together in small groups. Bangert *et al.*'s meta-analysis (1983) revealed that individual teaching in secondary education hardly led to higher achievement and had no influence whatsoever on factors like the self-esteem and attitudes of pupils.

Evaluation studies of special programmes to stimulate working in small groups reveal that some of these have a positive effect on lower-attaining pupils. Generally speaking, from other reviews of research on the effects of cooperative learning it appears that there is no conclusive empirical evidence to support the positive influence of this type of work on performance. Vedder (1985) explained the lack of an unequivocal positive influence of group work by the possible fact that the way in which pupils work together allows for insufficient cognitive stimulation.

In concluding this review of study findings on instruction effectiveness the results of research syntheses carried out by Herb Walberg will briefly be given. In an article in *Educational Leadership*, the results of a meta-analysis of thousands of individual studies were presented. These findings are summarized in Tables 3.3, 3.4 and 3.5. Fraser *et al.* (1987) gave a synthesis of 134 meta-analyses, which together comprised 7827 individual studies. Some of their findings are summarized in Table 3.6. Specific variables included in the main categories in Table 3.6 that correlate highly with achievement are: quality of teaching, $r = 0.47$; amount of instruction, $r = 0.38$; cognitive background characteristics, $r = 0.49$; feedback, $r = 0.30$.

A remarkable conclusion that Walberg draws from the research syntheses he carried out is the statement that the findings apply to all types of schools and all types of pupils. Walberg expresses this in the saying, 'what's good for the goose is good for the gander'. He does add that this especially applies to the more powerful factors (that is, the factors that correlate the most with levels of performance). When we look at these powerful factors, for instance the top five listed in Table 3.3, and the teaching methods and learning strategies that scored highest in Fraser *et al.*'s meta-analysis, it seems that highly structured learning or direct teaching, which emphasizes testing and feedback, again emerges as the most effective teaching form. Yet in Walberg's research syntheses forms of individual teaching and teaching adapted to fit the specific needs of pupils, as well as working together in small groups, come quite strongly to the fore. He even supports 'open teaching', in which cooperation, critical thinking, self-confidence and a positive attitude are important objectives. His own and other meta-analyses reveal that

Qer Source.

Table 3.3 *The effectiveness of teaching methods*

Method	Result
Reinforcement (reward and punishment)	1.17
Special programmes for the educationally gifted	1.00
Structured learning of reading	0.97
Cues and feedback	0.97
Mastery learning of physics	0.81
Working together in small groups	0.76
Experimental teaching of reading	0.60
Individual pupil instruction	0.57
Adaptive teaching	0.45
Tutoring	0.40
Individual maths teaching	0.35
Posing meaningful questions	0.34
Diagnostic methods	0.33
More individual teaching	0.32
Individual maths teaching	0.32
New physics programmes	0.31
Teacher expectations	0.28
Computer-assisted learning	0.24
Step-by-step constructed lessons	0.24
Advance planning of lesson material	0.23
New maths programmes	0.18
Biology lessons with pupils doing their own research	0.16
Streaming	0.10
Class size	0.09
Programmed learning	−0.03
Streaming pupils	−0.12
Teaching time	−0.32

Based on Walberg (1984). The size of effectiveness is reproduced in tenths of one standard deviation.

Table 3.4 *The influence of the family, peer group, class and media on achievement*

Method	Result
Homework that is checked	0.79
Class morale	0.60
The involvement of the family with homework	0.50
Home situation	0.37
Homework assignments	0.28
Socio-economic status	0.25
Peer group	0.24
Watching television	−0.05

Based on Walberg (1984). Results are reproduced as correlations.

Table 3.5 *The influence of background characteristics of pupils*

Characteristic	Result
Intelligence	0.71
Development (in stages as differentiated by Piaget)	0.47
Motivation	0.34
Self-concept	0.18

Based on Walberg (1984). Results are reproduced as correlations.

Table 3.6 *Effects of teaching and pupil characteristics on performance tests*

Factor	Result (correlations)
School characteristics	0.12
Social background characteristics of pupils	0.19
Teacher characteristics	0.21
Teaching characteristics	0.22
Pupil characteristics	0.24
Instruction method	0.14
Learning strategies	0.28

Based on Fraser *et al.* (1987)

open teaching has no adverse consequences for cognitive achievement, while there is a positive influence on creativity, social behaviour and independence. In the meta-meta-analysis of Fraser *et al.* individualizing emerged as a less powerful factor ($r = 0.07$).

No matter how impressive the huge data files upon which the research syntheses are based may be, there are limitations to the findings. Every time simple correlations are presented it cannot be ruled out that a particular correlation reflects the influence of a third variable, which in these simple analyses cannot be made visible. This problem exists partly because it can be assumed that many of the individual effectiveness predictors are correlated among themselves. And where this problem applies to the general analyses it can by no means be assumed that this is not also the case with many of the individual studies upon which the syntheses are based.

Finally, with regard to this survey of instructional effectiveness it must again be pointed out that within the scope of this book only a broad summing up of the most important research findings is possible. Even if the conclusion is that a few prominent characteristics of effective teaching can be distinguished – the amount of instruction and a structured approach – that apply to any given teaching situation, it should certainly not be forgotten that with a less general treatment all types of nuances exist that are linked to differences in subjects taught, pupil characteristics, school type and educational goals. For a review in which these nuances are well expressed see Brophy and Good (1986).

SUMMARY AND CONCLUSIONS

Five types of educational effectiveness research were discussed in this chapter. The fact that various sub-disciplines of educational science all address effectiveness questions indicates the centrality of these questions in educational enquiry as a whole. The five effectiveness-related areas of research examined in this chapter were:

1 Research on equality of opportunity in education and the significance of the school in this.
2 Economic studies of education production functions.
3 The evaluation of compensatory programmes.
4 Studies of effective schools and the evaluation of school improvement programmes.
5 Studies of the effectiveness of teachers, classes and instruction procedures.

The first two research traditions focused on 'material' school characteristics (such as teacher salaries, building facilities and teacher/pupil ratio). The results were rather disappointing in that no substantial positive correlations of these material investments and educational achievement could be established in a consistent way across individual studies.

In-depth process studies connected with large-scale evaluations of compensatory programmes pointed out that programmes which used direct, i.e. structured, teaching approaches were superior to more 'open' approaches.

The research movement known as 'research on exemplary effective schools' (or, briefly, effective schools research) focused more on the internal functioning of schools than the earlier tradition of input–output studies (summarized under 1 and 2 in the list above). These studies produced evidence that factors like strong educational leadership, emphasis on basic skills, an orderly and secure climate, high expectations of pupil achievement and frequent assessment of pupil progress were indicative of unusually effective schools.

Research results in the field of instructional effectiveness are centred on three major factors: effective learning time, structured teaching and opportunity to learn in the sense of a close alignment between items taught and items tested.

Although all kinds of nuances and specificities should be taken into account when interpreting these general results they appear to be fairly robust, as far as educational setting and type of students is concerned. The overall message is that an emphasis on basic subjects, an achievement-oriented focus, an orderly school environment and structured teaching, which includes frequent assessment of progress, is effective in the attainment of learning results in the basic school subjects. In the next chapters more specific information will be given about the research findings and the way they should be interpreted.

Chapter 4

A Closer Look at School Effectiveness Research

INTRODUCTION

In Chapter 3 I dealt with the various trends in educational effectiveness research; in this chapter educational effectiveness studies that specifically look at the effects of the factor school and individual school characteristics will be more closely considered. This school effectiveness research has most in common with the type referred to in Chapter 3 as 'studies on effective schools and the evaluation of school improvement programmes'. The term school effectiveness research implies a much broader spectrum of types of study than 'studies on effective schools'. In the latter, exceptionally high-achieving schools are identified and then examined to see what characteristics distinguish them from lower-attaining schools. Here, the term school effectiveness research is used not only for this type of study, but also for studies that investigate, using a random sample of schools, (a) whether there are differences in achievement and (b) whether these differences can be attributed to specific characteristics. Thus several research types discussed in Chapter 3 are incorporated. In actual research practice, all sorts of hybrids are also encountered. Recently developed techniques for multi-level research make it quite possible to include in one study both school characteristics and classroom (instruction) characteristics as effectors of achievement.

In this chapter a number of existing review studies of school effectiveness research are summarized, and then a schematic description of twelve fairly well known British and American effectiveness studies is given. In Appendix 1 four studies are closely focused upon to show in more concrete terms how school effectiveness research is designed and which problems are encountered. Obviously, apart from these research-methodological aspects, each section gives much attention to the substantive results that the review studies and individual projects revealed. Next, a schematic overview is given of twelve Dutch school effectiveness studies. These studies are described in more detail in Appendix 2. In the concluding section an assessment is made of the state of the art of school effectiveness research.

A REVIEW OF REVIEW STUDIES

With regard to school effectiveness research it has sometimes been jokingly remarked that there have been more reviews published than actual original study reports. Certainly when the quality of the studies under review is looked at this is not altogether far from the truth: the number of empirical school effectiveness studies from which generalized conclusions can be drawn is still rather modest. English-language review articles include Anderson (1982), Cohen (1982), Dougherty (1981), Edmonds (1979), Murmane (1981), Neufeld *et al.* (1983), Purkey and Smith (1983), Rutter (1983), Good and Brophy (1986), Ralph and Fennessey (1983), Kyle (1985), Sweeney (1982), Borger *et al.* (1984) and Levine and Lezotte (1990). Reviews in Dutch have been produced by, among others, Van der Grift (1987) and Scheerens and Stoel (1987). In what follows, I will strongly draw upon the influential review article of Purkey and Smith (1983) and the research synthesis of Borger *et al.* (1984).

Purkey and Smith distinguish four types of school effectiveness research: studies among so-called outliers, that is to say among extremely high- or extremely low-attaining schools; case studies; evaluations of school improvement programmes; and 'other studies'.

Outlier Studies

In the study of outliers a school is first looked at to see whether it has performed better or worse than one would assume on the basis of the characteristics of the pupil population. By means of regression analysis one is able to tell which pupil background characteristics affect achievement, on the basis of which one is then able to predict the achievement level of the school. If a school clearly comes out above this predicted level, it is assumed this is because of specific structural, curriculum or teaching characteristics. Purkey and Smith (1983) discuss nine outlier studies, all related to primary schools. While results vary from one to another, it appears that many similarities can also be found. The prevailing common effectiveness characteristics were good discipline, teachers' high expectations regarding pupils' performance and an emphasis on educational leadership (a school head who is actively involved with stimulating and monitoring activities related to teaching, rather than simply acting as an administrator or business manager). However, the interpretation of these results is undermined by weak research techniques, such as very small samples (between two and twelve schools) and shortcomings in the identification procedure of the outliers (because the effects of important background characteristics like socio-economic status were insufficiently neutralized). There is also criticism of the comparison criterion of the outlier studies. By comparing extremely 'good' schools with extremely 'weak' ones the effects of the school differences are magnified out of proportion; in this context it is better to compare the more positive respondents with the average schools. It can also be added that whenever the effectiveness of extreme schools is compared over several points in time, one is almost sure to find minor effects in later measurements as a result of the regression-towards-the-mean phenomenon.[1]

Case Studies

The seven case studies used by Purkey and Smith (1983) include well-known ones such as those of Weber (1971), Brookover et al. (1979) and Rutter et al. (1979). (An eighth study discussed by Purkey and Smith is ignored here because this was, in fact, an evaluation study.) It should be remarked that classifying Brookover et al.'s research project as a case study does not do it justice: no fewer than 159 schools were involved here!

The school factors that emerged from these case studies as positively influencing effectiveness are summarized in Table 4.1. There was little consistency in the standards used to decide whether or not a factor could be considered important. Sometimes this only rested on the subjective opinion of the researchers, without any kind of quantitative basis.

---

[1] The regression-towards-the-mean phenomenon appears whenever two groups are selected on the basis of unreliable measurements. Certainly as far as extremely high- or low-scoring groups are concerned, during selection (because of the unreliable nature of the measurements) capitalizing on chance will occur.

Table 4.1 *The most important school characteristics that emerged from seven case studies*

	Author						
	Weber	Venesky and Winfield	Glenn	Cal. State	Brookover and Lezotte	Brookover et al.	Rutter et al.
No. of schools	4	2	4	–	8	159	12
Strong leadership	X		X	X		X	
Orderly climate	X		X				X
High expectations	X		X	X	X	X	X
Frequent evaluation	X		X	X			
Achievement-oriented policy		X		X		X	X
Cooperative atmosphere		X	X				X
Clear goals for basic skills			X		X		
In-service training/staff development		X		X			
Time on task					X	X	X
Reinforcement						X	X
Streaming						X	X

From Purkey and Smith (1983).

From Table 4.1 it is apparent that there is remarkable consensus on the importance of school factors, such as strong leadership (mentioned four times), orderly climate (three times), high expectations (six times), achievement-oriented policy (four times) and time on task (three times). Purkey and Smith state that the case studies are open to the same research-technical criticism that was applied to the outlier studies. Bearing in mind the earlier remark made on the study of Brookover *et al.*, this study should be seen as a forceful exception to this unfavourable rule.

Programme Evaluations

Purkey and Smith (1983) discuss six evaluation studies in which most of the programmes assessed were compensatory ones. In three studies in Michigan, factors that from earlier studies appeared to be related positively to achievement were implemented in three schools. After one year these three experimental schools appeared to perform slightly better than the control schools. This result confirms once more the so-called five-factor model (see Chapter 1).

Van der Grift (1987, pp. 25–7) discusses the evaluation of three American school improvement programmes: the New York City School Improvement Project, the Rising to Individual Scholastic Excellence Project in Milwaukee and the New York Local School Development Project. In these projects the – by now familiar – effective school characteristics comprised the basis of the reforms. From the evaluations it appears that in each of the three project schools much better progress in achievement level was realized than in schools not involved in the project. Later in this chapter the evaluation of school improvement programmes that were greatly inspired by school effectiveness research results is looked at more closely.

Other Studies

Under the category 'other school effectiveness studies', Purkey and Smith deal with two large-scale surveys: the comparative study of Coleman *et al.* (1981) of public and private schools and the Safe School Study of the American National Institute of Education (NIE). Coleman *et al.* (1981) concluded that private schools do better than public ones and this was attributed to such factors as less school absence, more homework, more academic subject matter and greater demands made on achieving. From the NIE's Safe School Study it emerged that school characteristics associated with greater safety were also associated with better performance. Clear-cut rules, high staff morale, strong leadership and pressure for achievement appeared to be the factors that positively influenced the objectives of safety and a high achievement level.

Research Synthesis of Borger et al. (1984)

Borger and his co-authors have attempted to establish a more quantitative synthesis of school effectiveness research results. They analysed 24 studies and 24 review articles. The 24 studies conformed to the criteria that (a) data at school level were available and (b) achievement data were used as the operationalization of effectiveness. Seven of the 24 studies were case studies, and there were five outlier studies. The researchers concluded that no single school characteristic stood out as being exceptional in determining effectiveness.

Instead of this, eight factors were chosen that, from multiple studies, appeared to be linked to achievement. These were: leadership, school climate, teacher–pupil relationships (including the variable 'high expectations of pupil achievement'), curriculum/instruction (comprising the emphasis on basic skills, effective net learning time, homework, streaming, length of lessons and clarity on achievement), financial resources, physical environment, evaluation and characteristics of family background (socio-economic status, race and attitudes towards education).

Quantitative synthesis of studies, which regarding organization and methodology are just as divergent, is an extremely difficult exercise. In their quantitative summary Borger *et al.* appeared to get no further than tallying how often a particular school characteristic was studied and how often the characteristic concerned appeared to have a positive link with achievement (see Table 4.2). How a 'positive link' was interpreted exactly was not explained. Nevertheless, the review in Table 4.2 confirms the large degree of shared consensus on a limited number of factors, the same factors that emerge from the more qualitative reviews.

Table 4.2 *Number of positive relationships between school characteristics and achievement*

Factor	Number of studies including the factor	Number of positive associations with achievement
Leadership	18	18
School climate	14	13.5
Teacher–pupil relationship	17	15
Curriculum/teaching	19	17
Evaluation	5	5
Physical characteristics	5	1
Financial resources	5	4
Pupil socio-economic background	9	8

Based on Borger *et al.* (1984). Inconclusive findings were counted as 0.5.

Table 4.3 A schematic summary of twelve American and British studies of school effectiveness

Authors	School type	Number of schools	Dependent variables	Analysis level	Analysis	Independent variables + effect size	Between-schools variance	Variance explained by variables in model
Rutter et al. (1979)	Secondary	12	Exam results, behaviour, criminality, absenteeism	School, individual pupils	Rank correlation, regression analysis	Overall process characteristics explain 1.6% of the variance in exam results		
Brookover et al. (1979)	Primary	159	Learning achievement, reading and number, self-image, self-confidence	School	Regression analysis	School climate explains 6% of the variance in average achievement, when controlled for background characteristics of pupils: school structure explains 4% in average achievement		85% of the between-schools variance is explained by the various categories of independent variables jointly
Mortimore et al. (1988)	Primary	50	Learning achievement, reading, number, verbal reasoning, behaviour, attitude towards school, self-image, attendance	Pupils	Multi-level analysis	Intake characteristics, environmental variables; 'positive' school characteristics (in terms of correlations with dependent variables): educational leadership, involvement of deputy head, involvement of teachers, consensus among teachers, structured lessons, intellectually challenging teaching, work-centred setting, a limited number of focal points each lesson, optimum communication between teachers and pupils, record-keeping, parental involvement, positive climate	Net between-schools variance in achievement (%): reading 9, number 11, writing 13, oral language skills 27, behaviour 10, absenteeism 5.6, self-image 8.7, attitude towards school 7–12. Net between-schools variance in progress varied from 20 to 24% in reading, number and language	

Table 4.3 *continued*

Authors	School type	Number of schools	Dependent variables	Analysis level	Analysis	Independent variables + effect size	Between-schools variance	Variance explained by variables in model
Schweitzer (1984)	Primary	16	California achievement test	School	Correlations	Educational leadership r = 0.58 Emphasis on basic skills r = 0.12 Orderly and safe environment r = 0.59 High expectations of learning achievement r = 0.79 Frequent evaluation r = 0.68		
Brimer et al. (1976)	Secondary	44	Exam results in physics, literature, history	School	Multiple regression analysis, analysis of variance	*Mixed ability groups* In 1st, 2nd and 3rd year: r = 0.02 4th and 5th year: r = −0.49 for physics and r = 0.12 and −0.44 for literature and history, respectively *Teacher guidance* (not significant) *more informal structure of year groups:* r = −0.23 *Pressure for achievement* highly positive as well as highly negative correlations with the dependent variables *Relatively unstructured and informal school organization* r = −0.24		
Spade et al. (1985)	Secondary	4000 pupils	Mathematics achievement	Pupils	Multiple regression analysis	Maintaining order r > 0.10 Streaming r > 0.10 Individualized instruction (n.s.) Communication with school adviser r > −0.10		

Table 4.3 continued

Authors	School type	Number of schools	Dependent variables	Analysis level	Analysis	Independent variables + effect size	Between-schools variance	Variance explained by variables in model
Wolf (1977)	Secondary	127	Reading achievement	School	Regression analysis	Evaluation of pupil achievement $r = -0.16$		
Evertson et al. (1978)	Secondary	9	Language and mathematics achievement	Class	Regression analysis	Achievement bias, positive significant effect for mathematics		
Coleman et al. (1966)	Primary and secondary	4000	Language and number skills, practical knowledge, natural sciences, social sciences and humanities	Pupils	Regression analysis, analysis of variance	Teacher characteristics, peer group characteristics, inputs, socio-economic status of pupils	8.9% (explained by three categories of school variables)	
Madaus et al. (1979)	Secondary	52	Standardized achievement test, exam results	Pupils, classes	Regression analysis	Class characteristics explain 16.8% of variance in exam results and 5.2% variance in school achievement. Important school characteristics: achievement pressure; pupils subscribing to 'academic values'; learning time; high expectations	40.5% variance between classes	

Table 4.3 continued

Authors	School type	Number of schools	Dependent variables	Analysis level	Analysis	Independent variables + effect size	Between-schools variance	Variance explained by variables in model
Teddlie and Springfield (1984)	Primary	76	Norm-referenced test in basic skills	School	Factor-analysis correlations	*Teacher variables* Expectations $r = 0.22$ to 0.54 *School head* The degree to which the head believes parents are achievement-directed $r = 0.33$ The degree to which the head works together with teachers $r = 0.28$ Has high expectations $r = 0.49$ Is absent $r = -0.30$ The degree of parental support for the head $r = 0.26$		
Gray et al. (1983) (re-analysis by Aitkin and Longford, 1986)	Secondary	18	Number of O levels	Multi-level	Variance components analysis	Intelligence $r = 0.74$ School size (not significant)	27% uncorrected for intake characteristics (IQ), 7% corrected for intake characteristics	

A CLOSER LOOK AT TWELVE STUDIES

Review studies in the field of school effectiveness research remain somewhat superficial. A certain amount of generalization cannot be ruled out if one wishes to integrate research results. It is obvious, for instance, that closely linked characteristics like evaluation, monitoring, reinforcement and feedback can be lumped together. However, when we make a comparison with meta-analysis in the field of effective teaching research it is noticeable that here precise data are stated on the size of the correlations between instruction characteristics and achievement.

With a view to initiating a more quantitative synthesis, twelve British and American school effectiveness studies were closely analysed. A description of these twelve studies is included in Table 4.3. It was my intention, on the grounds of the basic data from these projects, to gauge (a) the proportion of the total variance in learning achievement that can be explained by the factor school, and (b) the effect size of individual school characteristics, also preferably expressed as percentage explained variance in learning achievement.

This attempt at synthesis was a sobering experience. After reading the reviews in which the same effectiveness-enhancing school characteristics are summed up every time, one has the impression that a response to the question 'What makes schools effective?' is child's play. Ralph and Fennessey (1983) are the only reviewers to point out the risk that repeated broad summing up of a limited number of studies (to which, moreover, all manner of criticism of research technique can be applied) conjures up myths. It is necesary to look more precisely at the research on school effectiveness. When that happens, such as in the analysis of the twelve projects selected here, then apparently:

- there is broad divergence between the various effectiveness studies;
- this divergence is on points like school type (primary/secondary education), selection and operationalization of independent variables (there are few standard instruments), choice of dependent variables (sometimes it is education level attained, sometimes examination results, sometimes scores from general cognitive skills tests, sometimes test data in a variety of subjects), level of analysis (school/class/pupil), and the statistics by which the effect is expressed (correlations, explained pupil variance, explained between schools variance, whether or not there are significant differences between means);
- basic quantitative data are often missing from the publications, such as the size of the between-schools variance.

In view of this ambiguity the attempt to reach a quantitative synthesis was abandoned. One is therefore limited to giving the descriptive data from the chosen projects, as outlined in Table 4.3.

In response to the data in Table 4.3, and the wide divergence between studies, the following conclusions can be drawn:

1   The impression often created, that the second generation of school effectiveness studies would reveal that schools differ from one another far more than the Coleman Report suggests, is not true. In the study of Coleman *et al.* a 'net' (corrected for pupils' background characteristics) between-schools variance of 8.69 per cent of the total variance was found. In recent school effectiveness studies like those of Gray *et al.* (1983) and Mortimore *et al.* (1988) net between-schools variances of 7 per cent and about 10 per cent respectively were found. In a classic second-generation school effectiveness study like that of Rutter *et al.* (1979) a variable comprising all the process characteristics included in the study appeared to explain only 1.6 per cent of the pupil variance in examination results.

2 Even when we employ more practical standards than 'percentage of variance accounted for', the results of recent school effectiveness research, when compared to those of older effectiveness studies (Coleman, Jencks), are by no means spectacular. Purkey and Smith (1983, p. 428) argue that the difference in achievement level between the lowest 20 per cent and the top 20 per cent of a number of schools ranked in order of merit for effectiveness would amount to some two-thirds of a standard deviation. This conforms with the estimate of Jencks *et al.* (1972) on the basis of first-generation effectiveness studies. It should also be pointed out that it often happens that an extremely effective school, populated by pupils with a lower socio-economic status, does not achieve the average attainment level of an average school with middle-class pupils.

3 By putting the above findings on more recent effectiveness research into perspective with regard to earlier studies, I do not intend to say that the school effects found are of little consequence. A difference in average attainment level between an effective and non-effective school of two-thirds of a standard deviation is no small result; it implies a lead or falling behind of almost an entire school year for the average pupil. In Chapter 5 we shall return to interpretation of the size of school effects.

4 Because one cannot achieve a quantitative synthesis regarding the effects of individual school characteristics on the basis of the data given in Table 4.3, one is left with little choice other than to determine with the 'naked eye' what are and what are not important characteristics. This 'eyeball' analysis leads to a reaffirmation of the list of characteristics that emerged from other review studies, especially with regard to achievement-directed policy, positive expectations of pupil achievement and structured teaching. However, there are a few discords, such as a negative correlation between frequency of evaluation and achievement (found by Wolf, 1977) and a positive correlation for the degree to which the school head does *not* work with the staff (Teddlie and Stringfield, 1984).

A BRIEF SUMMARY OF FIVE EVALUATIONS OF SCHOOL IMPROVEMENT PROGRAMMES

From the overview of effective schools research it emerges that research findings have a certain coherence, but at the same time there are reasons to remain cautious about the way findings are to be interpreted. In following chapters this message will be further amplified. Nevertheless, the United States has moved quite quickly to adapt the findings of the research in the form of school improvement projects. In 1983, Miles *et al.* located 39 effective school programmes in 25 states, involving no fewer than 875 school districts. There is an impression that not all these projects have been systematically evaluated and, even if they have, most of the evaluations are not of sufficient quality for their reports to have been published in academic journals.

Clearly different from this is the report on the evaluation of the Cardiff School Improvement programme (Reynolds *et al.*, 1989). This report will not be summarized here but will be saved as case material for Chapter 7. Five evaluations of improvement programmes inspired by effective school research will now be briefly described.

The Effective Schools Project in Jefferson County, Kentucky

In this project (see Miller *et al.*, 1985), ten schools worked continually for one year on implementing practically the most prominent findings of effective schools research. For this purpose a manual drawn up by Brookover, entitled 'Creative effective schools', was used. The participating schools had subscribed voluntarily to the project. The contents of the programme included pointers for class instruction, inspired by research into effective teaching, and for working towards an optimistic, achievement-oriented attitude for the entire teaching staff and an educationally oriented interpretation of the school leadership. During the implementation of the reforms an external school guidance adviser played an important role, and refresher courses and training were given to the teachers so that learning material could be directly related to the specific circumstances of a particular school. The evaluation findings of the project reveal that in a year the ten schools achieved noticeably better results in reading and number work than the remaining 77 primary schools in the area (the project schools averaged a 12 percentile point advance, while the others averaged 4 percentile points). Miller *et al.* (1985) point out that the implications of these findings should be placed into perspective, given the voluntary status of the ten schools, the possible working of the Hawthorne effect[2] and the lack of evidence to show whether the positive effects became stabilized, i.e. whether the school improvement programme was continued after its introduction.

The Knoxville City Schools Proficiency Test Project

This project (see Achilles and Lintz, 1986) was implemented in six secondary schools (three comprehensives and three high schools). The programme was made up of a number of specific didactic approaches (such as study skills training, working in groups and peer tutoring, i.e. pupils who teach one another), structured instruction forms (such as using progress tests, feedback and incentives), a clear contribution from the school head to the project and the stimulation of parental involvement in education. In addition, specific steps were taken to foster the actual implementation of the programme.

A check on the implementation was part of the evaluation programme during the project's first year. The effectiveness of the programme was established by measuring language and mathematics achievement. A quasi-experimental design was applied, whereby the pupils from the six experimental schools were compared with pupils from similar schools where no school improvement programme had been implemented. The findings were analysed using covariance analysis, with initial measurements in language and mathematics as covariables. The findings revealed that the experimental schools performed significantly better than the control schools.

Project Rise in Milwaukee

Project Rise took place in 18 primary schools (see McCormack-Larkin, 1985). The programme was inspired by findings on the effectiveness of school climate, curriculum, instruction, school organization, evaluation and the involvement of parents in education. What is particularly noticeable about the description of the programme is the emphasis on a positive achievement-oriented attitude from school heads, teachers, pupils and parents. For example, pupils ran academic pep rallies and teachers were lectured on how to fight against having defeatist views on the learning ability of disadvantaged pupils. Other characteristics of the programme were educational leadership, i.e. strong support from the head for learning and achievement, highly structured teaching and frequent achievement testing.

The learning results of the 18 project schools in reading and number were compared for nine years with the average achievement of all primary schools in the city. In the years before the programme the project schools consistently fell behind the city average. During the five years the project was implemented (up to and including 1984), this trailing behind was largely removed.

---

[2] The effect that comes from the extra attention that schools receive by participating in an experimental programme.

The Effective School Programme of the Mid-continent Regional Educational Laboratory in Kansas City

In this project (see Toft Everson *et al.*, 1984) research findings on school effectiveness, effective instruction and strategies for educational innovation were worked into a so-called staff development programme. The objectives of this programme are described as: becoming acquainted with relevant research findings; acquiring diagnostic skills to examine the existing school situation so that a comparison with the characteristics of effective schools can be made; learning to select strategies in order to deal with shortcomings that have been established by the diagnosis; developing school leadership according to the findings of effective schools research; implementing relevant findings and composing an evaluation system. Staff development was in the form of in-service training and took place at each school.

The programme was aimed at primary, comprehensive and high schools. The review quoted above also reports on a process evaluation in one of the school districts involved, after the programme had been running for one year. Among other things it was established that consensus had increased between teachers themselves and between teachers and school heads on the importance of effectiveness-promoting school characteristics. At class level, the method of teachers observing one another as part of a self-evaluation procedure was acknowledged to be an important change. An increase in the use of learning goals and the testing of pupils' progress was also recorded. The first results of a product evaluation indicated an increase in achievement progress in the project schools compared to the pre-project years in the same schools.

Evaluation of an Anonymous School Improvement Project

This evaluation study, described by Purkey (1984), investigated how far a school improvement programme in a particular school district corresponded in practice with the literature on well-known effectiveness-promoting characteristics. Particular attention was given to six measures at school district level that, according to Purkey and Smith (1983), would promote school effectiveness. These were: (a) encouraging the schools to experience the district board as a supporter of the improvement programmes; (b) stimulating innovative activities that could be tackled jointly by teachers and school heads; (c) offering maximum freedom of policy to schools to implement their own school improvement programmes; (d) stimulating staff development activities in which all personnel from a school could participate; (e) stimulating and encouraging initiatives and leadership at board, headteacher and teacher levels; (f) stimulating improvement programmes that related to the school as a whole.

Using case studies of six high schools it was established whether these measures had indeed been taken. The findings indicate that this was *not* the case. According to the evaluation study the school district initiative to implement an effective school programme was not taken seriously by the school, there was no appropriate infrastructure to realize the effectiveness-promoting measures and systematic long-term planning was missing.

From the descriptions of this limited choice of school improvement programmes it seems that in most cases use was made of both research findings on effective school characteristics (meso level) and findings on effective instruction (micro level). In these school improvement programmes, in fact, attempts were made to bring into practice an integrated effectiveness model. The information provided by the evaluations of these programmes only bears upon the programmes as a whole. The contributions of specific schools or instructional characteristics to improving the learning results were not determined.

The quality of the descriptive evaluations varies a great deal. The reports upon which the descriptions were based often gave few details of the research methods and techniques employed. One particular problem that arises when adopting the results of school effectiveness research in the form of integral school improvement programmes is implementation. Most programmes attempted to adopt research findings on innovation and implementation processes. This led to a phase-at-a-time approach and a strong emphasis on the involvement of all teachers in realizing the improvement programmes.

A MORE COMPREHENSIVE DESCRIPTION OF FOUR MAJOR AMERICAN AND BRITISH SCHOOL EFFECTIVENESS STUDIES

In Appendix 1 four school effectiveness studies are described in more detail. These are the studies by Brookover *et al.* (1979), Rutter *et al.* (1979), Schweitzer (1984) and Mortimore *et al.* (1988). These four case studies illustrate in the first place that there is a lack of theory in school effectiveness research. Brookover *et al.* come off best on this score; the projects of Rutter *et al.* and Mortimore *et al.* follow a more inductive approach by relating large numbers of variables to school achievement. Working with large numbers of independent variables and measuring several dependent variables sometimes leads to the use of quite arbitrary procedures to determine whether a certain school characteristic matters or not. Second, these documented projects give a picture of the complexity of school effectiveness research. Third, these studies confirm the importance of school characteristics that have emerged from reviews and research syntheses. This applies to the study of Mortimore *et al.*, even though some interesting new process factors are revealed there; for instance, with regard to the importance of the age (in months) at which children commence school and the emphasis on delegating educational leadership to deputy heads and other staff.

So far in this chapter the state of the art of American and British school effectiveness research has been looked at from the available review studies, by schematic description of twelve research projects, five evaluations of school improvement programmes and four case studies. Before going more deeply into an interpretation of all these data and fully considering the practical implications for the education field, in the following paragraphs I will discuss Dutch school effectiveness studies.

REVIEW OF DUTCH SCHOOL EFFECTIVENESS STUDIES

Dutch school effectiveness studies have a shorter history than the American and British research discussed above. From the overview given in this chapter it will be clear that all projects that can be classified as school effectiveness research were carried out in or after 1984. However, there is some similarity with evaluation studies of compensatory programmes in the Netherlands that took place slightly earlier in the mid to late 1970s.

In Appendix 2, Dutch studies that have some common ground with effective schools research, but which cannot really be regarded as such, are considered briefly, followed by a review of 16 Dutch school effectiveness studies. Here, the design and results of these studies are summarized in a similar format to that used to summarize schematically the American and British studies. Table 4.4 summarizes basic data on 16 Dutch school effectiveness studies.

From the data in Table 4.4 it can be noted that the average between-schools variance in Dutch research is some 11 per cent of the total variance. This compares with the percentages found in American and British studies. In Table 4.5, using the same primitive mode as that in the research synthesis of Borger *et al.* (1984), by means of 'tallying' I have indicated how often in the Dutch studies a particular school characteristic had a positive effect (no matter how this effect was expressed). From this review of Dutch school effectiveness research the following concluding comments can be made.

First, even more than in the documented American and British studies, the vulnerability of the school effectiveness research stands out. Even with long-term and exhaustive studies like those of Meijnen (1984), it appears difficult to draw unambiguous conclusions on effectiveness-promoting school characteristics. 'Many variables, little research consensus', 'a lack of clarity in

Table 4.4 A schematic summary of sixteen Dutch studies of school effectiveness

Authors	School type	Number of schools	Dependent variable	Analysis level	Analysis	Independent variables + effect size	Between-schools variance	Variance explained by variables in model
Meijnen (1984)	Primary	24	Intelligence, language and number performance	School, pupils	Analysis of variance, cluster analysis, correlations	A mix of formal subject teaching and teaching geared to specific characteristics of sub-groups of pupils is more effective than pure task-related or pupil-centred teaching	In the lower grades the between-schools variance was between 7 and 10% (IQ level). In the top grades this was 7–23% (for the dependent variables intelligence and achievement)	
Van Marwijk Kooij-von Baumhauer (1984)	Secondary	25	Exam results, attitude towards school	School	Mainly correlations	The following school characteristics correlated 0.40 or more with at least 3 dependent variables: earlier achievement; denomination of school; level of urbanization; positive expectations of pupils' achievement; average number of pupils sent out of class		
Stoel (1986), Knuver (replication; 1988)	Secondary	255	Exam results, % pupils that go on to higher education, % resits	School	Correlations	No school characteristic correlated significantly with all effect criteria; in the replication study the following variables correlated significantly with school achievement in both studies: the regular giving of homework; % full-time teachers (−); number of pupils (−); level of urbanization (+); frequency of meetings (−); individual forms of teaching (−)		

Table 4.4 continued

Authors	School type	Number of schools	Dependent variable	Analysis level	Analysis	Independent variables + effect size	Between-schools variance	Variance explained by variables in model
Tesser (1986)	Secondary	335	Attained education level	Pupils	Correlations	The following independent variables correlated significantly (P < 0.05) with the dependent variables in one out of four school types: degree of consensus among teachers (− 0.14; HAVO) parental involvement (0.14; HAVO) pupil guidance (0.17; VWO) achievement-oriented school policy (0.13; VWO) % problem pupils (− 0.15; HAVO) changes in teaching staff (0.18; HAVO)		
Roeleveld (1987)	Secondary	1047	Attained education level	Pupils	Analysis of variance, regression analysis	Secondary school types (6 categories)	After correcting for intake characteristics, schools account for 7–13% of total variance	
Van der Grift (1987)	Primary	321	General achievement test, final primary achievement school test (CITO)	School, pupils	Correlations, regression analysis		Educational leadership accounts for 12% of variance in pupil achievement after controlling for socio-economic status	
Bosker and Hofman (1987)	Primary	72	Language and reading achievement, attained education level at 12	Schools, pupils	Variance component analysis	Achievement-oriented attitude and experience of teacher explains 53% of the variance in mean number attainment in schools and 82% of mean language attainment	28% for number, 8% for language	

Table 4.4 continued

Authors	School type	Number of schools	Dependent variable	Analysis level	Analysis	Independent variables + effect size	Between-schools variance	Variance explained by variables in model
Van der Hoeven-van Doornum and Jungbluth (1987)	Primary	376	Attained education level	School level	Analysis of variance	Significant effect of the covariable (average socio-economic status of pupils), and the variables denomination and area; school climate and instruction characteristics together explain only 1% of the variance		
Vermeulen (1987)	Primary	17	Standardized achievement test	School level	Correlations	Only the variable 'orderly and secure school climate' correlated significantly ($r = 0.34$) with achievement; other school effectiveness predictors had no significant effect		
De Jong (1988)	Primary and secondary	58 primary 50 secondary	Intelligence, vocabulary	Pupils	Analysis of variance, regression analysis, factor analysis, analysis of covariance	*Academic emphasis* had a significant effect on intelligence level. *Pupil-centred* approach to teaching had no significant effect. *Streaming* had a negative effect on numerical IQ but a positive effect on verbal reasoning. *Amount of homework* correlated: 0.51 with verbal reasoning 0.40 with numeracy	Between-classes variance median: 40.5%	
Brandsma and Knuver (1988)	Primary	205	Number test	Schools, pupils	Variance components analysis	Corrected for covariables socio-economic status, intelligence and sex. Five variables together explained one-third of the between-schools variance: course followed by teacher (negative); whole-class traditional teaching has a positive effect; staff stability; involvement of a school guidance service (negative); level of educational reform (negative)	12.4% after being corrected for effect of covariables	37% of the between-schools 4.6% of the variance

Table 4.4 continued

Authors	School type	Number of schools	Dependent variable	Analysis level	Analysis	Independent variables + effect size	Between-schools variance	Variance explained by variables in model
Blok and Eiting (1988a)	Primary	158	Language tests	Pupils	Intra-class coefficient	Average i.c.c. = 0.125		
Blok and Eiting (1988b)	Primary	107	Reading and writing scores (from national assessment study)	Schools	Covariance structure analysis (LISREL)	Age/experience teachers 0.31 % working-class pupils −0.23 % ethnic minorities −0.53 % pupils in the sixth year that have resat a class 0.25 denomination 0.28 degree of homework (n.s.) degree of differentiation (n.s.). Figures reported are significant path coefficient		65%
Van der Werf and Tesser (1989)	Primary	184	Head's advice on secondary school type for primary school pupils	School, pupil	Random coefficient regression model (VARCL)	Significant effects of structural characteristics, such as: % working-class pupils, ethnic minorities, class size etc. Significant effects for two 'effective school variables': high expectations and high aspirations. Significance of one 'effective instruction characteristic', namely structured teaching	3.5% of the total variance is explained by differences between schools after correcting for pupils' socio-economic status	
Hoeben (1989)	Primary	219	Test split into reading, number and general knowledge	School, pupil	Analysis of covariance, regression analysis, covariance structure analysis	Teacher estimates of level of control and evaluation of pupils' progress had relatively little effect on performance		Instruction characteristics explained 7% of the total variance

Table 4.4 continued

Authors	School type	Number of schools	Dependent variable	Analysis level	Analysis	Independent variables + effect size	Between-schools variance	Variance explained by variables in model
Scheerens et al. (1989)	Secondary	1960 in 17 countries	Mathematics achievement	School, class, pupil	Variance components analysis, VARCL	Significant regression coefficient in more than 10 countries: pupil expectations of their own school career; teacher expectations of pupil achievement; opportunity to learn; amount of homework (7 positive and 3 negative associations)	For the Netherlands: MAVO 9% HAVO/VWO 13% LTS 40% LHNO 27%	For the Netherlands: 71%

Table 4.5 *Synthesis of Dutch school effectiveness research*

School characteristic	Number of studies with positive effect	Total number of studies
Teacher's experience	3	3
Changes in staff	2	3
Private/state education	3	3
Positive expectations of pupil achievement	4	5
Frequent evaluation	2	6
Achievement-oriented policy	4	6
Teacher cooperation/consensus	1	3
Child-centred approach	0	2
Opportunity to learn	1	2
Structured teaching	1	1
City/rural school	2	3
Orderly climate	2	4

the interpretation of hundreds of correlations' and 'compromises in the intensity of data-collecting procedures because of financial considerations' are a few of the sentiments used to express the methodologically vulnerable character of the studies discussed here. Regarding data collection, it is noticeable that in most Dutch school effectiveness studies information on school characteristics was almost always gathered by using written questionnaires. More intensive methods, like direct observation, which are used in the study of Mortimore *et al.* (1988), for example, have hardly been applied to Dutch school effectiveness research.

Second, Dutch studies reflect the lack of theoretical basis that has already been spotted in American and British effectiveness research, despite the fact that a few studies (Meijnen, 1984; Van Marwijck Kooij-von Baumhauer, 1984) have tried admirably to find links when conceptualizing from several sub-disciplines.

Third, differences can be observed in the choice of both dependent and independent variables in Dutch studies compared to British and American effectiveness research. In the latter, tests and test data on language and number achievement dominate, while in Dutch research more use is made of variables like 'schooling achieved' and 'education level attained'. Possibly this has something to do with the more pronounced tradition for testing in the UK and USA, and with the fact that the differentiated system of secondary education that still exists in the Netherlands lends itself well to having a differentiated scale to determine education level. In non-Dutch research the chosen independent variables or school characteristics converge more around ten factors that in a variety of contexts can be associated with effectiveness. In Dutch research it is more hit and miss: first select from a large number of variables what correlates more or less with achievement, then analyse it further.

Fourth, the impression from the documented Dutch research is that the links repeatedly found in other studies are only recognized quite weakly. In this connection Vermeulen's (1987) replication of Schweitzer's (1984) study is revealing, but even in the other studies it seems that variables like 'frequent evaluation' and 'educational leadership' show few consistent associations with achievement. 'Educational leadership' even correlates negatively now and then with educational achievement. As a possible explanation of these results one could think of a more amicable, as opposed to a more managerial, concept of a school head in Dutch schools, and a still fairly weakly developed evaluation tradition in education.

SUMMARY AND CONCLUSIONS

A Growing Body of Substantive Knowledge

Despite all the problems in carrying out school effectiveness research that have been documented in the preceding sections (and in Appendices 1 and 2) it is fair to say that there is a growing consensus on a list of school and instructional characteristics that have been shown to matter as far as reaching relatively high educational outcomes is concerned. Levine and Lezotte (1990, pp. 9–10) call these characteristics 'effective school correlates'. As the main categories of these they propose the following list: a productive school climate and culture (comprising items like 'an orderly environment', 'faculty cohesion and collegiality' and a 'school-wide emphasis on recognizing positive performance'), focus on student acquisition of central learning skills, appropriate monitoring of student progress, outstanding leadership (among other things: superior instructional leadership, frequent, personal monitoring of school activities and high expenditure of time and energy for school improvement actions), salient parent involvement, effective instructional arrangements and implementation (among other things: effective teaching practices and coordination in curriculum and instruction) and high operationalized expectations and requirements for students.

A somewhat more concise, but rather similar, listing of effective school characteristics will be used as the basis for formulating a comprehensive model of school effectiveness in Chapter 6.

The Need for More 'State of the Art' School Effectiveness Studies

From the overview of research studies in the previous sections (and particularly the more extensive descriptions of research projects in Appendices 1 and 2) it becomes evident that carrying out a 'proper' school effectiveness study is not an easy matter. By a 'state of the art' school effectiveness study I mean a study that:

- taps sufficient 'natural' variance in school and instructional characteristics, so that there is a fair chance that they might be shown to explain differences in achievement between schools;
- uses adequate operationalizations and measures of the process and effect variables, preferably including direct observations of process variables, and a mixture of quantitative and qualitative measures;
- adequately adjusts effect measures for intake differences between schools (e.g. in previous achievement and socio-economic status of pupils);
- has units of analysis that allow for data analyses with sufficient discriminative power;
- uses adequate techniques for data analysis – in many cases multi-level models will be appropriate to do justice to the fact that we usually look at classes within schools, pupils within classes and perhaps even schools within specific types of environments;
- uses longitudinal data.

Apart from being difficult, a fully fledged state-of-the-art school effectiveness study is also a time-consuming affair and a demanding organizational effort. In fact, studies that more or less meet these requirements have been quite exceptional. As pointed out above, the Mortimore *et al.* (1988) study is probably the best example; other 'big' effectiveness studies are the Brookover *et al.* and Rutter *et al.* studies (both from 1979) and the Louisiana School Effectiveness Study (Teddlie and Stringfield, 1984; Teddlie *et al.* 1987; Stringfield and Teddlie, 1990).

Although certain more specialized research approaches to school effectiveness (to be listed below) are also needed, it is quite important that there be more state-of-the-art studies, preferably in different parts of the world and in different educational systems and cultures. Only in this way can the emerging substantive explanatory models of school effectiveness be further tested and refined.

A Lack of Theory

As was remarked in the reviews of research studies above, school effectiveness research has followed a very inductivist approach. Often research studies have not been very far removed from the caricature of a fishing expedition for significant correlations between all kinds of school organizational and instructional conditions on the one hand and achievement test data on the other. This has led to a state of affairs where we have some knowledge on the question of what works in education but precious few answers to the more fundamental question of why effectiveness correlates influence educational outcomes as they appear to do. It seems obvious that the next phase in studying school effectiveness phenomena should give more attention to conceptual and theoretical aspects, since only in this way can progress be made in really understanding school effectiveness, in refining research studies and ultimately in improving practice. At the same time one should be aware of the enormous difficulties in formulating an encompassing theory of school effectiveness. For one thing, such a theory would have to be interdisciplinary and try to integrate sociological, psychological, managerial, economic and educational insights into the functioning of schools. Second, such a theory would be about the functioning of schools as a whole within different and changing contexts, so that one might wonder whether the complexity of the object of theorizing would not be altogether over-whelming. In Chapter 2 certain available theoretical 'building blocks' for school effectiveness modelling were reviewed.

When considering school effectiveness theory we have two distinct objectives: one is the formulation of a (preferably contextual and necessarily multi-level) *causal* model about good and bad functioning of schools; the other is the establishment of a more dynamic theory on how to *improve* the functioning of schools. The additional questions that are central in the latter theoretical ambitions are: which 'vehicles' or 'levers' from the former causal model are most suitable to improve schools and which strategies should be used to work these 'levers' in the most effective and efficient way?

More Specific Research Questions

In addition to the state-of-the-art effectiveness studies referred to above there are some developments in directing school effectiveness research towards more specialized questions. Behind these developments lie more refined models of school effectiveness that differentiate between various settings or contexts of schools, and various sub-groups of pupils. These will be discussed in the next chapter under the headings 'differential school effectiveness' and 'environmental contingencies'.

Broadening the Arsenal of Research Methods

The majority of school effectiveness studies are correlational as opposed to experimental, which means that the influencing or 'independent' variables cannot be actively manipulated and the random assignment of units to treatment conditions is out of the question. This implies that the validity of school effectiveness studies depends on the natural variability of the phenomena that are the object of investigation. The strength of this type of research arrangement is the 'real life' nature of the findings (as opposed to the sometimes 'artificial' appearance of results from laboratory experiments), its major weakness the lack of control over all kinds of non-measured influences on the effect variables. In many situations there is no alternative and one simply has to make the best of designing a correlational effectiveness study (see the above ideal-type description of a state-of-the-art effectiveness study).

There are some alternative research approaches, which to a degree are the consequence of new developments in conceptualizing school effectiveness. Computer simulations may serve as a bridge between more elaborate conceptual models of school effectiveness research and empirical research. Clauset and Gaynor (1982) provide an early example of the use of systems analysis in the design of school effectiveness models. More recent attempts at simulating organizational processes by means of computer models are also relevant in this respect. International databases and specifically designed comparative international school effectiveness studies are particularly useful in determining the generalizability or the contextual specificity of school effectiveness models (see, for example, Scheerens *et al.*, 1989). Presently there are various attempts, at the OECD among other organizations, to design international comparative studies of educational performance.

The *rapprochement* of the world of school improvers and the world of school effectiveness researchers offers new possibilities to rigorously evaluate school improvement programmes that attempt to bring into practice school effectiveness models. In some situations it might be possible to carry out these evaluations by means of a reasonably well controlled quasi-experimental or even 'truly' experimental design (an example of the latter is being conducted by Bosker *et al.*, 1990).

Finally, it is important that naturalistic case study approaches continue to be used to study school effectiveness. Theory building need not be based exclusively on abstract models that are partly adapted from other fields of social scientific research, but can also be 'grounded' in hands-on experience with practical school improvement efforts.

Chapter 5

The Significance of the Research Findings

INTRODUCTION

In the previous chapters the various types of educational effectiveness research were described and the most important findings summarized. Before going deeper into the implications the research findings have for the teaching field, I will try to answer certain basic questions on the research findings presented so far. These questions are concerned with the meaning of the available research results:

- Do the effectiveness measurements used in school effectiveness studies really cover the 'quantity and quality' of the output? (This question will be referred to as the problem of the educational validity of school effectiveness measures.)
- Are the school effects found in the studies actually large enough to be of practical significance?
- How stable is school effectiveness – in other words, are schools that produce exceptionally good results in one year just as effective in the following years?
- Do the data provide sufficient points of application for a policy on making schools more effective, and should that mainly be effected at teaching level, within the classroom, or at school management level?
- How robust are the school effectiveness research results with respect to different sub-groups of pupils and different contexts?

This chapter deals with each of these questions separately.

THE EDUCATIONAL VALIDITY OF SCHOOL EFFECTIVENESS MEASURES

The most used effect measurements are tests in pupils' native language, arithmetic and mathematics. In addition measurements of the education level reached by pupils by a certain set date are employed. Whenever we view effectiveness in terms of (sufficient) quantity and quality of the learning results we can ask whether this criterion is sufficiently represented or 'covered' by the already-mentioned measurements. The answer to this depends on the view of the sort of objectives that education has to achieve. A few important differences in emphasis are the position ascribed to non-cognitive educational goals, the importance of academic knowledge versus functional skills, and the importance of subject-related educational objectives versus more general cognitive skills.

Although there is a strong inclination to use tests that measure cognitive basic skills, non-cognitive aspects, such as the way school is experienced, self-image and self-confidence of pupils, were also measured fairly frequently. Fraser *et al.* (1987, p. 206), in their meta-analysis, point out that school and teaching characteristics that reveal a relatively high correlation with cognitive achievements also correlate with 'affective' teaching results. There are, however, differences in emphasis: for instance, smaller classes have more influence on the affective than on the cognitive field of education outputs.

The question of whether the educational validity problem is satisfactorily resolved by the choice of specific effect measures also depends on the area of application in which the effectiveness question is asked. In other words, those financing education will certainly be interested in measurement of returns, such as the percentage of successful pupils from a certain cohort group in a certain school type. Parents of pupils will obviously want to know the average achievements in certain key subjects, as well as details of the overall results of a certain school. In theory, researchers should be able to specify a separate causal model for every effect measure. Moreover, teachers – with an eye to using effect measures to modify their own teaching – would no doubt have use for curriculum or subject-related testing. Assessors of nationwide innovative projects would prefer to choose general, curriculum-free, cognitive skills testing (Slavenburg, 1986).

It is therefore obvious that the question of covering for 'sufficient quantity and quality of output' in specific effect measures will be answered differently from different positions.

CONSIDERATIONS ON SIZE OF EFFECTS

As already described in Chapter 2, school effectiveness research as a reaction to studies like those by Coleman and Jencks is largely motivated by an inspiration to demonstrate that schools in fact do matter. The remarkable thing about this is that later school effectiveness studies pointed to hardly greater differences between schools (in terms of explained variance) than Coleman and Jencks had done, yet titles like 'Schools can make a difference' conveyed a message that was altogether different from that of the earlier studies. There obviously exists a lack of clarity on the way measurements express the significance of school effects.

The first cause of misunderstanding that can crop up when interpreting the size of school effects is to lose sight of the fact that the concern is always with comparative and not absolute effects. How far schools differ one from another with regard to output is studied, and obviously not how far it matters whether pupils attend school or not. No matter how obvious this may sound, it seems that the implications of this are not always properly realized. It is quite possible that there are only small differences between effective and non-effective schools, while the average level of education in a country is still very high. In this context, Japan can be used as an example (Scheerens *et al.*, 1989). If formally established educational objectives, operationalized as standard attainment tests, were available, this would make effectiveness assessment less dependent on comparison with other schools. A second problem in interpreting the size of school effects and the influence of individual characteristics on the output is that the indicators used to express these effects are not always that revealing. For instance, the statistical significance of correlations between school characteristics and achievement is dependent on the number of research units. When effects are expressed as 'percentage variance explained by schools' it is not immediately clear whether these are to be interpreted as large or small.

When we look at school effectiveness research in the Netherlands, for example, it seems that the average variance between schools amounts to 11 or 12 per cent of the total variance. This percentage hardly deviates from the results of the American and British studies discussed in the previous chapter. So, whenever the question arises of what specific school characteristics contribute to these differences between schools, it appears that these specific characteristics can account for no more than 11 or 12 per cent of the total variance. The effect of school characteristics that account for some 3 per cent variance in pupil achievement can thus be expressed as 25 per cent of the between-schools variance. Expressing effect size in this way is possibly more appropriate because it expresses the contribution of the school characteristic in question to what can be explained at school level at all.

A third point that must be remembered when interpreting the size of school effects is that schools will make more of a difference when testing skills primarily learnt at school, as compared to testing skills that, to some extent, can also be learnt at home. The differences between schools are thus always greater for subjects like maths than for a subject like tuition in one's own language. More insight into the significance of school effects of a certain size can be gained when we express the size of effects in a way for which certain scientific norms exist (even if these norms are little more than relatively arbitrary agreements). Thus, in a school effectiveness study we can compare the average score of the least effective 20 per cent of schools with the average score of the most effective 20 per cent and express the difference in proportion to one standard deviation. Differences between 0.2 and 0.5 standard deviations are regarded as small, those between 0.5 and 0.8 as average and above 0.8 as large (Cohen, 1977). Purkey and Smith (1983) came to the conclusion that in both older (Coleman, Jencks) and newer school effectiveness studies the difference in average achievement between the 20 per cent least effective and the 20 per cent most effective schools amounted to 0.67 standard deviations. According to Cohen's standards of measurement this is an effect of average size. More insight into the *practical* significance of school effectiveness is gained when the relevant difference can also be expressed in money or time. Thus, the difference of 0.67 standard deviations is compared to an entire school-year's difference between the average pupil in the most effective schools and the average pupil in the least effective schools. In a similar manner, Rosenthal and Rubin (1982) demonstrated that effects which in terms of explained variance on the output variable were relatively . small still signified a considerable difference in scale points on the dependent variable.

Taking everything into consideration, the conclusion is that school effects that at first glance appear to be modest can have great practical significance when looked at more closely (see also Reynolds and Reid, 1985, p. 191). At the same time we should realize that the greater part of the variance in achievement is determined by difficult to influence background characteristics of pupils, such as parental milieu and intelligence. Moreover, instruction variables that directly intervene with the learning process of pupils, such as opportunity to learn, are more strongly linked with achievement than school characteristics like school climate and how a school is run.

THE STABILITY OF SCHOOL EFFECTIVENESS

With regard to the stability of school effectiveness, the general concern is whether effectiveness remains a constant characteristic of schools no matter how it is measured, how it is determined (at what class level) and when we do this. In the previous section various effect measurements were mentioned. Here the stability across years and across grades at one point in time will be dealt with. Bosker and Scheerens (1989) give the ranges shown in Table 5.1.

Table 5.1 *Range of stability estimates of school effects*

	Primary education	Secondary education
Stability in time	0.36–0.65	0.70–0.95
Stability across grades	0.10–0.65	0.25–0.90

After Bosker and Scheerens (1989).

From Table 5.1 it appears that there is some stability across calendar years, so that effectiveness appears to be a fairly permanent school characteristic. The stability across grades appears significantly less. In primary education, where classes are attached to specific teachers, this can be seen as an expression of the variety in effectiveness of teachers within one school.

THE CAUSAL INTERPRETATION OF RESEARCH RESULTS

Research into school effectiveness involves more than determining the achievement level of a school and then doing a comparative study to see whether it can be regarded as an effective school or not. To start with, only looking at average levels of achievement can lead to misleading conclusions if the more or less favourable educative starting level of the learning population is not taken into account. A school consisting largely of pupils from the lower socio-economic groups can produce excellent results, but the average level might still be below that of a school with middle-class pupils. In research terminology this is expressed as the adjusted average score for a certain test, where the adjustment is for the background characteristics of pupils that can influence learning performance.

The key question is: what characteristics do effective schools have that are missing in non-effective schools? For this, schools are compared not only for output but also for process characteristics, such as organization, curriculum and instruction. Whenever it is established that certain curriculum, organization and instruction characteristics are more emphatically present in schools with a relatively high, rather than a relatively low, output, one is inclined to conclude that these characteristics are the cause of the differences in effectiveness. It is tempting to connect such causal interpretations to the results of effective school research. Yet, in a strict sense correlations do not allow for unequivocal pronouncements on causes and effects; that could only be done if effectiveness determinants could be put to the test in experimental research. Nevertheless it is difficult to leave out causal interpretations with regard to effectiveness-promoting school and instruction characteristics. Apart from limitations that arise from the correlative nature of school effectiveness research, interpretation of the results is limited because of the lack of a theory that could explain *why* certain school characteristics are related to high levels of performance.

When, for the sake of convenience, we assume the five-factor model of school effectiveness (educational leadership, orderliness, high expectations of pupil achievement, emphasis on basic skills and frequent assessment), the following critical questions can be asked of the causal status of this model.

It is not clear whether high expectations of pupil achievement should be seen as a cause or effect of high levels of achievement. It is not implausible that there is a reciprocal influence between expectations and achievement: an optimistic atmosphere stimulates performance and the increased level of achievement heightens expectations again. With such mutual influencing, the obvious question is 'what comes first?' and whether this can be brought about by a particular line of policy.

There is something tautological about emphasizing the learning of basic skills and at the same time largely making use of tests to measure these skills as effectiveness criteria. It stands to reason, one might say. Yet this link cannot be regarded as completely trivial because it might appear to be fruitful when an important role is given to basic skills in education. This criticism applies less when more general cognitive skills tests are used, because training for these sort of tests is less likely.

There is uncertainty surrounding the primary point of application of effectiveness-promoting school characteristics. Orderliness, achievement-orientation and positive expectations are sometimes seen as characteristics of a school's general climate and at other times as characteristics of successful school leadership. These characteristics can be defined at both school level – as aspects of management and organization – and teacher level (individual class management). The question is whether effectiveness is largely determined by characteristics as defined at school level or by similar characteristics at class level, or by both. From multi-level analyses of existing data sets, it emerges that class characteristics have a stronger link with performance measures than school factors (Scheerens *et al.*, 1989).

These limitations on the causal status of the best-known school effectiveness model are similarly restricting as far as *making* schools effective is concerned: in other words, in converting research results into guidelines for educational practice. There have been initiatives to reach a more integral causal reconstruction of the findings of effective schools research, and these are discussed in later chapters. For the time being it must be concluded that the central question, of which causal interpretations can be given to the relationship between school characteristics and achievement, has not been fully answered.

The research-technical strength or weakness of the studies is relevant to the question of how certain one can be about school effectiveness research findings. The general view is that school effectiveness research is a difficult and complicated type of study in which one can almost always find something to criticize. Most reviewers stick to the fact that all forms of effectiveness research have their weaknesses, but given the degree of convergence argue for the robustness of the findings.

DIFFERENTIAL SCHOOL EFFECTIVENESS

Usually in school effectiveness research overall effect measures are used, i.e. aggregated performance measures of all pupils in a particular grade. A refinement in the design of school effectiveness studies is to examine performance measures for different sub-groups of pupils, for instance girls versus boys, pupils with higher versus pupils with lower socio-economic status (SES), white versus black pupils, etc. This approach has been described as 'differential school effectiveness' (Nuttall *et al.*, 1989). Following this line of inquiry different authors came up with different conclusions. On the basis of massive meta-analyses, Walberg (1984) states that the factors enhancing educational productivity work equally well for different sub-groups of students. Mortimore *et al.* (1988), in examining sex differences, found that, 'in general, schools which had a positive effect in promoting reading progress for one sex also tended to have a positive effect for the other' (p. 210). But in a minority of schools effects on reading progress were positive for boys and negative for girls. Nuttall *et al.* (1989) found evidence for differential school effects with respect to sex and ethnic background, implying, for instance, 'that some schools narrowed the gap between boys and girls or between students of high and low attainment on entry, whereas some other schools were found widening the gap' (p. 774). Jesson and Gray (1991, p. 246) found some evidence of differential effectiveness: pupils of different attainment levels did slightly better in some schools than in others. It should be noted that 'differential effectiveness' is a general term that carries various meanings.

The most basic meaning of differential effectiveness is the well established fact that schools with a more privileged population of pupils (higher socio-economic status, more 'cultural capital') generally reach higher average achievement than schools with less favourable entrance characteristics in their student population. This amounts to an unadjusted comparison of achievement levels between sub-groups at one specific point in time.

A more interesting conceptualization of differential school effectiveness is the comparison of the performance of sub-groups of pupils within schools over time. In this way it can be established whether schools that are effective in raising the level of, for instance, girls are also effective in raising the achievement level of boys. In this case school effects are examined by adjusting for previous performance and by differentiating sub-groups. Additional statistics that are relevant when following this approach are the variance in specific sub-group differences between schools and the covariance of several sub-group differences (see Nuttall *et al.*, 1989, pp. 773–4). These statistics tell us respectively the degree to which schools vary in sub-group differences (some being more egalitarian than others) and whether schools that are differentially effective with respect to certain sub-groups (e.g. boys versus girls) are so to more or less the same degree for another division of the student population (e.g. high versus low SES). Again, these statistics are particularly interesting when they can be examined longitudinally, i.e. when they are compared over several points in time.

These two meanings of differential school effectiveness (which could be labelled as the unadjusted cross-sectional approach and the adjusted longitudinal approach) are restricted to specific interpretations of the actual *effects* of schooling as compared to the processes that affect high or low school performance. In terms of an input–process–outcome model these views are limited to a comparison of the consistency and the differentiation of output measures (in the case of the unadjusted cross-sectional approach) or input–output relationships (in the case of the adjusted longitudinal approach) when comparing sub-groups of pupils. A third, and more comprehensive, meaning of differential school effectiveness is concerned with input–process–output relationships. In this case the central question is whether the organizational and curricular arrangements that work for one sub-group of pupils are also beneficial for another sub-group of pupils. So, for instance, one might want to investigate whether the five-factor school effectiveness model would work equally well in schools with a majority of students from higher socio-economic backgrounds and in schools with a predominantly middle-class population of students. According to this third meaning the study of differential school effectiveness amounts to a study of the generalizability of school effectiveness models across different sub-groups of the student population. From the existing research examples it appears that the level of the sub-group of students coincides with the school level; in other words sub-groups are not contrasted within schools but only between schools. This is because the 'process' or 'treatment' factors in school effectiveness research are usually defined at school level. If different treatments for specific sub-groups within schools were taken into account, differential school effectiveness would have progressed to the aptitude–treatment interaction paradigm from instructional psychology. Presently, this level of sophistication has not been realized in empirical school effectiveness research.

Examples of empirical studies that reflect the input–process–output approach to differential school effectiveness studies are those by Teddlie *et al.* (1987), Firestone and Wilson (1987) and Hallinger and Murphy (1986). Usually these studies are presented under the heading of 'contextual differences in school effectiveness'. But since 'context differentiation' here would mean nothing but a between-school difference in socio-economic status of the student population, these studies would be more properly categorized as a particular approach to differential school effectiveness. Teddlie *et al.* (1987) found that teachers and principals in effective low-SES schools held high present, but more modest future, educational expectations, while teachers in effective middle-SES schools held very high present and future educational expectations.

Effective low-SES and effective high-SES schools also differed with respect to the overtness of the display of a reward structure. Principals in effective low-SES schools spent a greater proportion of their time developing and maintaining external rewards than principals in effective middle-SES schools. A third difference that Teddlie and his co-authors found was that principals in effective low-SES schools spent more time assisting teachers in academic matters than principals in effective middle-SES schools. A final difference was the greater frequency of contacts between teachers and parents in the effective middle-SES schools. Hallinger and Murphy (1987), who reported similar results, interpret this difference as protection of school life against the intrusions of the less educationally inclined low-income community. In the case of effective high-SES schools the greater frequency of contacts with the local community is seen as taking advantage of high parental expectations for success.

SCHOOL EFFECTIVENESS AND ENVIRONMENTAL CONTINGENCIES

Closely related to the input–process–output approach to differential school effectiveness discussed in the preceding section is the concept of environmental or contextual influences on school effectiveness. The only real difference is the replacement of a population characteristic as the 'contextual' factor by a genuine environmental factor, for instance secondary versus primary schools, urban versus rural schools, private versus public schools or schools within a particular national educational system compared to schools from other countries. Again the basic question is whether input–process–output models of school effectiveness, such as the five-factor model, or Walberg's model of educational productivity, are robust with respect to context differentiation or require context-specific modifications. The hypothesis that school effectiveness models depend on environmental conditions is supported by the general notion of contingency theory from the field of organizational science. Basically, contingency theory states that the effectiveness of organizational structures depends on the fit with environmental characteristics (congruence thesis) and the consistency of internal organizational configurations (configuration thesis).

Apart from its theoretical background, adding the notion of 'environment' to school effectiveness studies – like the concept of differential school effectiveness – requires a refinement of the school effectiveness research agenda. Examples of research studies that have addressed the environmental issue are those by Firestone and Herriott (1982), Firestone and Wilson (1987) and Scheerens *et al.* (1989).

Firestone and Herriott found that effective secondary schools employed a broader mission, namely to excel in all subjects, than effective primary schools, which strongly emphasized basic skills. Although Firestone and Wilson (1987) found similar patterns of relationships between managerial style, teaching practice and achievement when comparing primary and secondary schools, they established that high school principals were not influenced by the student body composition in terms of socio-economic status, whereas primary school principals used tighter control when SES was lower. Scheerens *et al.* (1989) compared predictors of mathematical achievement in seventeen countries. Variables that were related to the construct of high expectations of educational achievement and opportunity to learn appeared to be quite consistent in showing a positive correlation with achievement across countries. They also showed that the patterns of between-school variances and between-teacher variances differed drastically among countries.

In comparing private and public sector schools, a majority of authors conclude that private schools generally do better, although the issue is still being debated. Explanations of how this alleged superiority of private schools comes about are still hypothetical. Coleman *et al.* (1981) claim that Catholic schools in the United States are superior because they demand more homework, maintain better discipline and require advanced courses. Hallinger and Murphy (1987) say that parents in private school environments are more supportive and active in promoting the well-being of the school. An interesting development in the comparative research on private and public sector schools would be to compare effective private and effective public sector schools, according to the kind of outlier design Teddlie *et al.* (1987) used in comparing effective low-SES and effective middle-SES schools.

SUMMARY AND CONCLUSIONS

Critical questions that should be addressed in interpreting the significance of the findings of school effectiveness research concern the following issues:

- Do the effectiveness measurements used in school effectiveness studies really cover the 'quantity and quality' of the output? (This question was referred to as the problem of the educational validity of school effectiveness measures.)
- Are the school effects found in the studies actually large enough to be of practical significance?
- How stable is school effectiveness; in other words, are schools that produce exceptionally good results in one year just as effective in the following years?
- Do the data provide sufficient points of application for a policy on making schools more effective and should that mainly be effected at teaching level, within the classroom, or at school management level?
- How robust are the school effectiveness research results with respect to different sub-groups of pupils and different contexts?

The answers to these questions can be summarized as follows:

- The generally chosen effect measurements for school effectiveness research allow sufficiently for the cognitive domain of educational objectives; depending on the reply to the question of whether one regards these objectives as the most important educational goals, appreciation of the educational validity of school effectiveness research findings may vary.
- While school effects are not large in absolute terms, their practical implications can often be demonstrated.
- There is some evidence that effectiveness is a relatively constant characteristic of schools across the years, while the stability of effectiveness across grades is rather low.
- The causal status of the relationships found between school characteristics and effect measures is relatively small because of the correlative nature of the research, a lack of theory and insufficiently sharp-edged conceptualization.
- With regard to the robustness and generalizability of school effectiveness research findings across sub-groups of pupils and across environments the research evidence is still rather limited. In order to detect evidence on differential school effects fairly sensitive analyses and rather extensive data collection are required, and the same is true when comparing the differential effects of different school contexts. School effectiveness models appear to be fairly robust as far as factors like opportunity to learn, structured teaching and high expectations of pupils' achievement are concerned. The evidence on context-specific and group-specific findings is, as yet, insufficient to warrant any definite conclusions. It should be emphasized, however, that studies aimed at uncovering these differential effects are quite important and might well be seen as the next stage in the development of school effectiveness research, where more refined models are the overall objective.

When one overviews all the empirical research that has been summarized in this part of the book, a 'mixed' feeling remains about the significance of what has been achieved in this field. On the one hand the sheer number of empirical studies (particularly with respect to instructional effectiveness) is overwhelming, and there appears to be a fair amount of consistency in the evidence on the relevance of a few general factors (achievement orientation, effective learning time, opportunity to learn and structured teaching). On the other hand, however, there are quite a few methodological weaknesses in most of the studies that have been reviewed.

Empirical school effectiveness research repeatedly has to battle with the complexities inherent in research in natural settings. Another drawback is that the connection with what is available in the domain of theories and conceptual models (see Part One) appears to be minimally utilized in the practice of current school effectiveness research.

Considering this state of affairs it seems particularly hazardous to begin discussing the practical relevance of these research findings. Nevertheless, that is what will be done in the third part of this book. Although practical recommendations are by no means of the nature of cookbook recipes or blueprints, the position is taken that the available research evidence is sufficient to try to integrate it in the form of ideas and principles that, it is hoped, will inspire educational practitioners to use them in ways that will suit their own purposes. In Chapter 6 the substantive educational effectiveness research findings will be integrated into what is termed a 'practical theory' of school effectiveness. In Chapter 7 the dynamics of making such a theory 'work' are the focus of interest, under the heading 'levers for enhancing school effectiveness'.

PART THREE

PRACTICE

Chapter 6

What Makes Schooling Effective? A 'Practical Theory' of School Effectiveness

INTRODUCTION AND SUMMARY OF EARLIER CHAPTERS

The question about school effectiveness can be answered in the same way as the question about quality in education: by the statement 'effectiveness must be apparent', which is analogous to the statement 'quality must be apparent' (De Groot, 1986). In other words, quality cannot be inferred from intrinsic characteristics of processes. Effectiveness is apparent from education results. These can be measured in terms of the percentage that succeed or as an average test score. In school effectiveness research the extent to which schools differ from one another in levels of achievement is studied. In order to reach an honest comparison and to ascertain what can actually be seen as a school's contribution to achievement, favourable or less favourable starting characteristics of pupils should be controlled for. This can be achieved only when schools with similar starting situations are compared to one another. Another method of making a fair comparison is to register carefully the starting situations of the pupils in, for example, intelligence and socio-economic background, and to neutralize the influence of these on achievement with the help of statistical techniques. When schools are compared to one another in this way, it appears that the differences between effective and less effective schools can be as much as an entire school year for the average pupil. This means that average pupil X at effective school A is a year ahead of average pupil Y at non-effective school B (assuming that pupil X had the same favourable or unfavourable starting situation as pupil Y). Even though this is perhaps a somewhat rosy example because extremes are being compared, even an effect that only amounts to half of this is still important enough. Thus we can conclude that meaningful differences in effectiveness exist between schools. Effective schools research is concerned not only with the question of whether schools vary and by how much, but also with the question of what these differences can be attributed to. What school characteristics are different in effective and non-effective schools when the influence of differences in starting situations of pupils is eliminated?

In various research traditions different categories of school characteristics have been linked to differences in results. Economists and educational sociologists concentrated initially on the material and personnel provisions of a school. The results of this research were less than spectacular. Only for the characteristic 'average experience of teacher' was there often – but by no means always – a correlation with achievement that was of any consequence. Educational psychology looked particularly at characteristics concerned with teacher behaviour, instruction methods and the way lessons were structured. From this research characteristics like 'effective net learning time', 'correspondence between what is taught at school and the content of tests and exams' and 'highly structured learning' emerged as being important. In the more recent research tradition of 'effective schools' research the emphasis is more on the influence of curriculum and organization characteristics defined at school level. Characteristics that emerge from this type of research as probable determinants of effectiveness are strong educational leadership – that is, a school head who is actively involved with the content, form and assessment of what is taught – a secure and orderly school climate, emphasis on acquiring basic skills, high expectations of pupil achievement, which involves high demands to achieve, and frequent assessment of pupils' progress.

There are certain problems in interpreting these results. It is unclear whether 'high expectations of pupil achievement' should be seen as a cause or result of high levels of actual achievement. Moreover, from the research findings it is unclear whether these characteristics should be largely traced back to school management or are more in the nature of a general 'mentality' of a school. Finally, a possible point of criticism is that it is small wonder that emphasis on basic skills appears to be an important school characteristic when achievement is largely measured in terms of attainment in basic skills like language and arithmetic.

A more integrated conceptualization is needed when judging the proper merit of school effectiveness research findings. It would be even better if the research results could be geared to more general explanatory principles; in short, the theoretical basis of school effectiveness research could be improved. The curious thing about this area of research is that the approach has been highly inductive and empirical. That is to say, by correlating all kinds of variables with achievement, slowly and by fits and starts a general consensus has evolved on 'what works' in education. 'How it works' and 'why it works' are questions that still do not come sufficiently to the fore. But some insights are available from an eclectic use of theories developed in various disciplines. Most important in this respect are ideas about incentive structures, organizational facilitators of conditions of effective induction, coordination in schools and evaluation–feedback–reinforcement cycles (see Chapter 2).

In this chapter a more integrated summary of research findings will be presented. This will be done by means of a specific structure in which various organization levels are differentiated. While this model does not presume to be a school effectiveness theory, components that can be geared to existing theories will be identified. The model also provides a structured framework for the various school characteristics included in the research discussed in earlier chapters, the most important of which will be dealt with in more detail in the concluding section.

TOWARDS AN INTEGRATED MODEL OF SCHOOL EFFECTIVENESS

In this section a synthesis will be made of the research results and theoretical insights discussed in Parts One and Two. Assumptions regarding ways in which effectiveness-promoting characteristics could mutually strengthen one another are made explicit. According to scientific research these assumptions are still inconclusive. In addition – as is apparent from earlier chapters – more certainty exists about some effectiveness-promoting, school and instruction characteristics than about others. From Dutch school effectiveness research, for instance, an unambiguous confirmation of the five-factor model has yet to emerge, and the negative findings from this research have had the upper hand until now. This limitation has to be kept in mind during the following discussion. Finally, synthesis leads almost inevitably to generalization. Statements are made that research generally confirms, but all kinds of specific variants and contextual conditions are ignored. In short, the integrated model of school effectiveness is a hypothetical model that does not lend itself to being used as a precise prescription for educational practice. Instead it may provide practitioners with some ideas that they might adapt to their own situations.

Taking all the other research findings discussed earlier, my reply to 'What makes schools effective?' would be as follows:

1   The determination to achieve better results.
2   Maximization of actual net learning time.
3   Structured teaching.

These factors are very simple. The message comes down to the fact that there is more chance of succeeding when there is a serious commitment to succeed. More instruction leads to more results and the best teaching technique available should be used, which is structured learning or direct instruction.

Besides the three core factors there are a few supplementary ones that can be regarded as a back-up:

1 School organization and management inwardly focused on creating favourable preconditions for effective class instruction.
2 School organization and management externally focused to safeguard favourable preconditions for effective instruction.
3 Environmental stimuli to motivate the school to be effective.

These conditions presuppose a multi-level structure as depicted in Figure 6.1, in which there are three management levels: the classroom, the school and the context of the school.

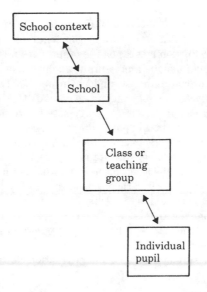

Figure 6.1 A multi-level model of schooling

In interpreting the principles of the structure in Figure 6.1 with regard to content, it is best to look from low to high or from inside to outside. Thus we start with the instruction characteristics that are the most beneficial for the learning of individual pupils. These are at class or teaching group level and are realized through the teacher and the methods he or she uses. School characteristics at 'above class level' can largely be regarded as 'facilitators' of conditions for effective instruction: order in the classroom is fostered by order in the school building; frequent testing of pupils' progress is fostered by the presence of a school testing policy etc. A second school-level category of conditions that can be differentiated in relation to classroom level can be imagined as 'buffers'. Buffers are organizational and management conditions that ensure that the primary production process can run undisturbed.

An interpretation of this sort of buffer can be given by referring to the alternative effectiveness criteria discussed in Chapter 1. Requirements such as continuity, consensus and solidarity have to be fulfilled at an acceptable level in order to ensure that the work does not lead to extreme uncertainty and a lack of job satisfaction. At the same time these conditions should not be goals in themselves to the extent that actual work suffers.

In Figure 6.1 there is a box representing school context or school environment. Under this heading hide various aspects. Contextual aspects that can be related to school effectiveness include:

1 Demographic and socio-economic characteristics of the city, neighbourhood or area where a school is situated.
2 Specific characteristics of the school itself, such as its size, type (primary or secondary school) and characteristics of its pupil population – the percentage of foreign pupils, for instance.
3 Governing bodies of the school, such as a school board, teaching inspectorate, local education authority and central government.
4 Relevant 'stakeholders' in the school's vicinity, such as local industry, secondary schools and consumers of education or their representatives; parents in fact.

In effective schools research conducted so far, little thought has been given to context characteristics 3 and 4. However, it seems relevant to consider these characteristics as important interpretations of the context box of Figure 6.1. The relationship between school and context can again be imagined in terms of favourable conditions on the one hand and buffers to protect the educational production process on the other. Favourable context conditions relevant to school effectiveness would include a pressure for achievement from a higher administrative level, e.g. the local educational authority, and an inspection focused on assessing education output. For buffers between production process and the environment the alternative effectiveness criteria discussed in Chapter 1 can be referred to once more. Acquiring resources and ensuring a sufficient yearly intake of pupils are in themselves elementary conditions in order to reach production. In more abstract terms, the background to the creation of these sort of buffers lies in the principle of reducing uncertainty created by the environment. The important issue of education as relevant to the needs of the labour market may be seen as a specific aspect of this general principle. While this is perhaps primarily an issue for school bodies governing the school, deregulation in higher and intermediate vocational education implies that schools themselves are also confronted with this.

In subsequent sections the bare outlines of an integrated model for school effectiveness as mentioned above will be fleshed out, by justifying the previous choices and by dealing in more concrete terms with the most relevant school and instruction characteristics.

CONCEPTUAL STRUCTURE

In this section the most important choices and assumptions of the integrated school effectiveness model are again enumerated. The model is called *integrated* because it attempts to relate the research results of the various disciplines with one another. In particular it tries to act as a link between conditions for effective instruction (micro level) and conditions for organizational effectiveness (meso level). In the organization-theoretical debate, in which the position is taken that effectiveness is not an unequivocal concept, a clear stand has been taken by choosing *productivity* as a central effectiveness criterion. Alternative effectiveness criteria, such as safeguarding resources and continuity and consensus in the organization, are conceived as a means with regard to productivity. In the model the school is not seen as a closed unit but as a system in *open interaction with the environment*. An implication of this is that external favourable and hindering conditions for school effectiveness are distinguished. Another is that the possibility that internal school conditions that promote effectiveness can be somewhat different in different contexts is accepted. While the model is technologically inclined and not meant to propagate a particular educational ideology, it is not free from value judgements since most school effectiveness research only tests cognitive basic skills, and it cannot be ruled out that the model would be altered if entirely different learning results, for instance at a social or affective level, played a more central role.

School organization philosophers associate the effective schools model with a bureaucratic form of organization (Lotto, 1982). Effectiveness-promoting characteristics, such as strong leadership, a general focus on basic skills and frequent assessment, are conceived as characteristics of a hierarchical, mechanical and formal structure. The criticism is also made that 'schools are not like that'. Teachers are quite autonomous and formal behavioural practices stand little chance; in short, the school is too much a loosely coupled entity of ideas and individual professionals to behave according to an effective school model. As long as this vision is not substantiated by research findings, it provides no serious competition for the established effectiveness model of empirical research. However, when we interpret the model further – for instance, with regard to a concept like 'instructional leadership' – the organizational realities of schools must be taken into account.

A FURTHER DESCRIPTION OF EFFECTIVENESS-PROMOTING SCHOOL AND INSTRUCTION CHARACTERISTICS

So far in this chapter, an as yet empty structure of an integrated school effectiveness model has been sketched. It will now be fleshed out by insertion of the various substantive findings from empirical school effectiveness research and theory development.

At the micro level of the classroom attention is drawn to the following instruction characteristics: structured learning, effective learning time and opportunity to learn. At the meso level of school organization the following characteristics are discussed:

- pressure for achievement;
- aspects of instructional leadership;
- recruiting of qualified staff;
- evaluative potential of the school;
- financial and material characteristics of the school;
- organizational/structural preconditions;
- school climate.

With regard to school context, attention is given to specific characteristics of the school and its surroundings and to external stimuli that could activate more effectiveness. The characteristics mentioned above are supported to various degrees by empirical research. The effect of certain characteristics is fairly convincingly demonstrated, while others are as yet no more than plausible suppositions. In order to rule out as far as possible any misunderstanding on this point, in Table 6.1 the empirical basis for each of the characteristics has been qualified.

Structured Teaching

The general principle of structured teaching is the use of multiple didactic interventions to support the learning process. Examples of these include: making clear what has to be learnt (formulating learning objectives); splitting teaching material into manageable units for the pupils and offering these in a well-considered sequence; much exercise material in which pupils make use of 'hunches' and prompts; regularly testing for progress, with immediate feedback of the results. Mastery learning is a didactic approach that includes these principles of structured teaching.

The idea of structured teaching is probably most suited to the more typical school subjects in primary schools, especially in regard to reproducible knowledge. This is also the research setting from which the relevant results have largely come. Nevertheless, it appears that learning at secondary school level as well as the learning of higher cognitive processes, such as problem solving, can also benefit from a structured approach. At these levels a modified form of structured teaching is generally applied: the steps through the subject matter are larger,

Table 6.1 *The degree to which the most important school and instruction characteristics relevant to effectiveness have been confirmed by empirical research*

Characteristic	Multiple empirical research confirmation	A reasonable empirical basis	Doubtful empirical confirmation	Hypothetical
Structured teaching	x			
Effective learning time	x			
Opportunity to learn		x		
Pressure to achieve		x		
High expectations		x		
Pedagogic leadership			x	
Assessment ability			x	
School climate			x	
Recruiting staff				x
Organizational/ structural preconditions			x	
Physical/material school characteristics		o		
Descriptive context characteristics			x	
External stimuli to make schools effective				x
Parental involvement		x		

x, a meaningful influence; o, a more marginal influence.

testing is less frequent and more opportunity is given to practise and apply problem-solving strategies independently.

Adaptive instruction (adapting subject matter over time and in the way it is presented to the level of pupils) can be seen as a specific form of structured teaching. From the research literature it is difficult to gain a clear view of the usefulness of instruments to achieve adaptive instruction. The effect of placing pupils in streamed groups is in general not that important, even though exceptionally gifted pupils can benefit from homogeneous groups. The empirical basis for this pronouncement is generally doubtful because research findings on streaming are not unequivocal.

Structured teaching comprises a number of quite common principles that in educational practice can be reached via various routes. Standard textbooks can be screened to see how far they accommodate the basic principles of structured teaching. Another vehicle for this type of learning could be the 'planning behaviour' of teachers – preferably as a coordinated activity for all staff of a primary school or secondary school department. One can also think of various types of computer-assisted learning because these approaches offer a lot of scope for exercises and testing of subject matter.

Conditions at school level that can help to strengthen structured teaching include:

- a coordinated and considered choice of methods that enhance structured teaching;
- a school information system that helps staff to test frequently and to record and use the test results;
- a test service system (like a computerized test or item bank) or a pupil monitoring system as part of a school information system;
- special programmes in which high cognitive skills are systematically practised, such as study proficiency programmes.

Effective Learning Time

To increase effective learning time at school four different aspects have to be considered:

1 Extending the institutionalized time spent on learning by giving more lesson time, making the school week (Saturday morning school) and the school year (fewer holidays) longer.
2 Giving homework or more homework.
3 Increasing the effective learning time without changing the institutionalized learning time.
4 Increasing the learning time for a certain subject by reallocating the total learning time among all subjects.

Obviously, there are clear limitations for increasing the official learning time and one can even expect a counterproductive result from a certain increase. In economics jargon educational achievement is a diminishing-returns function of instructional time. Levin (1988) presented data from which it appeared that lengthening the school day by an hour (half an hour for both reading and number) led to an average progress in reading and arithmetic of respectively 0.7 and 0.3 months. From this same review it seems that instruction forms like tutoring and computer-assisted learning led to remarkably greater results.

Effective net learning time should be established per pupil. By adopting such an approach it appears that whole-class teaching can be superior to individualized teaching, simply because with the latter the teacher has to divide his or her attention in such a way among pupils that the net result per pupil is lower than with whole-class teaching. In studies where effective teachers are compared to less effective ones, it appears that for the former 50 per cent of their teaching time is spent on interactive instruction, 15 per cent on organization and management duties and 35 per cent on inspecting and monitoring pupils' work (Stallings and Mohlman, 1981). Obviously effective learning time in school is directly affected by order. When there are disciplinary problems the time needed for organization and management greatly increases, while at the same time pupils' concentration becomes less.

Another aspect of effective net learning time is expressed by the concept *curricular emphasis*. Great differences exist between schools in the time spent on certain subjects. Goodlad *et al.* (1984) found that the time spent in American primary schools on the subject of arithmetic varied from 3.8 to 5.5 hours per week.

Pupil motivation is an influencing factor in effective net learning time. By attempting to stimulate the motivation to learn among pupils, teachers can indirectly increase effective net learning time. Methods here include a challenging and inspiring presentation of subject matter and working with punishment and reward. From the studies of Mortimore *et al.* (1988) it emerges that positive reinforcement in particular – the frequent praising of pupils – positively influences achievement.

At school level methods that enhance effective net learning time are:

- Working with an explicit school curriculum document and motivating staff to draw up work and lesson agendas.
- Explicitly putting forward 'increasing effective learning time' as an important intermediary objective on the road towards more effective teaching.
- Maintaining the achievement standards required of the pupils. In school effectiveness research it is regularly found that high expectations of pupil achievement are associated with better school achievement. Clearly, there is nothing more negative for the teaching results of a school than a defeatist attitude to pupils reaching levels of achievement that fit their abilities. The right amount of appeal to pupils to 'give it all they've got' has a lot to do with stimulating the willingness to learn and thus with the effective net learning time. Conditions at school level that encourage maintaining the achievement standards teachers require of the pupils are providing resources that enable regular tests of pupil achievement (test service systems, pupil monitoring systems) and a target policy to counter a defeatist attitude among teachers. Here one can think of methods like team discussions and counselling, initiated by the school head.
- A specific policy from the school management team directed at maintaining discipline and order in the school. An orderly atmosphere in a school building is more conducive to order in the classroom than chaos and uproar. A particular aspect that can play a role here is to curtail improper leave of absence. An elementary source of help for this is a proper register of absenteeism. An automated absentee registration system could be useful.
- Finally, reducing the number of lessons cancelled has a direct bearing on a school's effective learning time.

Opportunity to Learn

In education, learning objectives are specified and made concrete in two ways. First, a didactic specification occurs, leading to a number of teaching assignments that have to be carried out in order to reach mastery of the learning goals. Second, an assessment specification takes place in which learning objectives become operationalized as tests and examinations. Opportunity to learn is the extent to which the didactic specification relates to the assessment specification – how far what is being tested has been taught during lessons. Opportunity to learn stands or falls by the presence or absence of a valid and authorized assessment specification, such as a final test, which provides a good coverage of the learning objectives and which is officially recognized.

In secondary education national examinations should fulfil this function. In view of this starting point it is not exaggerating to propose that 'good' education is dependent on a valid and standardized test and examination system. When this is absent it is not even possible to indicate what good education is. Van der Linden (1987) has pointed out that the present secondary school examination system in the Netherlands does not meet these requirements by any means. Studies show that the more opportunity pupils have to practise course material and skills covered by a school-leaving test or examination the better the performance reached on average. For some (Van der Linden, 1989) this is even a reason to recommend teaching for tests as a desirable didactic principle. In view of the above this is a consistent line of reasoning. However, what must be emphasized again is that the starting point is an adequate test and examination system, which implies among other things the availability of so many assignments that the opportunity to practise letter for letter a specific examination assignment would be very small.

Practical school measures to encourage opportunity to learn all point to a screening of the entire test and examination assignments and to having this information in mind when selecting course material and exercises.

So far the instruction characteristics that emerge from the research literature as promoting effectiveness have been discussed. The conditions at school level that could promote the applicability of these micro-level instructional characteristics have been indicated in each case. These conditions can be summarized into three types: specific policy, activating consensus with regard to this policy, and tools and measures at school level that make it easier to implement effective instruction characteristics. The *teacher* has not been mentioned very much in the exposition; it should be emphasized, however, that the teacher is the most important 'producer' of the basic conditions for effective instruction.

In the following section on pedagogic conditions that promote effectiveness, conditions at school level are specifically dealt with. These are political pressure for achievement, aspects of educational leadership, the evaluative potential of the school, the school climate, recruitment policy, organizational and structural preconditions and selection processes.

PRESSURE FOR ACHIEVEMENT

In Chapter 1 attention was given to approaches to effectiveness in organizational theory. It emerged that productivity, which is interpreted here to mean effectiveness, is not the only possible definition of effectiveness. Other values that an organization can aspire to are: survival by safeguarding sufficient resources and basic materials; a large measure of cohesion and motivation among personnel; and stability and continuity. These alternative effectiveness criteria are summed up here as productivity back-up criteria; that is, it is assumed that to a certain degree a compromise must be reached in order to allow an organization to be as productive as possible. At the same time there is an awareness of the possibility that these back-up criteria can become objectives in themselves to the extent that productivity suffers.

In dealing here with pressure for achievement as an overt choice in school policy, no mono-maniac preoccupation with achievement is implied because the importance of back-up criteria is recognized. However, a specific bias in overall school policy to achieve the highest possible teaching results is seen as an important basic condition for actually realizing effectiveness. It depends on the particular circumstances of a school what emphasis should be given to the support criteria. It is understandable, for instance, that where a school's intake is dropping owing to demographic trends, the necessary investment will be made in recruiting, advertising and school marketing – in a broader sense the last of these could include advertising and product and consumer awareness.

Specific forms of school policy that, given the above-mentioned restrictions, may be called achievement-oriented are:

- recording annual 'attainment' figures in terms of percentages admitted to the various types of follow-up education, average test and examination results, data on drop-outs;
- using these mentioned figures in conjunction with a school policy for the immediate years ahead, and informing the education consumers (pupils) and their representatives (parents);
- placing 'attainment' on the agenda at staff meetings and in talks between the school head and individual staff;
- employing achievement pressure as a criterion when recruiting new teaching staff;
- implementing resources, including testing systems, that make it easier to introduce an achievement-oriented policy.

When discussing educational outcomes and educational productivity one ought to be specific about what types of results are actually meant. The simplest response to this is when overall measurements of results, such as the output or performance of pupils with regard to school-leaving examinations, are assumed. The possible criticism that such an interpretation of production criteria causes more important educational objectives, such as cooperative behaviour, independence and tolerance, to disappear from view is only partly relevant. In the first place examination systems only express what society expects from a specific school type. Whenever certain quantifiable dispositions that can be noted as achievements in education are *not* included in the examinations, the conclusion is that these objectives obviously do not have the highest priority. Moreover, these other educational objectives can be aspects that are not measurable or not teachable and there is a risk of lapsing into indoctrination. In both cases the exclusion of such educational objectives from a definition of productivity need not weigh too heavily (Doddema-Winsemius and Hofstee, 1987).

In school effectiveness research practice, productivity is mainly regarded as the result of testing basic skills like own language, arithmetic and maths. Is it then the intention, in order to follow in the footsteps of this restriction in research practice, to establish an achievement-oriented policy in the sense of 'back to basics'? To start with, the principle dealt with here is 'content-free'. It is established that an emphatic commitment to achieve a certain output is important for its actual realization, but the sort of output concerned is left open. Second, examination programmes and subjects included in final tests give a clear idea of the total areas in which educational attainment should be measured. By recognizing the importance of basic skills within this context, a broader area is defined than elementary basic skills. Third, with regard to the emphasis on achievement in school subjects, a similar differentiation can be made to that between productivity bias and support values. Objectives like 'being able to work with others' and 'can work independently on assignments' can be seen as support conditions for acquiring school knowledge.

ASPECTS OF EDUCATIONAL LEADERSHIP

The review studies on the type of leadership associated with school effectiveness give a picture that strongly corresponds with priority considerations in respect of whether or not to have an achievement-oriented school policy. Effective school heads are differentiated from average ones by the fact that they do not simply 'mind the shop' – in itself no mean task – but are also geared towards achieving high teaching results and, in order to realize this, are prepared to become actually involved with the teaching. In research where 'educational leadership' is compared to 'average school leadership', the latter is distinguished by an emphasis on administrative and management duties and striving for what is here identified as support effectiveness criteria, such as a harmonious relationship with the immediate environment, order and maintenance of the smooth running of the organization. With the average school head, however, these criteria are more goals in themselves than they are interpreted as being conducive to effectiveness or productivity. School heads who comply with the educational leadership description are strongly focused on the primary function of educating; that is, on the achievement of learning goals by pupils. Their entire management style is determined by this, without their losing sight of the importance of support criteria. In the way they interact with the world outside the accent is on acquiring facilities in order to make effective instruction possible, for instance by gaining resources or by persuading parents of pupils of the importance of certain conditions in the home for encouraging learning at school. With regard to staffing, a well considered recruitment policy is exercised, aimed at building up a homogeneous teaching staff. Pedagogic school heads carry out an active policy in appointing teachers to groups of pupils. Moreover, they encourage organizational and structural conditions that make consensus possible on the (achievement-oriented) mission of the school, and put every personal effort into making sure this consensus is achieved. Pedagogic school heads also assess what their teachers are doing, by, for instance, having talks with them about their work and about pupil performance or observing lessons.

Next, the pedagogic school head is active as far as the choice of teaching methods and resources is concerned. In view of the fact that he or she largely steers a course with a compass of information emanating from records of pupils' progress, frequent assessment is quite important. At the same time he or she will go all out to acquire and implement the necessary tools for this, as well as storing the information and making it readily available.

At first glance the description of 'educational leadership' conjures up an image of a show of management strength: not only the routine work necessary for the smooth running of a school, but also active involvement with what is traditionally regarded as the work sphere of the teachers. A basic requisite for educational leadership is time management, so that back-up and routine assignments leave sufficient time for the more pedagogic tasks. Nevertheless, this leadership does not always have to come down to the efforts of one main leader. From the school effectiveness research of Mortimore *et al.* (1988) it emerges that deputy heads in particular fulfil educational leadership duties. Delegation can go further than this level: it is desirable that, given the consensus of a basic mission for the school, there is as broad as possible a participation in the decision-making. In the end certain effects of pedagogic leadership, such as a homogeneous team, will fulfil a self-generating function and act as a substitute for school leadership (according to Kerr's (1977) idea of 'substitutes for leadership').

At the same time there are structural impediments to achieving this sort of school leadership. Images of school organization as determined by the professional autonomy of teachers, and as being a 'loosely coupled' system, illustrate clearly the limitations of this type of school leadership. Moreover, certain restrictions could arise in carrying out an effective personnel policy owing to the terms and conditions by which teachers are employed. And last but not least, the entire functioning and motivation of teachers will be dependent on their satisfaction with national education policy and by the 'cost–benefit analysis' of the burden of teaching responsibilities on the one hand and reward and public regard for the profession on the other. Ways to remove these stumbling blocks should be sought both inside and outside the school.

Internally, educational leadership implies a certain depreciation in the professional autonomy of teachers. Where schools are labelled 'professional bureaucracies', pedagogic leadership serves to strengthen the bureaucratic component. At the same time this type of leadership appeals to professional values like competency and a greater consumer awareness. More involvement from the school head in what the teachers are doing need not be demonstrated in the form of directives from above; a more acceptable form for professionals, such as collegial support, can be chosen (Firestone and Wilson, 1987). In other words a certain encroachment on professional autonomy need not infringe on the professional status of the teaching profession. Deregulation, inspection and reward for output are external conditions that can support school effectiveness-oriented educational leadership.

THE EVALUATIVE POTENTIAL OF THE SCHOOL

Assessment emerges at every level of the school effectiveness model as a necessary consequence of an effectiveness-oriented policy. At classroom level assessment is one of the basic characteristics of structured teaching. At school level assessing pupils' progress and the way teachers function is one of the pillars of educational leadership. In the discussion of 'opportunity to learn' the importance of proper final testing and examinations has already been pointed out. When I deal later with the relevant contextual characteristics of school effectiveness, the implications of periodic assessment and inspection at the national level will be examined more closely.

In discussions on the governability of organizations in the public sector it is often stated that these avoid rational planning and control because the results are not quantifiable. This view when it involves schools does insufficient justice to psychometric developments with regard to testing. The techniques to measure educational output are certainly there; that not enough use is made of them is another matter (Van der Linden, 1987).

In management theory, evaluation is an elementary requirement for effective management. In organizational and management theory debates the question is frequently raised as to how far rational operative models can be applied to complex organizations. As far as schools are concerned the characterization of a school as a professional bureaucracy can again be referred to. One of the features of this is that autonomous professionals cannot stand having their work assessed, particularly when the assessment is of their personal ability to function. Consequently, in schools there is a certain resistance to evaluation. Organizational preconditions to assessing the entire school spectrum and conditions to make use of evaluative results within the school's policy are often insufficient. The extent to which schools succeed in (a) actually utilizing the technological potential of educational assessment and (b) overcoming organizational stumbling blocks for evaluation is identified by the term 'the evaluative potential of the school' (for a further discussion see Scheerens, 1987). It is quite likely that schools will differ in their evaluative potential and in the relevant research literature there are indications that this has implications for effectiveness. Schools can increase their assessment ability by:

- using methods (schoolbooks) that incorporate testing;
- making more use of standardized school progress tests within the framework of whole-school evaluation;
- making use of data banks, testing systems and school management information systems;
- institutionalizing talks on teaching performance between the head and individual staff;
- allowing staff to follow in-service courses on educational evaluation;
- making use of tools for self-evaluation, also identified by the term 'school-based review';
- creating minimum organizational prerequisites for implementing and utilizing evaluation, such as periodic meetings between staff or departments.

Finally, I will make a few remarks on the attainability of matters like 'educational leadership' and 'increasing the evaluative potential of a school'. Both may be regarded as aspects of rational management. Both infringe up to a point on the professional autonomy of teachers and both pull the school organization in the direction of a bureaucratic organization model because formal authority is confirmed and there is a certain formalizing of relations (for instance, in the form of specific agreements on producing assessment data). Such developments can expect resistance within schools. Increasing the evaluative potential of a school can be seen as the first step towards educational leadership. By school management focusing on assessment results, by, for instance, regularly talking with staff about tests and examination results, discussions on objectives can gain a concrete basis and interminable dialogue – a well-known experience in the process of drawing up a school curriculum – can be avoided. In short, working towards increasing the evaluative potential of a school appears to be a good starting point for achieving effectiveness-enhancing conditions at school and classroom level.

THE SCHOOL CLIMATE

In the school effectiveness literature a number of desired characteristics, including an emphasis on basic skills, high expectations, frequent assessment, and order and a secure setting, are presented sometimes as characteristics of educational leadership and at other times as characteristics of school climate. In my opinion, associating these characteristics with school leadership is more practical because then one is referring to a concrete 'actor' who has certain opportunities to achieve one thing or another. The term 'school climate' stresses the point that the relevant, desired characteristics ought to have broad support within a school structure. Consensus on an achievement-oriented 'mission' of a school, a joint effort to create an orderly atmosphere and involvement in assessment activities are the central characteristics of an effectiveness-promoting school climate. School climate also expresses the fact that these desired characteristics of a school can be of a long-term nature. Because school climate refers more to the resultant manipulation of other school characteristics than to a direct manipulable characteristic of schools, it will not be discussed any further. Our interest, after all, is largely in malleable conditions.

STAFF RECRUITMENT AND STAFF DEVELOPMENT

Technological resources, like structured teaching and assessment tools, may be significant in making schools more effective but the key to school effectiveness lies with those who have to teach. In an earlier section I dwelt on the demands that are made by a pedagogic school leadership. Earlier, the fact that teachers must 'carry' the effectiveness-promoting instruction characteristics was dealt with.

A specific personnel policy is thus an important tool for making schools more effective. In the largely theoretical situation of a school having to recruit its staff entirely from scratch, first an instructionally focused school head would have to be appointed, whereupon he or she could then draw up as homogeneous as possible a group of teachers. From the conditions discussed above, certain points for attention when selecting staff can be elaborated upon. As well as the obvious criteria, such as competency and experience, attitude towards an achievement-oriented educational philosophy should be noted, together with familiarity with the principles of structured teaching and methods of assessment, and willingness and ability to work together with colleagues. Certainly the desired characteristics can, within the framework of staff development, be brought about via coaching from the school head and in-service training. Another approach which is, for instance, carried out in the Netherlands consists of refresher courses offered at national level. It must be noted, however, that existing employment regulations, such as the 'last in, first out' principle and automatic promotion, do not encourage the pursuit of an effective personnel policy.

ORGANIZATIONAL AND STRUCTURAL PRECONDITIONS

From the instruction and school characteristics dealt with, four aspects can be suggested that make intervention in the organization structure desirable (by organization structure, the breakdown of the organization into departments and functions, and the more enduring relations between units, is meant):

1 High demands placed on the school management, who form a 'multi' management consisting of the head and deputy head(s) – this is particularly desirable as schools become bigger.
2 Demands made on consultations about teaching duties at school, in view of the need for consensus on educational aims and the dialogue that obviously goes with the implementation of instruments like assessment systems and the introduction of computers for management and instruction purposes; formalized staff discussion and departmental meetings can meet these needs.
3 The use of information systems, to institutionalize flows of information from one stratum of the organization to another.

4   The growing need for specialist education technology know-how can create new staff functions, such as system controller or pedagogic staff worker.

In school organization models, such as the ones developed by Marx (1975), particular attention is given to formalized consultation as a response to the increasing individualization of education. In later references, inspired by Marx's work, schools with a well-developed consultation structure were considered to be more resilient to all manner of outside intervention, such as imposed mergers (Gooren, 1989). In the school effectiveness model presented here such organizational and structural conditions are seen as having a buffer function, which to a certain extent must be complied with, in order to make the primary production process of the organization relevant to society's needs on the one hand, and to protect it from various distractions on the other. So although in school effectiveness thinking consultation is largely seen as function-related, it also has a role in an organization's power to survive and where possible in the motivation and job satisfaction of the teachers.

SELECTION PROCESSES

Schools can vary in the severity of their internal selection processes. Aspects of this include the policy with regard to resitting a class, recommending a 'lower' level of secondary education or identifying primary school children for special education, and whether or not a conservative policy is followed in putting candidates forward for central written examinations. This factor has not been mentioned here as a characteristic that would promote school effectiveness, but as something that is important for interpreting achievement and output data. In measuring output the selection factor is often taken into account because the number of graduates is divided by the number of the relevant pupil cohort or because pupils who leave between times gain a score for a variable like 'education level reached'. However, whenever test data at the end of training serve as an effectiveness criterion, differences in selection during training are usually not taken into account. This can lead to misleading interpretations with regard to the relative effectiveness of schools (Bosker and Scheerens, 1989).

PHYSICAL AND MATERIAL SCHOOL CHARACTERISTICS

For the sake of completeness attention will be given to certain school characteristics that have often been studied, but from which no significant or unequivocal correlation with teaching results has been found. This category includes school building, size of school, facilities, classroom size and expenditure per pupil.

Now and then it has been established that favourable *physical characteristics of a school building*, such as the amount of light, fresh air and an acceptable level of noise, are positively linked to achievement and negatively to vandalism (Chan, 1979; Goldman, 1961). From most of the studies, however, it appears that the age and state of a school building are hardly important (Anderson, 1982; Bridge *et al.*, 1979).

The extent of the *facilities* available in a school, such as a library, an assembly hall or a gym, hardly ties in with differences in achievement between schools. Various researchers have pointed out that how the facilities are *used* is more decisive than their actual presence.

The results of studies on the effects of *school size* are not unequivocal; the link with cognitive performance is tenuous. In Dutch research (Stoel, 1980; Van Marwijk Kooij-von Baumhauer, 1984), a negative link was found between school size and the way pupils experience school. Economic studies on the efficiency of increasing school size are anything but clear cut in that there is a lack of consensus on how big a school should be. What is valid is that very small schools are more expensive than large ones.

With regard to *class size*, there are again conflicting research findings. The most plausible is that within the range of 20 to 35 pupils class size has little effect on pupil attainment; only when classes are clearly smaller can this produce advantages.

Educational economists obviously have often been preoccupied with studies on the effect of differences in *expenditure per pupil*. From various review studies it seems that there is no reason to suppose that high expenditure has a favourable effect on educational output (Hanushek, 1986). An explanation for the inconsistency and lack of effect of this school characteristic is that the margins by which schools vary on these points are simply too slight to lead to any significant effect. Only with much larger differences in size, expenditure and facilities could one expect significant effects.

In the construction of the integrated school effectiveness model presented earlier, context characteristics were differentiated, along with instruction characteristics at classroom level and school level organizational characteristics. These will be discussed in the ensuing sections under the headings of descriptive environmental characteristics and 'active' efficiency-enhancing stimuli.

DESCRIPTIVE CHARACTERISTICS OF THE SCHOOL AND SCHOOL ENVIRONMENT

Certain characteristics are not easy to manipulate, but nevertheless affect levels of achievement. To begin with, the composition of the school population plays a role. High numbers of disadvantaged pupils and ethnic minorities push down the performance of the entire pupil population. Because the central concern here is with the 'construction' of effective schools no further attention is given to these contextual characteristics. A second specific school characteristic is the denomination of schools and differences between private and state schools. From various American and Dutch studies it emerges that independent schools have higher levels of achievement on average (a recent example is the research of Blok and Eiting, 1988b). These study results have been criticized because the differences could largely be attributed to the differences in socio-economic status of the pupil populations. An explanation for the better attainment levels in independent and private schools is looked for in greater parental involvement with the school and a larger consensus between parents and school personnel on teaching goals.

A third category of specific school characteristics concerns the geographical setting of a school: rural, inner city or suburb. The effects of these contextual characteristics on teaching output can, however, be explained away by the differences in background of the pupil populations – even though this does not apply entirely to absenteeism, which in large cities is greater than in rural schools.

An interesting, fairly recent development in school effectiveness research aims at establishing whether well-known effectiveness-promoting school characteristics work in the same way in schools with various contextual characteristics (see Chapter 5). The results of this type of study do not refute the importance of the effectiveness-promoting school characteristics already discussed, but do indicate a number of interesting nuances. For example, Firestone and Herriott (1982) established that in secondary education the factor 'accent on basic skills' was more broadly interpreted than in primary education – broad in the sense that effective secondary modern schools had an explicit mission to excel in all subject fields. Firestone and Wilson (1987) found that in effective secondary schools, especially schools with a relatively high socio-economic status pupil population, more emphasis was placed on the supportive aspects of school leadership as opposed to the more controlling ones than in primary schools with a majority of low socio-economic status pupils. Teddlie *et al.* (1987) established that in schools with relatively low socio-economic status pupils school heads had to appear much more obviously as initiators of educational reform than heads of schools with a high SES composition. The latter school heads could delegate more to teachers and leave more of the stimulating influence to parents.

EXTERNAL STIMULI TO MAKE SCHOOLS MORE EFFECTIVE

Schools are subject to the same kind of mechanisms as every organization in the public sector. This means that there will be a greater preoccupation with acquiring inputs and extending services than with an efficient production of outputs. Means of cutting through the dominant reward structure include privatization, deregulation and output financing. With privatization, educational institutes would be subject to market mechanisms and therefore forced to work more efficiently. Deregulation offers schools more opportunities to acquire resources independently and if necessary more freedom to modify the internal reward structure. Here it would be going too far to discuss all the variants and the advantages and disadvantages of privatization and deregulation (see, for instance, Boorsma, 1984). Suffice it to say that a government could adopt these practices in theory, with a view to stimulating efficiency within education. That this has been considered by the Dutch government can be witnessed from its White Paper 'The school on the way to 2000' (Ministry of Education and Science, 1988).

One instrument that forces educational institutions to concern themselves more with the quality and quantity of output is output financing. It is conceivable that output financing could be applied on the basis of certain indicators of the quantity of educational outcomes (proportions of exam passes, for instance). Not only results to do with quantity should be heeded, however, but also the level of knowledge and skills acquired by pupils; otherwise a lowering of standards could occur. This would be a very bad side-effect of output financing of educational institutions. Implementation of output financing in primary and secondary education would probably have no more than marginal significance. One could imagine that schools with high levels of achievement – taking the starting situation of pupils into account – would be rewarded with extra facilities. Less probable is that the survival of these sorts of schools would be made dependent on producing sufficient qualifying output.

A less harsh method that could be implemented to stimulate schools' output would be an assessment-centred government policy. Examples of this include working with official final goals for the various school categories, national assessments and working with so-called education indicator systems (educational statistics providing evidence on the quality of education). National assessment programmes and indicator systems produce data on the state of education at a national level, and this information need not necessarily be used for official intervention in specific schools. Nevertheless, it can be assumed that even such a school-transcending application would encourage a greater inclination towards output in education. Results from national assessment programmes can at least lead to debate in the media, so that various societal groups could be brought together to make demands on the quality of education.

Taken one step further, assessment results of indicators could be used in part to control schools; the government could do this with those schools where it was the administrative authority. For other types of schools, local authorities or school governing bodies could use the relevant data, let us say, to exchange ideas with schools on the achievement produced. In this connection the schools inspectorate should be mentioned. It is anticipated that the inspectorate could fulfil its duty of monitoring standards better if it had more concrete evaluative data on schools. (For a more detailed discussion on implementing educational indicators see Scheerens (1990).)

The *involvement of parents* in education is an environmental condition that appears to be beneficial to the quality of education. This is largely to do with the home situation backing up the conditions that promote learning at school. Another aspect is parental demands on the school itself. Parents of children can be considered as representatives of education consumers. In theory parents are important stakeholders in the schools their children attend and their demands could be an important external stimulus to urge schools to be effective. In practice, however, the situation is different. In the organized education field pupil and parent bodies play a subordinate role (Leune, 1987). Moreover, parental involvement greatly depends on socio-economic background – this basically means that involvement is absent where it is most needed.

It would seem desirable that the government – especially if it wants to be seen as watching from the sidelines – encourage education consumers to play a stronger role in making demands on schools. The data that become available from the evaluation-centred policy should be made accessible and usable to the education consumer. This could be done, for instance, by making public the academic performances of schools and publishing results in local media, as currently happens in the United Kingdom. Forms of privatization, such as voucher systems, are often mentioned as a stimulus to encourage education consumers to become more involved with the quality of education.

In any discussion of external impulses for schools to work effectively, cultural aspects play a role. One such aspect is how far the quality of education is really an issue in society. In the Netherlands at present the reply to this would be 'not much', although it is conceivable that the significance currently placed on the word 'schooling' by private industry could create a movement in the opposite direction. Another social/cultural aspect that should be mentioned in this context is how the teaching profession is valued. There is of course a financial or economic side to this. In the Netherlands it is acknowledged that teachers have a heavy work load, but at the same time it has been established that there is no room at all to make the teaching profession more financially attractive.

SUMMARY AND CONCLUSIONS

In this chapter the results of various types of effectiveness research have been drawn together into one general model. The main formal characteristics of this model are that effectiveness-promoting conditions at various levels – the classroom, school and school environment – should be seen in relation to one another. The relationship in question is interpreted to mean that high-level conditions reinforce low-level conditions.

At classroom level the factors considered most important are structured teaching, effective learning time and opportunity to learn. At the meso level of the school organization the following characteristics were discussed:

- pressure for achievement as an explicit choice in school policy;
- aspects of instructional leadership;
- recruitment of qualified staff;
- evaluative potential of the school;
- financial and material resources of the school;
- school climate.

In addition, several organizational and structural preconditions that are thought to enhance effective policies and effective classroom practices were discussed. These comprise multiple leadership functions when schools grow bigger; opportunities for consultations among teachers (such as department meetings); the use of information systems; and (possibly) new specialized staff functions, such as system controller or pedagogic staff worker. As relevant descriptive characteristics of schools and school settings, the following variables were discussed:

- composition of the student population with respect to socio-economic status and number of pupils from minority groups;
- religious denomination of schools and the distinction between private and public schools;
- geographical setting (rural, inner-city or suburban);
- school size;
- incentives for higher administrative levels to improve the performance of schools;
- involvement of parents and demands made by educational consumers.

The integrated model thus consists of:

1 A multi-level formal structure.
2 The general principle that higher-level characteristics are seen as facilitators of lower-level conditions, as a specific interpretation of the nature of cross-level relationships.
3 Substantive findings; that is, the most important variables that have emerged from various types of educational effectiveness research.

With respect to this summary of research evidence some general observations must be made. First of all, the model implies a normative choice, namely to accept the fact that school effectiveness research findings generally depend on cognitive outcomes in basic school subjects. As pointed out above, the model could become different if other types of educational outcomes were considered.

Second, the empirical evidence for the various effective school and classroom characteristics varies. Some factors have repeatedly been confirmed and reconfirmed in empirical studies. Others depend on little more than conjecture (see Table 6.1).

Third, most of the factors described in this chapter are considered to be malleable; that is, they can be actively manipulated by teachers, school heads or administrators. In practice, attempts to change these factors are often improvement programmes in which several of the factors are manipulated at the same time. The next chapter is dedicated to school improvement efforts that are inspired by the results of school effectiveness research.

Chapter 7

School Improvement: Levers for Enhancing School Effectiveness

INTRODUCTION

In this book an attempt has been made to make sense of the many research findings concerning school effectiveness, by carefully evaluating their validity, by trying to relate the findings to theoretical constructs and models, and by interpreting them in terms of a 'practical theory' of school effectiveness. School effectiveness is seen as both an intriguing area of academic study and an important source of inspiration for improving educational practice. With respect to this practical interest the key question is: to what extent does school effectiveness research and theory offer concrete and specific guidelines for school improvement?

In Chapter 6 I attempted to integrate and interpret the major research findings into a description of factors that should be considered as effectiveness-enhancing. For several reasons this process did not produce a viable blueprint for school improvement.

- First, as was explicitly shown in Table 6.1, the research evidence is inconclusive and conclusions on the positive influence of several major factors are still rather tentative.
- Second, in several parts of this book the 'differential' nature and contextual specificity of school effectiveness research has been emphasized, which implies that local applications of the 'practical theory of school effectiveness' should be adapted to situational characteristics.
- Third, between school effectiveness models – no matter how sophisticated – and the application of such models in educational practice there must be a process of educational change. It goes without saying that every insight that has been gained in the field of strategies of educational innovation and school improvement is needed to bridge the gap between theoretical school effectiveness models and practical applications.
- Finally, comprehensive models of school effectiveness have not yet reached a sufficient level of sophistication to establish clearly the *order of influence* of the variables, in the sense of which variables actually precede others causally' (Creemers and Reynolds, 1989, p. 340).

In this chapter I will consider several broader categories that could be manipulated as levers for enhancing school effectiveness. Generally, available school effectiveness models include three main categories of factors that could be thought of as 'kicking an improvement process into life':

1 External influences that come into contact with the school.
2 The internal self-renewing capacity of schools.
3 Technological developments.

These three approaches correspond to the level of school context, the level of school organization and the primary process of teaching and learning at classroom level. They also roughly resemble Bennis *et al.*'s (1969) well-known distinction between power-coercive, normative re-educative and rational-empirical innovation strategies. In the integrated model of school effectiveness discussed in Chapters 2 and 6, the key factors that determine these various potential 'causes' for school effectiveness research have their place in the context and process dimension (see Figure 2.1).

Joyce (1991) follows an approach that is somewhat similar. He mentions five 'doors to school improvement':

- *Collegiality*: 'developing cohesive and professional relations within school faculties and connecting them more closely to their surrounding neighbourhoods'.
- *Research*: 'helping school faculties study research findings about effective school practices or instructional alternatives'.
- *Site-specific information*: data collection and analysis by schools.
- *Curriculum initiatives*: introducing changes within subject areas.
- *Instructional initiatives*: organizing teachers to study teaching skills and strategies.

Joyce's categories 'collegiality' and 'site-specific information' correspond to the development of the internal self-renewing capacity of schools, whereas 'research', 'curriculum initiatives' and 'instructional initiatives' can be subsumed under technological developments.

A general response to Creemers and Reynolds's question about the 'order of influence' of variables has been implied in the earlier discussion of the metaphor of schools as 'nested layers'. The primary causes of educational achievement are to be defined at the level closest to the individual learning processes of pupils (i.e. the classroom level), whereas school organization and the local environment contain increasingly removed supportive conditions.

Examples of external and internal stimulants of school improvement that will be briefly examined in this chapter are: changing the external incentive structure of schools; human resource development; changing the school culture; and increasing the evaluative potential of schools. Restructuring the school's curriculum and creating conditions for effective instruction will be discussed within the context of their functions as technological 'levers' to improve education. The discussion of these approaches culminates in the recommendation that all school improvement projects should be comprehensive in two ways: they should be directed to all levels of the functioning of educational organizations, and should combine various levers for enhancing effectiveness. The chapter concludes with brief sketches of some comprehensive school improvement projects.

It should be noted that the entire area of improvement strategies and processes will not be discussed here. For this subject the reader is referred to several excellent publications in this series that concentrate on this specific area (most notably Fullan, 1991; Hargreaves and Hopkins, 1991).

LEVERS FOR ENHANCING SCHOOL EFFECTIVENESS

Tinkering with Incentive Structures

In the previous chapter, privatization, deregulation, output-financing of schools and 'evaluation-centred' educational policy-making were mentioned as instances of altering the incentive structure of schools. The overall intention of these measures is to 'force' schools to become more efficient, i.e. to produce better results at lower cost or at least to reach higher achievement levels with the same budget. Public choice theory, as discussed in Chapter 2, supplies the scientific background to these approaches.

During the past decade many European countries have used some of these ideas in their educational policies (Scheerens, 1992). Although making schools more autonomous is the feature that is explicitly emphasized in propagating these policies, there are also certain centralizing tendencies. In the UK, for instance, the 1988 Education Reform Act brought increased autonomy to individual schools, in the sense of financial control and devolved management, but at the same time a national curriculum and a massive centralized assessment programme were announced. These changes in national education policies coincided (although the relationship is more than coincidental) with a continued contraction in national budgets for education from the early 1980s, and the fact that at that time right-wing governments were in power in many European countries.

It should be noted that current policies to make schools more efficient that are somehow inspired by the market metaphor combine several rather different ingredients:

- enhancing the managerial and financial autonomy of schools in order to enhance their responsiveness and allow them to be run more like private enterprises (e.g. by means of block grants and forms of privatization);
- instances of output control (national assessment, educational indicator systems, output finance);
- stimulating educational consumerism (by making schools publish achievement data and strengthening the position of educational consumers in school governance).

The first and third ingredients can be seen as true steps to enhancing the functioning of market mechanisms in education, whereas the second, evaluation-centred educational policy is more like a surrogate for control by the market. Furthermore, despite the overall objective of improving the functioning of local educational markets (a tendency towards decentralization) the whole enterprise is centrally orchestrated. Usually schools are not really eager to become more financially autonomous and, apparently, educational consumerism does not grow by itself, but must be externally stimulated. This could be viewed as a contradictory element in this approach to educational improvement. The way the pros and cons of this approach are seen strongly depends on one's evaluation of the nature of schools as professional organizations. When emphasis is placed on the positive elements of this image of schools, such as professional responsibility and the intrinsic motivation of relatively autonomous professionals, many of the market-inspired policy measures will be judged as counterproductive and even harmful. When stress is put on the negative side of professionalism, such as unresponsiveness to external changes and client demands, immunization against external control and resistances to rationalization and innovation of work processes, market-inspired changes could be seen as the only way to awaken the educational province from its alleged lethargy.

Apart from its merits, the *feasibility* of externally changing the incentive structures of schools remains an important question. The inventiveness and resourcefulness of schools to counter and use to their own advantage even compelling central policy measures should not be underestimated. For instance, in one British local education authority (LEA), schools produced a lot of 'process' data about their internal functioning in addition to the achievement data they were forced to publish. The additional data were used both for marketing purposes (to attract pupils on grounds other than previous outcomes) and for self-evaluation processes.

Two final remarks about the practice of publishing school outcome data to stimulate consumers to 'vote with their feet' about a school's continuity should be made. The first is that publishing raw, unadjusted test or exam results paints a distorted picture of a school's effectiveness. As in school effectiveness *research*, the concept of value added (i.e. achievement measures adjusted for entrance behaviour, previous achievement or socio-economic back-ground) is of vital importance. Second, even valid performance data for schools are likely to enforce inequalities in education, since choice mechanisms will be affected by inequalities among consumers to use performance data properly.

The Self-renewing Capacity of Schools

The concept of schools as professional bureaucracies indicates why schools are slow to change and, at the same time, shows the 'natural' way to improve their functioning: through recruitment and training of professionals. This is a complex and slow endeavour. From many of the process characteristics of school effectiveness models, it is quite evident that factors such as instructional leadership, high expectations for pupils' achievement, an orderly climate and a shared achievement-oriented mission strongly depend on the attitudes and skills of the staff. The question that must be considered here is what triggers heads and teachers to behave according to these effectiveness-enhancing characteristics.

Traditionally, facilitators of educational innovation have focused on socio-psychological aspects of the functioning of school teams. This was inspired by the human relations approach in organizational science. The concept of enabling schools to improve themselves was considerably broadened in the International School Improvement Project (ISIP), in which school improvement was depicted in terms of mutually reinforcing processes of school-based review, supportive educational leadership, external support, educational policy measures at national level, and professional development of teachers and school administrators, e.g. by means of in-service training (Hopkins, 1987, pp. 193–6).

The process orientation of school improvement has remained, however (Creemers and Reynolds, 1989), with particular emphasis being placed on consensus building and participatory decision-making. In my opinion the literature on educational innovation and school improvement has indicated that the self-renewing capacity of schools is currently more like the desirable end-state of considerable investment on the part of educational support agencies than like an intrinsically powerful lever for enhancing school effectiveness. The most promising feature, reinforced within the framework of the ISIP, appears to be school diagnosis or school-based review, as a first step in making schools learning and responsive organizations (in a later section on enhancing the evaluative potential of schools, more attention will be given to school self-evaluation). Yet the process of developing and implementing a procedure of school-based review is (rightly) depicted as an educational innovation project in itself, and requires external support.

The Failing Technological Revolution in Education

Process factors at the core of the school effectiveness model presented here (see Figure 2.1) are concerned with the technology of the primary process of instruction. Direct instruction, mastery learning and stimulation of meta-cognition (i.e. learning to learn) are all factors in a structured approach. Educational technology is interpreted here both in the broad sense of systematic ways to achieve educational objectives (i.e. a plan for the school curriculum) and in the narrow sense of the application of electronic devices such as audio-visual media and computers.

Again, the question is whether technological innovation could be considered a primary lever for enhancing school effectiveness. Although improvement at the instructional level is clearly essential for attaining better educational achievement, the answer is negative: it is very unlikely that the availability of advanced educational technology will set improvement processes in motion. For one thing, laboratory-designed educational technology should be adapted to local conditions. Another factor is that professionals will tend to be critical of methods that 'mechanize' part of their work. Even in the event of a positive reception of new technology, teachers will need time to develop a sense of 'ownership' (as the school improvement people say) of the new methods.

Economists tend to compare education to agriculture in expressing the observation that a technological revolution in education has failed so far. In the 1960s some utopians believed that radical changes could be brought about by the use of audio-visual media. In practice a lot of expensive material remained locked in cupboards. Similar visions were outlined with respect to the influence of the computer in education (see Pogrow, 1983). Although the availability of computers in schools has sharply increased during the past decade (Pelgrum, 1990), the computer as a teaching medium (computer-assisted instruction rather than learning how to program a computer) is still applied only in a very modest way in most countries. Experts in the field of computers in education are still doubtful about the chances that the amazing range of technological possibilities will ever be implemented in the field of education on a large scale (Moonen, 1990).

The view that new technology would be a primary lever for school improvement corresponds to the research, development and diffusion (RDD) approach, a type of innovation strategy that has long since lost its appeal for educational innovation theorists. Nevertheless, if it is accompanied by careful implementation strategies, a revival of RDD might be applauded. In my opinion, technological inputs could give substance to process-oriented school improvement, just as carefully designed changes in incentive structures could add a facilitating *contextual* element.

An intriguing aspect of improving the general technology of a school (i.e. the school curriculum) can be seen in instances of curriculum planning at school level. Since the second half of the 1970s, elementary and secondary schools in the Netherlands have been encouraged to develop so-called 'school working plans' (general school curricula). The experiences have not been very encouraging. In many instances 'paper' plans were developed that bore little relationship to the actual teaching at classroom level. Frequently, schools did not progress much further than endless discussions about general teaching aims. Evaluations revealed that there was no relationship between the use of school working plans and educational achievement (Van der Werf, 1988). It is interesting to compare the Dutch experiences in this field to the more recent efforts in the UK with respect to school development plans (Hargreaves *et al.*, 1989). The ways in which school development planning (SDP) in the UK differs from the Dutch work with school working plans (SWP) are probably reasons to be more optimistic about the success of the former approach:

- SDP is enforced by a pre-specified national curriculum, whereas the development of SWP was not;
- SDP starts out with an audit or diagnosis of the current state of affairs, whereas in SWP the approach started with an attempt to formulate general objectives, which in the next phase had to be put into operation;
- SDP is a more comprehensive approach, including in-service training and staff development planning, while SWP was only curriculum planning;
- in SDP a lot of systematic attention is given to implementation and frequent (formative as well as summative) evaluation; this was generally not the case with SWP;
- SDP includes school management development, whereas SWP did not.

Enhancing the Evaluative Potential of Schools

The centrality of evaluation in school effectiveness models has already been discussed in previous chapters. The question that should now be addressed is whether evaluative or diagnostic activities are feasible starting points for school improvement processes. In theory, it makes a lot of sense to assess the current situation and determine strengths and weaknesses of organizational functioning, as an initial step in deciding upon priorities for improvement. One of the advantages of this approach is that, provided the initial assessment or diagnosis is structured and empirical, the discussion of innovation targets can be concrete and specific. In this way, abstract 'goal clarification games' can be avoided in the initial phase of, for instance, school development planning. This does not mean that the formulation of overall educational aims should be avoided, but rather that the meaning of more global and abstract educational ideals can be directly referred to the reality of the current functioning of the school.

In accordance with the integrated model of school effectiveness, the evaluative potential of schools refers to evaluation activities at various levels. At the classroom level the frequent testing of student progress lies at the heart of structured instruction. At the meso level of the school organization, school-based review could be seen as a vital prerequisite to organizational learning. Finally, at the level of the school's direct environment, consumer demands for objective information and accountability requirements from higher administrative levels also press for evaluative data on certain key aspects of the school's functioning.

Whether in practice evaluation can indeed fulfil its potential to be a primary lever for enhancing school effectiveness depends on the satisfactory resolution of several issues. First, it should be recognized that teachers and schools often resist evaluation activities (often for very good reasons, as when the evaluation's validity is doubted or when there are doubts about the proper use to be made of the evaluation results). This means that the very least that should be done is that the initiators should provide information on the purposes, methods and use of evaluation procedures. Second, school evaluations can be divided into two major categories: those initiated for accountability purposes and those meant for self-reflection and improvement.

A balance must be struck between the extremes of feeling threatened by external accountability demands on the one hand, and non-committal, uncritical, subjective self-evaluation on the other. The tension between divergent functions of school evaluations is one of the reasons why evaluation-centred school improvement is rightly seen as an innovation in itself. Schools should know the various possible functions and be familiar with the range of available methods and techniques. Incidentally, evaluation for accountability and evaluation for school improvement should not be seen as mutually exclusive categories. In most instances the main categories of data (i.e. process and outcome data) will be needed for both. There is also a common requirement for objectivity. One important distinguishing characteristic might be that evaluation for school improvement generally requires more detailed information on educational processes (along with data on student progress) than evaluation for accountability.

Third, school evaluation at the various levels of school organization requires certain skills: knowledge about data collection methods, techniques to retrieve, store, process and analyse data, possibly using computers for these functions, and skills of reporting and feeding back evaluation results. This implies that certain functionaries in the school will have to be trained in these skills. At the same time it is most likely that to some degree schools need to depend on external support agencies.

Finally, user-friendly technology for school self-evaluation must become available. In this respect, a lot of work has already been done on developing instruments for school-based review, school management information systems and pupil monitoring systems (for overviews see Hopkins, 1988, 1989; Voogt, 1989; Scheerens and Hopkins, 1992).

In summary then, it is believed that the evaluation-centred approach to school improvement has great potential. The degree to which a school's capacity for self-renewal can be identified depends strongly on appropriate evaluation mechanisms. At the same time it should be recognized that there is a lot in the operation of schools that depends upon practical experience, input regulation and professional routines. Therefore the rational ideal of organizational learning based on self-diagnosis and self-evaluation should not be extended to such a degree that it could stifle professional ingenuity and more informal processes of evaluation and feedback.

SCHOOL IMPROVEMENT AND SCHOOL EFFECTIVENESS RECONSIDERED

Quite differently from the usual slow percolation of social scientific knowledge into policy-making and practice, the results of school effectiveness studies have been readily adopted by practitioners, at least in the USA. As early as 1982, Odden and Dougherty mentioned that most states in the USA had implemented school improvement programmes that reflected features of the effective schools literature. Several authors have questioned why educational reformers appeared to be so eager to apply the insights gained from school effectiveness studies. Mackenzie (1983, p. 6) points at the common-sense appeal of the original five- or seven-factor models of school effectiveness. He also mentions that after the era of pedagogical pessimism induced by the work of Coleman and Jencks in the late 1960s and early 1970s, educational practitioners were ready for some more encouraging messages. Ralph and Fennessey (1983) doubt the objectivity and validity of school effectiveness research and suggest that from the very beginning the effective schools perspective has been a 'rhetoric of reform' rather than a scientific model.

At least two things are necessary to apply the results of school effectiveness research: research results and strategies for educational change. Reynolds *et al.* (1989, p. 802) demonstrate that traditions in the field of educational innovation are quite important for the adaptation of research results. They indicate that efficient use of school effectiveness research results for school improvement purposes in the UK was hampered, in the 1960s and 1970s, by a top-down quantitative orientation, and later, in the early 1980s, by a bias towards focusing innovations upon the individual teacher and a strongly qualitative orientation. In the Netherlands, apart from one major exception (the Education and Social Environment Programme of the city of Rotterdam), the educational support structure has been very slow in making use of school effectiveness research findings. Only quite recently was a start made, with various effectiveness-inspired school improvement projects (in the cities of Amsterdam, Rotterdam and Utrecht, and in the province of Friesland).

The two worlds of school effectiveness researchers on the one hand and school improvement facilitators on the other have different traditions and, although much progress has been made in recent years to bridge the gap between them, harmonious cooperation is still difficult (Creemers and Reynolds, 1989). Some of the grounds for this schism are:

- the quantitative orientation of researchers compared to the predominantly qualitative orientation of the school improvers;
- an interest in abstraction and generalization (large-scale research) versus an interest in local, situational factors that call for specific applications in each case;
- an objective versus a more engaged attitude;
- being attuned to different audiences, namely the scientific community of educational researchers versus educational officers and school personnel.

Apart from these perhaps somewhat exaggerated polar differences, the transition from research to school improvement practice is complicated by the fact that the research evidence is far from conclusive (providing no blueprints for effective schools). This situation makes practical application more difficult and easier at the same time: more difficult because the message of school effectiveness research still leaves a lot of uncertainty; easier because these very uncertainties give local administrators room to make use of their own expertise in assessing the potential for change in local situations.

Following these preliminary remarks about the relationship between school effectiveness research findings and the school improvement processes inspired by these research findings, a conclusion should be reached on effectiveness-oriented school improvement. None of the four levers for enhancing school effectiveness – changes in the incentive structure, internal capacity for change, technological innovation and increased evaluative potential of schools – can in itself be seen as a sufficiently powerful lever for enhancing effectiveness (see Joyce, 1991, for a similar statement). Changing the external structure of incentives by measures inspired by the market mechanism was shown to have possibly harmful side-effects. The self-renewing capacity of schools was unmasked as a desired end-state resulting from the heavy involvement of educational change facilitators, rather than a readily available means for improvement. Belief in the dynamics of technological innovations and rational planning applications was strongly tempered by earlier experiences and a certain inbred resistance of school organizations to this type of innovation. Enhancing the evaluative potential of schools, though an attractive 'stepping stone' to set improvement activities into motion, was, like the self-renewing capacity of schools, finally judged to be an object of school improvement, rather than a primary lever for enhancing effectiveness.

Despite these rather negative conclusions it is clear that school effectiveness research results and model building have something to say as far as school improvement is concerned. One general conclusion is that school effectiveness research findings provide the prevalent process and school-level orientation of school improvement with two additional perspectives: one is *content* (specific guidelines on to which type of instruction, leadership and environmental stimulants are important) and the second is environmental *context*, implying that school environmental factors on the one hand and technological classroom level factors on the other are important in making schools more effective.

More specifically, examination of four likely levers for enhancing effectiveness has led to the conclusion that school improvement should preferably use all four levers together, to make them into a mutually enforcing set of partial strategies for improvement. Combined with the multi-level notion in the integrated model of school effectiveness, this calls for school improvement projects that are directed to the principle of synergy in two ways:

- to work simultaneously at the levels of the classroom, the school organization and the relevant local school environment;
- to try to use several levers for inducing change at the same time: achievement stimulating incentives, training, recruitment and development activities, technological innovation, and more pronounced evaluation activities and facilities at the various levels of the school organization.

In the next section integrated approaches to school improvement will be illustrated by means of descriptions of recent school improvement programmes.

EXAMPLES OF INTEGRATED SCHOOL IMPROVEMENT PROGRAMMES

The programmes discussed in this section are termed integrated because they either use more than one lever for enhancing school effectiveness or are directed towards several levels of the organizational functioning of schools.

The Cardiff School Improvement Programme

The description of this school improvement project is based on work by Reynolds *et al.* (1989). The overall aim of the Cardiff School Improvement Programme was to change school organizational structure and to provide opportunities for the professional development of staff. Teachers were seen as school-based change agents. The content of the innovation conveyed via the teachers was inspired by the emerging school effectiveness literature of the late 1970s and early 1980s. The structure of the programme was described as follows:

1   The duration of the programme was initially two years, requiring the teachers involved to attend one day per week at University College Cardiff.

2   Course participants examined a range of pupil problems, learning difficulties, behavioural problems, etc. and studied the literature on how schools might be contributing to these problems, together with literature on school change strategies, group work skills and the organizational development approach of Schmuck and Miles (1971) and others.

3   Teachers were asked to undertake research (called a 'school-based study') into the effects of school factors and institutional functioning on pupils in their own schools, the research to be undertaken in close consultation with their colleague group in the particular schools. This study was to involve using the research literature, their own perceptions and those of their colleagues (and pupils where possible) in the school to diagnose intra-school factors that led to ineffectiveness and to suggest ways in which the school could become more effective.

4   Teachers were encouraged to liaise with their colleagues in school, both before and after the school-based study.

5   Teachers were kept in touch with the programme after they had completed the course by means of visits to schools by programme staff and by occasional reunions for four or five years following completion of the course.

The programme took place in 38 secondary schools, involving 43 teachers, among them five headteachers, who had completed the intensive two-year programme. After two years the impact of the participants' course experiences on their schools was evaluated. The evaluation at this stage consisted of interviews with the course participants themselves and their colleagues. Of the 43 teachers, 37 were reported by their colleagues as having changed in one or more positive ways (e.g. increased professional awareness and increased flexibility); 26 had generated one or more institutional changes. These institutional changes were categorized as:

- *developments in pastoral care and staff communication about problem pupils* (totalling 36 institutional changes, e.g. 'most disruptive pupils distributed to different registration groups', 'merit certificates introduced for years I and II');
- *developments in academic system or curriculum* (totalling 21 changes, e.g. 'new basic studies curriculum introduced for remedial department');
- *developments in monitoring and assessment of individual pupils or systems* (fifteen institutional changes, e.g. 'more monitoring of academic progress and behaviour of pupils by year tutors', 'departmental heads to include some evaluation of their departments in their reports');
- *closer liaisons with outside agencies* (eleven changes, e.g. 'more contacts with educational psychologists', 'education welfare officer more involved with head of lower school');
- *closer liaison with parents* (seven changes, e.g. 'year tutors now make home visits', 'parents' evening established for year V');
- *staff development communication* (three institutional changes, e.g. 'regular staff meetings introduced two or three times per term', 'voluntary seminars for staff introduced');
- *more pupil participation and autonomy* (two institutional changes: 'self-report for pupils included in pupil profiles', 'children allowed in school relatively unsupervised at lunch time');
- *other developments* (two instances of institutional change: 'more open management' and 'mixed staffroom established').

A further interesting evaluation finding was that headteachers and deputy heads initiated more school changes than other groups.

The follow-up investigation, seven years after the initial evaluation, revealed that a high percentage (about 80 per cent) of the institutional changes were either maintained or further developed. In schools where the course member who introduced institutional change was no longer in position this percentage was only slightly lower. In a sub-sample of schools, pupil outcomes were examined one year before the programme started and four years after its completion. A control group of 30 schools was used to provide comparative outcome data at the same points in time. The results showed that programme schools performed better on all three criteria (attendance, high academic achievement and basic academic achievement) than non-programme schools.

The authors attribute the success of the Cardiff School Improvement Programme to the following characteristics:

1. The assumption that the course members 'owned' the organizational changes in schools, because they were very much involved with school diagnosis and generating information strategies. It was also assumed that there was considerable involvement of the wider school staff, since a majority of the successful course participants fed back their study results to their colleagues.

2. Opportunities were given for *interaction* between the school effectiveness literature and the course participants' own practical knowledge (the school effectiveness literature was definitely not used as a 'recipe' for school improvement).

3. The strong involvement of teachers who held senior administrative positions in their schools.

4. The fact that incentives were provided to individual teachers in the form of degrees that were gained by completing the course.

5. The focus upon pupil problems and school organizational responses to these problems ensured that the programme was seen as relevant to the day-to-day needs of programme practitioners.

6. The fact that contact was maintained with programme participants by means of follow-up visits to participating schools.

7. Commitment from the sponsoring authorities.

8. Organizational changes were based upon a 'whole school philosophy of change, whereby all aspects of schools are changed to avoid the lack of synchronicity caused by partial institutional change' (Reynolds *et al.*, 1989, p.812).

9. The fact that individual participants acquired new influence in school because of their enhanced professional qualifications.

Examination of the Cardiff School Improvement Programme in terms of the earlier analyses of levers for enhancing school effectiveness and integrated school effectiveness models reveals that several of these levers were employed. From the programme description it becomes clear that empirical diagnosis of problem areas was quite important in the first phase of the programme. The attention that was given to providing incentives to course participants (in the form of specific degrees) relates to another category of measures to stimulate change. Furthermore, the programme clearly had a substantial content in its methods of structuring curricula and school organizations, which were inspired by the school effectiveness research literature. It was clearly not a 'content-free' process-oriented attempt at changing the self-renewing capacity of the school. The programme was also clearly directed at innovation on several organizational levels: the professional functioning of individual teachers, organizational and managerial conditions, and relationships with the school environment (most notably parents).

One of the major reasons for the programme's success, the degree of involvement of staff, has to do with innovatory strategies and the process aspect of school improvement, rather than with the content aspect (school effectiveness models) that is the focus of this book. This is worth noting since it underlines the point made earlier that effective school improvement requires both knowledge on content (school effectiveness models) and knowledge on school improvement and innovatory processes.

The 'Improving the Quality of Education for All (IQEA)' Programme

The second school improvement programme to be described is, at the time of writing, still in the planning stage. It is a design for a 'holistic' school improvement programme, which, in its first phase, involves three schools in the LEAs of Barking and Dagenham, Essex and Havering. Despite the fact that this programme has been neither implemented nor evaluated, it is referred to here because its holistic and integrated nature illustrates particularly well some of the notions on school effectiveness and school improvement that have been conveyed in earlier chapters. The description is based upon an article by Ainscow and Hopkins (1991).

The overall vision of the IQEA project is to produce and evaluate a model of school development and a programme of support that strengthens the schools' ability to provide quality education for all pupils. The cadre of people to coordinate the project in schools will consist of two coordinators from each project school, the appropriate local authority inspectors or advisers, and a project team of educational experts from the Cambridge Institute of Education.

An interesting feature, as far as innovation strategy is concerned, is that a contract will be drawn up between the various parties involved. The contract is meant to clarify expectations and to ensure the conditions necessary for successful development. In my opinion, such contracts may also be helpful in ensuring commitment to vital programme aspects (e.g. evaluation activities). A contract counteracts the free-floating, 'unengaged' nature that innovatory projects in education sometimes have.

School improvement in the IQEA project is described as an approach to educational change that is concerned with developing strategies for strengthening the school's organization, as well as enhancing outcomes for students and staff. The intention at the core of the project is to accomplish educational goals (including goals broader than cognitive achievement) more effectively. A further key focus of the project is the internal interaction of schools (teaching and learning activities as well as the school's framework for action, its role allocations, the use of resources that support the teaching and learning process, and the way in which people in school work together). Furthermore, the school is seen as the centre of change. This means that the situations of the schools, as well as contextual characteristics, are taken into account. This implies that school improvement efforts need to adopt a 'classroom-exceeding perspective; in other words, we begin from the classrooms and work outwards' (Ainscow and Hopkins, 1991, p.4).

This method of structuring school improvement activities corresponds with the nested layers model of school organizations described in Chapters 2 and 6. It is quite evident that effects directed at the primary process of teaching and learning are combined (and, it is hoped, enforced) by supportive conditions at the school level.

The project proposal lists a number of principles of school improvement, and these are worth citing:

1 The main focus for action should be on teaching and learning in classrooms, in order that *all* students develop 'the intellectual and imaginative powers and competencies' that they need in as personalized a way as possible.
2 Such classroom practice can only be sustained through on-going staff development.

3 Leadership should empower people (students, staff and community) to achieve their own and the school's purposes.

4 All members of a school community should actively build and share a common vision of its main purposes.

5 The school's current priorities should reflect its main purposes, its vision, and be generated through consultation.

6 Work on the current priorities should be based upon planning in order to manage the process of change.

7 The substance of staff development should be teaching skills, as well as the best available knowledge of curriculum content.

8 Collaboration is a necessary condition for staff development and school improvement.

9 Processes of improvement should be informed by monitoring, feedback and reflection on the part of students as well as staff and, of course, the school.

10 Successful policy implementation occurs when groups of teachers adapt educational ideas to their own context and professional needs.

From this list it appears that the project will employ several of the levers for enhancing school effectiveness: staff development, a strong accent on monitoring, feedback and reflection, a clear emphasis on teaching skills and curriculum content (to be seen as a more technological aspect of the project). Furthermore (as was the case in the Cardiff School Improvement Programme), individual participants are provided with opportunities to obtain university certificates, a feature that comes under the heading of providing incentives for school improvement activities.

The authors of the IQEA project design emphasize school culture as a vital factor in the improvement process. They see the culture of a school as 'a reflection of the norms and values of its members' and state that the types of cultures most supportive of school improvement efforts are those that are collaborative, have high expectations for both students and staff, exhibit a consensus on values, support an orderly and secure environment and encourage teachers to learn, take responsibility and work together. The emphasis on school culture in conjunction with the instructional focus calls for what the authors indicate as 'powerful and integrative implementation strategies that directly address the culture of the school'. Such integrative strategies require individual strategies (such as staff in-service training, school evaluation and development planning) and development of the internal infrastructure (e.g. the way in which teachers work together, the organization of learning and the management arrangements employed by the school).

The comprehensive and holistic nature of this school improvement project has been sufficiently illustrated in the above discussion. The authors expect that the various principles for school improvement will lead to synergy: 'together they are greater than the sum of their parts' (Ainscow and Hopkins, 1991, p. 4). This idea of synergism was also arrived at in this book when considering the possibilities of each separate lever for enhancing school effectiveness. A practical problem endemic to these integrative approaches is their complexity, the time and effort they require and the vulnerability that follows from these characteristics. Somehow a piecemeal approach to holistic school improvement appears to be needed, although this sounds suspiciously like a contradiction in terms.

The Rotterdam Homework Project

The Rotterdam Homework Project[1] came into existence when the Rotterdam City Council decided that secondary schools needed an extra incentive to develop explicit policies on

---

[1] I am indebted to Dr Jos G. G. Zuylen (project leader of the Rotterdam Homework Project) for providing a concise summary description of the main features of the project.

homework. One of the sources of this initiative was an important advisory report concerning the restructuring of the first phase of secondary education in the Netherlands, formulated by the Scientific Council for Government Policy in 1987, in which independent learning was seen as a means to fight inequality in education.

After considering (and rejecting) the idea of funding each individual school to develop homework policies, the City Council decided to assign a private educational consulting agency to develop and implement a special programme aimed at improving homework policies and practices. According to its developers the approach chosen in the Rotterdam Homework Project (RHP) was developed in educational practice as well as in theory. The practical situation in which this specific approach to homework was developed was a secondary school that was badly in need of a credible and appealing market strategy (after an unsuccessful merger the survival of the school was being threatened). The approach chosen was the implementation of 'homework-free' education, which meant that pupils no longer received assignments to do at home, but instead worked independently on former 'homework' tasks during school hours.

The first theoretical bases of the Rotterdam Homework Project were ideas developed in educational psychology of independent learning (Simons, 1989) and the application of meta-cognitive strategies in education (Willems and Van Hout Wolters, 1989). The core of these ideas is that pupils should be stimulated to use self-directed learning, for example by asking themselves questions, planning their assignments, making summaries, etc. Second, the Rotterdam Homework Project was inspired by school effectiveness models and school improvement approaches. From the school effectiveness literature, the idea of supporting essential changes at the micro level (classroom level) by organizational conditions at meso level (school level) was derived. The key aspects of the innovation at micro level are the general factors 'structured teaching' and 'increasing effective learning time'. At the meso level, instructional leadership and staff cooperation are emphasized. Evaluation is integrated into the approach to independent work on (homework) assignments.

As far as the implementation strategy is concerned schools have quite a few different options in how they may wish to participate. So, for instance, schools can choose between a homework-free approach and a more structured way to guide and counsel assignments that pupils take home. Once schools have made their choice for a specific option, a formal contract is made up between the schools and the consulting agency.

The essence of the innovation at micro level is relatively simple, though far-reaching. Teachers spend only one-third of a lesson on explaining and introducing new knowledge and skills; the other two-thirds consists of integrative assignments to pupils and independent work in which the pupils apply what they have learned. The approach to 'learning to learn' at school requires that teachers explain in advance of each assignment how the pupils are to go about carrying it out. In the case of homework assignments specific ways of doing them are agreed upon in advance for all pupils. As far as learning to learn at home is concerned, pupils use a special notebook to write down particular guidelines about the assignments (context specification, the way to tackle the assignments and the amount of time required for the various parts of the assignment). The project also has an option that includes the schools offering guidance to parents on the ways in which they can assist their children in doing homework assignments.

The contract that the participating schools sign specifies a sequence of phases that each school is to go through:

1 Informing the school about the project.
2 Analysing the situation at the school and confronting it with the core ideas of the project.
3 Choosing goals and objectives.

4 Preparation and organization of project activities by a specific task force (from the school's staff); this phase results in a concrete action plan.

5 Implementation and evaluation by school teams, assisted by the external consultants.

6 Institutionalizing the innovation.

7 Summary evaluation (school evaluations are aggregated by the consultants for the overall project evaluation).

Presently, 31 secondary schools take part in the project. The annual budget is 400,000 Dutch Guilders. The project will run for a period of three years. Evaluation data on the project are not as yet available.

In terms of the analytical frame of reference that was developed in earlier chapters, the Rotterdam Homework Project is of interest for its integrative approach (micro/meso integration). The project further combines a very specific substantive change of the primary process of schools with a specific process-oriented implementation strategy. Despite the high degree of influence individual schools have over the way in which they participate, and the fact that the implementation is carried out by the schools themselves, the project also has some aspects of a top-down, technology-oriented innovation (initiative of the City Council, explicit guidelines about changes in teaching strategies).

A fourth example of an integrated school effectiveness project is that of the Halton Board of Education in Ontario. This project builds upon the Mortimore *et al.* (1988) effectiveness study, described in Appendix 1. The main vehicle of this improvement project is what is called a school growth plan. The substantive areas this project focuses on lie at both the organizational level (cooperative planning) and the instructional level (e.g. classroom management and in-structional skills). For a description of this improvement project the reader is referred to Stoll (1991).

SUMMARY AND CONCLUSIONS

In this chapter several levers for inducing educational change were discussed and three examples of 'comprehensive' school improvement projects were given. The models of school effectiveness discussed in earlier chapters indicate several points of impact for school improvement. Public choice theory emphasizes modification of incentive structures. Taking this course of action in educational innovation corresponds with power-coercive innovatory strategies. Models of school organization, particularly the image of the professional bureaucracy, highlight staff development through training and in-service training. According to this per-spective, which is related to normative re-educative innovation strategies, educational change should come from within, although external educational facilitators are thought to act at least as catalysts, or even as the primary initiators of school improvement. School improvement through technological innovation and a more systematic use of evaluation corresponds with economic models of education production functions and a systems approach (cybernetics in particular). In terms of innovation strategies, this is the area of rational empirical strategies.

Another aspect of the school effectiveness models is the multi-level or nested layers image. Power-coercive strategies are associated with the level of the school environment; staff development and coordination improvement mechanisms are focused on the levels of school organization and individual professionals. Technological innovation is primarily associated with the classroom level.

The descriptions of modern school improvement projects indicate that approaches have been chosen that integrate several levers of school improvement, and that impact on several aggregation levels. Substantive school effectiveness models have clearly inspired the contents of school improvement programmes. The alleged gap between theoretical school effectiveness researchers and practical school improvers is also closing because of the increasing number of carefully evaluated school improvement programmes. Again, the potential of school-based evaluation as a bridge between the procedural orientation of school improvement experts and substantive knowledge of 'what works' in education should be mentioned. Evaluation and feedback are the elementary mechanisms by which the idea of schools as 'learning organizations' can be made real. In my opinion, the idea of providing school improvement programmes with a hard core of technological innovation is still insufficiently used. The Rotterdam Homework Project is a clear exception.

Chapter 8

Conclusion: The Future of School Effectiveness Research as a Guide to School Improvement

School effectiveness, particularly in association with the so-called school effectiveness *movement*, may have somewhat of a bad name for its 'faddish' nature. In this sense the observation can be made that the popularity of the term school effectiveness reached its peak several years ago. The question of whether the phenomena that are studied in school effectiveness research will stay high on the agenda of educational research and systematic educational reform must therefore be addressed. I will deal with this question in this final chapter by drawing some conclusions on the salience of what we already know in this field for educational practice and by examining the viability of educational effectiveness as a research programme.

WHAT DO WE KNOW?

The question about the salience of school effectiveness research findings for educational practice should be tackled in three ways:

1 By examining the available evidence.
2 By assessing whether the established facts make sense in terms of conceptual models and theories.
3 By examining which aspects of the models are amenable to active manipulation and measures to improve educational practice.

Since these questions have been dealt with extensively in earlier chapters only some illustrative evidence will be presented here; the main purpose is to draw up a balance.

Instead of repeating the summary conclusions of Chapter 6 on the available research evidence, I will cite some illustrative practical implications suggested by school effectiveness researchers. Brookover *et al.* (1979) make the following practical recommendations, based on their study of 159 primary schools in the state of Michigan: (a) maintain communal objectives that encourage higher achievement levels for all pupils; (b) consistently apply feedback and reinforcement in accordance with the mastery learning model. Mortimore *et al.* (1988) dedicate a whole chapter of their research report to practical implications, in which recommendations are also differentiated according to different groups of actors in the field of education.

Central government should be mindful that local education authorities do not stint on the costs of running school buildings. In addition, the government should provide facilities for *smaller classes* in the lower grades of primary school. *Teacher-training institutes* should take into account the essential factors generated by this study, particularly with regard to what is within the reach of teachers (structured lessons, intellectually stimulating teaching, a task-oriented environment, a limited focus with regard to subject matter presented during lessons, optimum communication, the maintenance of records, parental involvement, use of positive feedback and praising of pupils). *Local education authorities* should be able to do something with the finding – not previously mentioned here – that voluntary schools do better than state ones; for example, by trying to provide the latter with the leeway voluntary schools have. Moreover, LEAs could make infant classes smaller by making the top classes bigger if necessary.

The optimal school size that emerged from the study, two parallel classes for each age group, could be used by the LEA as a guideline. LEAs could also contribute to proper maintenance of school buildings and stability among the staff of a school, and provide support for newly appointed school heads, for the youngest children in each age group and for increasing parental involvement.

Teachers' unions should see the study findings, the researchers hope, as an incentive to focus more on the content of education (besides matters of terms and conditions) and in particular to do their utmost to achieve smaller classes and to react positively to the design of tools for measuring pupils' progress. *School heads* should be concerned with the study findings that relate to educational leadership, class size, involvement of the head and deputy head in school policy, consistency among teachers in the way the curriculum is interpreted, parental involvement, the maintenance of records of progress and the creation of a positive school climate. *Teachers* should be more aware of the importance of having high expectations of pupils' achievement. They should note the core elements of the study related to the way subject matter is taught, such as structured lessons, intellectually challenging teaching, a task-oriented environment, sharply focused subject matter during lessons and optimum communication between teachers and pupils during lessons (taking into account the balance between whole-class teaching and individual instruction).

Van Marwijk Kooij-von Baumhauer (1984), a Dutch school effectiveness researcher, concluded her study of secondary schools with the following recommendations:

- the departmental meeting is the most favourable organizational provision for schools, which have to deal increasingly with pupils who are unfamiliar with general academic secondary education;
- only candidates who have a proven record of inspiring and stimulating other teachers should be considered for the appointment of school principal;
- drab or indifferent schools should give attention to which aspects of the school are liked and disliked by teachers and staff;
- state schools should have a governing structure whereby the school is locally supported and also administered by a directly interested body in the area;
- it would be useful if the teachers' unions paid more attention to matters of educational philosophy, in order to help members create a clearer identity for their school;
- schools should be given the opportunity to split when their size becomes unmanageable or is considered unacceptable.

These recommendations include measures concerned with instruction at the classroom level (e.g. mastery learning), favoured organizational arrangements (deputy head, departmental meeting) and a positive climate and administrative arrangements at the supra-school level (e.g. providing public schools with a board comparable to the governing bodies of private schools). This leads to the formulation of integrated, multi-level models of school effectiveness research, such as the ones arrived at in previous chapters, where conditions on various layers of the school organization are seen as mutually reinforcing each other.

Such models, in a sense, are no more than structured summaries of relevant effectiveness-enhancing factors. In order properly to understand what they mean, one should look for underlying explanatory principles. My attempt to do so (Chapter 2) resulted in a kind of patchwork: bits and pieces of organizational and instructional theories and models appeared to be useful in explaining part of the integrated model used to summarize the research results. How far have we come in laying bare the essential mechanisms that make schooling effective? Is this perhaps an overambitious question, and should we be content with disjointed and 'eclectic' knowledge? In Chapter 2 a case was made for the central importance of evaluation feedback and reinforcement cycles at various levels of the organizational functioning of schools. In Chapter 7 evaluation was discussed as one of several feasible levers for triggering school improvement and enhancing effectiveness.

The cybernetic principle, which links evaluation, feedback and adapted action, is closely related to evaluation feedback and reinforcement cycles (in fact the latter can be seen as a specific instance of the former). There are several merits to an evaluation-centred explanation of school effectiveness findings. First, evaluation is central to the concept of effectiveness, which more or less implies that goal attainment can be assessed through evaluative procedures. Second, an evaluation-centred orientation implies a retroactive attitude to planning, which means that corrective actions are firmly rooted in the descriptive reality of a school's functioning. As studies on curriculum planning in education have shown, such types of retroactive planning may often work better than proactive planning, where efforts to reach agreement on operationalizations of 'grant' objectives frequently come to nothing. Third, improving evaluation procedures is a concrete and direct way to embark on a process of school improvement, although setting such a process in motion should be seen as an innovation in itself, involving technical requirements and facilities, specialized skills and – perhaps most importantly – certain attitudes that reflect a willingness to reflect on and be open to possibly critical assessment of one's own functioning. This last observation points at a fourth advantage of capitalizing on evaluation mechanisms, namely its connection with a more encompassing image of 'sound' organizational functioning, that of the school as a learning organization. Information processing and an open mind to the adaptations necessary to face environmental changes are central to this organizational image.

Morgan (1986, pp. 77–109) is emphatic in stating that merely improving information systems and review procedures may be insufficient or even harmful with respect to organizational effectiveness. Particularly when evaluation feedback and reinforcement cycles occur within a bureaucratic framework, such procedures will evoke defensive reactions that could inhibit rather than stimulate improvement. In his opinion the cybernetic principle, depicted as 'single-loop learning', should be elaborated to 'double-loop learning'. This involves an additional loop of reflecting on the norms of operational functioning that guided evaluations in the single-loop learning situation. To put it differently, Morgan states that effective organizations should have proficiency in 'learning to learn'. He goes on to sketch a management philosophy and an organizational structural configuration that together are conducive to this process of learning to learn. The managerial philosophy emphasizes: 'an openness and reflectivity that accepts error and uncertainty', 'recognition of the importance of exploring different viewpoints' and a participative approach to the planning process. The organizational structure that provides the best chances for such a management philosophy is characterized by redundancy and connectivity (which means that sub-parts or members of an organization are able to fulfil each other's functions), by the principle of requisite variety (meaning that the internal diversity of a self-regulating system must match the variety and complexity of its environment) and by capacity for self-organization.

The professional bureaucratic nature of schools has inherent characteristics that correspond to this ideal-type organizational structure (namely the redundancy aspect) and characteristics that appear to collide frontally with these principles (the idea of connectivity as opposed to the 'loosely coupled' nature of educational organizations). Furthermore, the idea of the learning organization seems to be specifically designed for organizations that operate within a dynamic, complex environment. Despite important changes in the environment of schools (owing to demographic changes, decentralization and deregulation, increased accountability requirements, etc.), it is still debatable how turbulent or relatively stable school environments (in industrialized countries) presently are.

So, the image of the learning organization as a more holistic construct to explain school effectiveness cannot be applied uncritically, although it opens up interesting areas for further analysis. Although the cybernetic principle is powerful as an explanatory mechanism behind the findings of empirical school effectiveness research, it is quite clear that we have not yet arrived at an encompassing theory explaining school effectiveness.

In Chapter 7 it was argued that school improvement programmes ought to be comprehensive, both in the sense of being operational at various levels of organizational functioning (management and the primary process of teaching) and in the sense of using various levers for evoking change (such as providing well-targeted incentives, training and organizational development and school self-evaluation). This position is akin to what Joyce (1991) calls 'comprehensive restructuring' and to a 'holistic approach to school improvement' as described by Hopkins (1990). Such a comprehensive or holistic approach is deemed necessary since every aspect of school functioning is connected with every other aspect. But a critical point that could be raised is that by trying everything at once one might end up by accomplishing nothing at all. What seems to be required is a careful sequencing of the various improvement-oriented activities. A global school diagnosis (see Scheerens and Hopkins, 1992) might be a likely first step. The results of this diagnosis could then be used for the planning of further interventions.

Approaching school improvement from the perspective of school effectiveness research – as has been done in this book – underlines two points: first, the importance of review and evaluation procedures (see above); second, the need to give 'substance' to improvement by gearing it closely to operational (or technological) innovations at the level of classroom instruction. Such measures could be seen as the hard core of improvement programmes, which, no doubt, should be accompanied by people-oriented strategies taken from the innovation and school improvement literature.

HOW CAN WE LEARN MORE ABOUT SCHOOL EFFECTIVENESS?

A first answer to this question should be that we can learn more about school effectiveness by careful analysis of serious and systematic efforts to improve school functioning. Once again the relevance of evaluation of school improvement programmes to furthering knowledge on school effectiveness should be emphasized. In addition, with respect to the future of school effectiveness research three specific types of studies can be distinguished: 'state-of-the-art' school effectiveness studies, foundational studies and fundamental studies.

State-of-the-Art School Effectiveness Studies

As pointed out in Chapter 4, fully fledged state-of-the-art school effectiveness studies have been quite rare. The requirements of such studies, also listed in Chapter 4, are quite heavy, not only from a research-technical point of view, but also with respect to organization and financial costs. Yet such studies are needed. Innovations in state-of-the-art school effectiveness studies that are badly wanted include quasi-experimental approaches, in which effectiveness-enhancing conditions are systematically implemented as treatments in natural settings and international comparative surveys.[1]

---

[1] In fact, initiatives on both types of study are presently being taken. Bosker and co-workers (Bosker and Harskamp, 1990) are presently working on a quasi-experimental school effectiveness project in the Netherlands, and an international group of researchers is preparing an international comparative school effectiveness project under the name ISERP (International School Effectiveness Research Project) – see Creemers and Reynolds (1989).

Foundational School Effectiveness Studies

By foundational school effectiveness studies I mean studies that are concerned with elementary conceptual issues, such as the stability of school effectiveness, with instrument development and with research-technological and methodological innovations. It is important that such issues be resolved in the best possible way, not only to support fundamental and applied research, but also to further empirical knowledge on the scope and integrity of the concept of school effectiveness.

In the majority of empirical school effectiveness research studies, the short answer to the issue of criterion choice is to use achievement scores in basic school subjects (reading, arithmetic, language) as the effect variables. Although a strong case can be made for this choice (Doddema-Winsemius and Hofstee, 1987; Scheerens, 1989; Hofstee, 1991), questions of criterion choice and justification of educational goals deserve more attention within the framework of a more fundamental school effectiveness research programme. Items on the research agenda that can help in overcoming some of the conceptual uncertainties implied in the above are:

● the study and application of methodologies for the justification of educational goals (Fischer, 1980; Lakomski, 1991; Scheerens, 1991);
● inventorization, quality assessment and (perhaps) enlarging the available instruments for measuring other than the more traditional school effectiveness criteria;
● comparative studies with respect to the question of whether schools that are strong in traditional cognitive effectiveness criteria are also strong in achieving non-cognitive outcomes (e.g. school well-being);
● studies that compare different adjustment procedures to determine 'net' effects of schooling.

Another important conceptual issue is to find out the degree to which school effects can be 'explained away' by teacher effects. Modern applications of multi-level analysis techniques are very well suited to fleshing out the differentiation between these two sources of variance in educational achievement.

The connotation of 'school effectiveness' has an element of duration and scope. That is, in order to call a school effective, high achievement levels should persist over time (stability) and effectiveness judgements should not be based on the functioning of just a partial segment of the total organization (scope). Ralph and Fennessey (1983, p. 690) say that exemplary schools should demonstrate consistently high achievement levels for more than a single grade and show good performance in all classrooms. Consistency of achievement over subject-matter areas (e.g. reading and arithmetic) is another instance of the scope of effectiveness within an organization.

Although a short-cut approach to the requirement of sufficient scope would be to state that performance at the final stage of the highest grade of a school represents the cumulative effect of all previous grades (Bosker, 1991), the consistency of achievement levels across (parallel) classrooms, grades and subject remains an interesting research area. The issue of 'scope' is closely related to the issue of school and classroom effects mentioned above. The supposition that school effectiveness is an attribute of the total organization is supported to the degree that achievement can be shown to be consistently high across organizational sub-units. A similar argument can be made with respect to stability of effectiveness over time. The available research evidence on these various types of consistency is still inconclusive and partly contradictory (a recent summary is provided by Bosker, 1991).

Another kind of foundational school effectiveness study concerns sub-group and context specificity of school effectiveness. This line of enquiry has been dealt with in Chapter 5 under the headings differential school effectiveness and context specificity of school effectiveness models. All these questions about consistency across organizational sub-units, sub-groups, subject matter areas and contexts are concerned with the robustness and integrity of the concept of school effectiveness as an organizational phenomenon. To the degree that consistency and generalizability claims cannot be maintained, the research directed to these issues is likely to yield specific information on partial, context-bound models of educational effectiveness.

Methodological and research-technical innovations that are important in the field of school effectiveness research include developments in the measurement of change by means of item-response modelling, applications of techniques for the analyses of multi-level data and of covariance structures (LISREL), and a systematic application of qualitative methods. Instrument development is particularly relevant to non-cognitive educational outcomes and school organizational phenomena related to an achievement-oriented policy, school climate and the evaluation potential of the school. These methodological issues will not be pursued further here (see Scheerens, 1991).

Fundamental School Effectiveness Studies

Fundamental school effectiveness research is closely tied to the further development of school effectiveness models and theories. The distinction between applied school effectiveness and fundamental school effectiveness research is seen as being based upon the theory-driven nature of the latter. In this case different labels may be used, since fundamental effectiveness studies are most likely to be generated from sub-disciplines in educational science, like educational psychology, curriculum studies or educational management and organization. The common core of such studies consists of causal models of educational achievement. A certain tendency of *rapprochement* among various sub-disciplines can be discerned; for instance, school and contextual factors are being included in micro-level models of optimal instructional conditions, and school management and organization studies more frequently try to link organizational variables with outcome measures. Seen from this perspective, the claim can be made with a certain degree of confidence that 'effectiveness-related' studies will remain high on the research agenda of educational science, even though specific labels like school or educational effectiveness may go out of fashion. Another unifying term to indicate this type of outcome-oriented educational research would be to speak of the search for *instrumental educational theory*, aimed at the explanation of process–output relationships in education.

An approach to further fundamental school effectiveness research that could be promising is the formalization of conceptual models and exploration of these by means of simulation techniques and the building of expert systems. Such approaches could be seen as bridging the gap between complex conceptual school effectiveness models and empirical research.

The idea that management and organizational conditions could be used to improve educational outcomes has been ridiculed by March (1978, p. 219; cited by Boyd and Crowson, 1985), who stated that 'changing education by changing educational administration is like changing the course of the Mississippi by spitting in the Allegheny'. Although organizational effects may indeed be relatively small the developments in the field of school effectiveness research indicate that such conditions, together with instructional conditions at the classroom level, provide very promising material for both educational research and the improvement of educational practice.

Appendix 1

Four Studies

In order to bring the reality of school effectiveness research more into focus and to make a further attempt to discover what the effectiveness-promoting school characteristics so often stated really mean, four studies are described in greater detail. These are the studies of Brookover *et al.* (1979), Rutter *et al.* (1979), Schweitzer (1984) and Mortimore *et al.* (1988). The first two were chosen for their familiarity and the relatively favourable opinion concerning their quality in most review studies. Schweitzer's study was chosen because a Dutch replication study has been carried out, which is described in Appendix 2. The study of Mortimore *et al.* was chosen because it appears to be the most exhaustive and advanced effectiveness study so far.

Each study description starts with a general characterization followed by a discussion of the methods, techniques and findings. In a concluding paragraph the impact of the data and the implications for practice are considered for each study.

SCHOOL SOCIAL SYSTEMS AND STUDENT ACHIEVEMENT

General Description

The study of Brookover *et al.* (1979) can be seen as a reaction to the findings of Coleman *et al.* (1966) and Jencks *et al.* (1972), who concluded that school characteristics, unlike the racial and socio-economic background of pupils, had relatively little influence on student achievement. In these earlier studies certain relatively easily describable school characteristics, which can be classified as *inputs*, such as the qualifications of teaching staff, facilities and financial resources were looked at in particular. Brookover *et al.* enlarged upon the stock of school characteristics by taking 'social structure' and 'social climate at school' into account. Social structure was defined as 'the interaction patterns which occur in a school' (p. 7). Social climate meant the entire norms, expectations and opinions on what is considered to be adequate teaching conduct, as well as the feelings that members of the organization have about their roles and those of other members of the school management.

Brookover *et al.* regard the social structure and the social climate of a school as intervening variables between the inputs and outcomes of the school as a social system; that is, these factors partly determine in which direction a school converts its resources and other potential into teaching results. The assumption here was that by taking these intervening variables into account, differences between schools in results could be better explained than in research where only input-outcome relations were looked at. Brookover *et al.* did not limit 'outcome' to achievement in main school subjects, but also covered more personal characteristics like 'self-image' and 'self-confidence' of pupils as well.

The research design can be defined as a correlation study involving 159 primary schools. Within this sample, schools were broken down into particular sub-groups, which were then compared to one another. Thus the total sample of schools was divided into a group of schools with a majority of black pupils and a group of schools with a majority of white pupils. The group of 'white' schools was then sub-divided into schools with an average socio-economic status (SES) of pupils' parents, and schools with a low socio-economic status regarding pupil population. A representative sample of schools in the state of Michigan (68 schools) was also used. In order to add depth to the correlation study, case studies were made of four schools with a low SES status, two 'white' and two 'black' schools, with each category including a relatively effective and a less effective school.

Research Questions

The central hypothesis being tested in the study was that characteristics of the social system of the school (structure and climate) largely explain the between-school variance in achievement and affective outcomes, when the differences in intake characteristics between schools have been taken into account.

A technical point that should be carefully noted here is that Brookover *et al.* analysed differences in mean achievement per school and worked out what percentage of the *variance between school averages* was explained by the differentiated input and social system characteristics. Because differences between schools (school averages) explain but a fraction of the total variance at pupil-score level (10–15 per cent, for example), the total variance percentages explained by individual categories of school characteristics are mainly small (4–6 per cent of the total variance, for example). In this study much higher variance percentages were explained by school characteristics, but this is largely because the variance being explained is not the *total variance* (pupil level), but the variance between school averages.

Design, Methods and Technique of the Study

Conceptual model The conceptual model central to the study of Brookover *et al.* and the main categories of variables are given in Figure A1.1.

Variables The composition of the pupil population was measured per school as the average socio-economic status (SES) of the social origin of pupils and the percentage of white pupils per school.

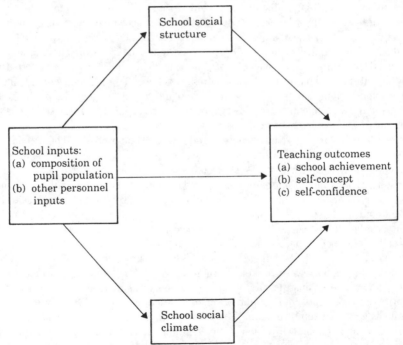

Figure A1.1 The conceptual framework used by Brookover *et al.* (1979)

Other personnel inputs were measured using seven variables: school size, average daily absenteeism, number of trained teachers per 1000 pupils, average number of years teaching experience per school, average time teachers have taught at the school in question, percentage of teachers with a higher qualification and average teacher salary per school.

The school social structure was measured by means of teacher's satisfaction with the school, parental involvement with the school (according to the opinion of head and teachers), differentiation, the percentage of the teacher's workday spent teaching (according to the school head's opinion) and how far the teaching could be characterized as 'open' teaching, i.e. the freedom of pupils to talk and walk about during lessons, whether pupils could sit where they wanted in class, the frequency with which pupils were allocated new places and how far the pupils were involved with the same or different learning tasks.

The school social climate was measured by means of fourteen variables concerned with the norms, expectations and feelings with regard to the school as experienced by teachers, pupils and heads. A distinction was made between 'pupil-climate variables', 'teacher-climate variables' and 'head-climate variables'. Pupil-climate variables were:

- sense of academic futility among pupils;
- the appreciation and expectations pupils had for education with regard to their own future academic career;
- the same for the education they were currently receiving.

The teacher-climate variables were:

- expectations of pupils with regard to their possibilities of following a university training;
- the same with regard to secondary school training;
- an inclination towards improving pupils' achievement level;
- teachers' perception of headteacher's expectations of pupils' school career;
- teachers' academic futility.

The headteacher-climate variables were:

- the degree to which parents are interested in their child's school career;
- inclination towards improving educational achievement;
- impression of the school's reputation;
- pupil achievement expectations.

It is possible to classify all these climate variables under the headings 'sense of optimism about pupils' school career' and 'sense of commitment to improving pupils' achievement'. Besides these categories of variables, which are seen in the study as effecting school achievement, there are dependent or endogenous variables that are supposed to be influenced by these variables. The dependent variables, or effect criteria, were:

- the average educational achievement per school in reading and number in the fourth year when measured by tests that were part of the Michigan School Assessment Programme;
- assessing academic self-concept, measured with the help of an existing and validated scale;
- pupil self-confidence, measured with the use of an instrument developed at the Johns Hopkins University.

Methods As has been mentioned, achievement measurements in reading and number were derived from an already existing data bank created by the Michigan School Assessment Programme. In addition, written questionnaires and interviews with pupils, teachers and headteachers were used. The questionnaires were administered by researchers and trained test assistants. Occasionally, observations were carried out to test the reliability of self-reporting. In one case, on the basis of observation data it was decided not to use certain assessment measures because they deviated too much from what occurred in reality (this was related to teachers assessing actual time spent teaching). For the case studies, use was made of participatory observation and unstructured interviews.

Data collection and analysis In many cases groups of variables within certain categories were combined. For this the raw scores of the original variables were first expressed in standard scores. Thus, for instance, in some analyses an index for the school population composition was used in which both racial and SES composition were combined.

The analyses were naturally geared towards determining the relation between the social system variables (independent variables) and the effectiveness criteria (dependent variables). For this three techniques were used:

- determining product-moment correlation coefficients;
- applying regression analysis in which the effect of the various categories of independent variables was estimated step-by-step;
- partitioning the explained variance as determined by regression analysis.

As has already been mentioned, data analysis took place at the aggregation level of the school. The data collected for the case studies were summarized into descriptions for each school.

Results

From analysis of the correlations between the various categories of independent variables it appeared that four out of five variables by which the social structure of the school was measured correlated positively and significantly with the input variables (correlations of 0.29–0.62). The climate variables were also correlated with both the input and the structural variables. Thus, for example, a high correlation (0.87) was found between the composition of the pupil population and the level of academic futility. Between the cognitive and non-cognitive dependent variables there were no significant correlations. In so far as one should see measured non-cognitive outcomes in this study as indicators of pupils' well-being at school, it appears that at the better-achieving schools pupils' well-being need not be high.

The main findings of the step-by-step regression analyses, in which components of the school social system (inputs, structure, climate) were related to cognitive learning results (reading, arithmetic), for the representative sample of 68 schools were as follows:

- when the inputs are first introduced into the regression analysis, this category of variables explains 75 per cent of the variance in school averages;
- when the structure variables are first introduced they explain 41 per cent of this variance, while introducing the climate variables first explains 72 per cent of the variance in school averages;
- when the climate variables are introduced after the input variables they explain 6 per cent extra of the variance in school averages; the structure variables in the same position explain 4 per cent extra variance;
- when the input variables are introduced after the climate variables they explain an additional 9 per cent variance.

In the sample of mainly black schools, climate and structure contribute more to the variances in school averages than in the representative sample.

From partitioning the contribution of the different categories of independent variables to the explained variance, it appeared that 8 per cent can be uniquely attributed to inputs, 6 per cent to climate and 4 per cent to structure. It is clearly a problem when interpreting the results of this study that the different categories of independent variables (inputs, structure and climate) correlate strongly with one another. In the homogeneous sub-samples the percentages of variance explained by structure and climate are noticeably greater (up to 30 per cent explained variance). The researchers concluded that the between-schools variance is determined not only by differences in intake, but also by climate and structure characteristics. As far as the relations with educational achievement of the individual variables within the main categories are concerned, the large effect of the variable 'academic futility' given by pupils ($r = 0.77$) was rather striking. Two structure variables that unexpectedly correlated negatively and only slightly positively, respectively, with achievement were open teaching and differentiation.

From the regression analyses in which self-image and self-confidence were the dependent variables, a larger 'unique' contribution emerged from the *climate* and *structure* variables (21 and 14 per cent respectively for the representative sample) than for the achievement score analyses. Moreover, the input factors appeared to be markedly less associated with self-image and self-confidence than with reading and arithmetic achievements (only 4 per cent unique explained variance in the representative sample). From the case studies it emerged that under the better-achieving schools headteachers and staff believed that improving educational achievement was a realistic and attainable objective.

Practical Implications

Brookover *et al.* succeeded in explaining 85 per cent of the between-schools variance in achievement with the variables from their social system model. If they had been able to explain variance at the level of pupils' achievement with their model, this percentage would have been much lower. They have merely shown that the between-schools variance is not determined only by intake differences, but that structure and climate also matter. Thus it remains difficult to determine whether climate and structure actually carry much weight with regard to individual pupil differences in achievement. The unique contribution to the explained variance is not overwhelming. Moreover, more fundamental criticism is conceivable regarding the operationalization of the concept 'school climate' in this study, and the interpretation of this operationalization as an independent effector of achievement. The climate variables are largely expectations of pupil achievement. Moreover, no distinction is made between more realistic and less realistic expectations. In other words, if at the better schools the staff have higher expectations than at the 'weaker' schools, one can see this as adequate assessment of the possibilities of one's own school.

In so far as the climate concept of Brookover *et al.* consists not only of optimism on achievement, but also of an achievement-directed policy, there is a practical implication to be extracted: that when a school opts for an achievement-directed policy and consistently carries it out, there will be an improvement in achievement levels. The optimistic side of the climate concept probably lends itself less to active manipulation (unless the management-trainers' guild see a future in higher-expectations therapy for headteachers).

Practical recommendations that Brookover *et al.* make are:

● maintaining communal objectives that encourage higher achievement levels for all pupils;
● consistently applying feedback and reinforcement in accordance with the mastery-learning model.

FIFTEEN THOUSAND HOURS

Background

The main motive underlying the study of Rutter *et al.* (1979) was to investigate whether the negative conclusions on the effect of school on learning achievement, as revealed by the studies of Coleman *et al.* (1966) and Jencks *et al.* (1972), might not be disproved if another category of school characteristics was taken into consideration. Similar negative conclusions on the effect of school when compared to the effect of social origin had also been revealed in British studies. The other school characteristics that were expressly incorporated in the study of Rutter *et al.* were classified under the heading 'process characteristics' of teaching, such as academic emphasis, the use of punishment and reward, etc. An important incentive when setting up the study was the consideration that as well as the choice of school characteristics, the methodology of the studies referred to above reinforced the fact that only an extremely limited school effect could be determined. Rutter *et al.* argued that larger school effects would be discovered when:

- curriculum-related achievement measurements (like exams) were used instead of general intelligence tests;
- longitudinal instead of cross-sectional research designs were used;
- school characteristics that in themselves had much between-schools variance were used;
- effect standards were more aimed at achievement levels than at differences between groups of pupils.

The general objectives of the study of Rutter *et al.* are sketched in the ambitions stated above. First, it was realized that the effect of pupils' background characteristics would have to be monitored in order to reach an accurate estimation of the influence of school characteristics. As well as the more traditional school characteristics included in the earlier generation of effectiveness studies – summarized here under the heading 'physical and administrative characteristics of the school' (such as the state of the school building and the division of pupils into classes) – a new category, 'process characteristics' of the school, was included. Examination data (not test data) were used as effect criteria and 'good behaviour', 'delinquency' and 'attendance' of pupils were included as additional effect criteria. Finally, an attempt was made to realize a longitudinal study design.

In the choice of process characteristics no particular theory of how schools function was presumed. The choice of variables was apparently determined by the need to give as complete as possible a picture of life in school. That choices were made is evident, but justification of the choices is not given in the study's report.

From the study's report it can be deduced that, by using a longitudinal design and an intensive description of school process characteristics, Rutter *et al.* intended to investigate: (a) to what extent schools differ in effects; (b) to what extent these differences in effects can be attributed to process characteristics.

Design, Methods and Technique of the Study

The design of this study was classified as longitudinal. In practice, this meant various things. First, the data collected at individual pupil level were obtained by means of a cohort design. In a previous study of 1970 all ten-year-olds in one London borough were tested. Of course, these pupils were then attending primary school. The data collected in 1970 about this group of pupils concerned intelligence, reading achievement, the extent of behavioural problems (according to the opinion of teachers) and details on family background. Pupils in the 1970 cohort who attended 20 non-selective secondary schools in London were then followed up (this involved two-thirds of the pupils in the borough register). In 1974 they were again tested for intelligence, reading comprehension and behavioural problems. At the same time supplementary data were collected on contact with the law (delinquency), country of origin and occupational status of parents. In a separate sub-study it was established that the cohort pupils did not differ significantly from their peers in the schools concerned.

Second, the longitudinal design meant that data were collected on *all* pupils in twelve of the 20 schools during their entire secondary-school period (twelve schools were decided on because data-gathering was too intensive to be carried out at all 20 schools). The most important measurement of secondary school attendance was the fifth year (for most pupils their last year at school). At that point the final outcome measurements of the study were carried out; for the cohort pupils this was in 1976.

The 'longitudinal' use of the cohort data (1970 and 1974) comes down to these data being used to correct the outcome measurements of 1976 for 'intake differences', or characteristics that pupils took with them to a school. While the study report refers now and then to 'school progress' this is *not* determined in the study. The repeated measurements at pupil level are not used to determine a learning gain per pupil, but only to estimate more clearly the influence of school on learning achievement. Where data have been established at other points during secondary schooling, these have been used to determine the *stability* of the characteristics concerned.

Four categories of variables were central to the study: intake measurements, process characteristics on the functioning of schools, outcome measurements and so-called environmental factors (summed up as background characteristics of schools). The intake measurements have already been mentioned in the discussion of the cohort study.

The following outcome measurements were applied to the study:

- pupils present during lessons – this was determined during a two-week period in the fifth year when pupils, absent or not, were registered, and a school mean was determined;
- pupils 'good behaviour' – a variety of data, like pupil self-assessment, teacher assessment and researchers' observations, were combined into a scale of 25 items which together represented both good and bad behaviour at school level;
- delinquency – this was measured as the total number of pupils who at the age of fourteen had come into contact with the police;
- examination results – a general achievement index was designed for the various levels within the English examination system.

The process data on the functioning of the schools were determined by various methods of data collection (interviews, structured observations) from various groups of respondents (headteachers, staff and pupils). This abundance of data was classified under several more general headings:

- academic emphasis, expressed for instance in the amount of homework and the total time each teacher spent teaching;
- teaching behaviour of staff (including class control);
- the use of reward and punishment during teaching;
- 'pupil friendliness' of the school;
- pupils' specific responsibilities (for instance, the degree of formal status class representatives have);
- staff stability;
- stability of a pupil's circle of friends;
- staff organization.

The environmental factors determined were:

- characteristics of pupil's own neighbourhood (mean socio-economic status);
- the balance of the school intake regarding intelligence, socio-economic status and ethnicity.

Finally, a fifth category of variables was taken into account: physical and administrative characteristics of the school; the state of the buildings; and the way pupils were divided into classes.

The data analyses of this study can be divided according to the two main research questions. Do schools differ in mean outcomes? If so, to what conditions (school characteristics and environment factors) can these differences be attributed? In order to establish accurately the differences between schools, differences in intake had to be monitored. Each outcome variable was first examined to see which of the intake variables (determined during the measuring points of the cohort study of 1970 and 1974) correlated most strongly with the outcome variable in question. Then an analysis of variance was carried out to see if differences between schools still remained after the effect of the most important intake characteristics had been taken into account. On the basis of these analyses of variance, corrected school averages per outcome variable were also established, because, for instance, a rank-ordering of schools per outcome criterion was established.

The relation between school characteristics and outcome criteria was established by determining the rank correlation between a particular school characteristic and the order of rank of schools for the criterion concerned (the order of rank was determined on the basis of the school averages, corrected for intake differences). If a particular school characteristic was categorical by nature, a non-parametric test was used in order to compare differences in orders of rank between (sub)groups.

As well as the main analysis, various manipulations were applied to the raw data in order to condense it into a limited number of combined measurements and indexes. Details of this are only partly mentioned in the study report and will not be summarized here. The same goes for the reliability checks applied to various instruments.

Results

After correction for language skills in the junior school and occupations of parents, the school factor still appeared to have a significant effect on the attendance criterion. With regard to behavioural problems, schools apparently varied considerably from one another. These differences only weakly related to a high proportion of entrants with behavioural problems, so that it can be concluded that schools really differed on this score. For the percentage of pupils that had come into contact with the law a similar conclusion was drawn, even if that was only for the sub-group boys (the delinquency rates for girls were very low).

The study of verbal reasoning indicated that pupils from this particular group of schools had lower achievement than the national average and lower than the average for the city of London. After checking for verbal reasoning skills (measured at aged ten), a significant main effect for schools still remained, which led to the conclusion that the twelve schools of the study also varied from one another on this criterion. From the rank correlation between the order of rank of schools (averages adjusted per school), as established for each of the four criteria, it appeared that schools that were 'good' in educational achievement had to cope with relatively few behavioural problems or absenteeism.

A school's physical and material characteristics, such as private/state, boys/girls, pupil/teacher ratio, streamed/unstreamed, size and age of the building, had little or no relevance for the criteria (attendance, good behaviour, examination results and delinquency).

Most sub-characteristics of the variable academic emphasis, such as attention to homework, total teaching time per week, class lesson preparation and positive expectations on learning achievement, correlated significantly and positively with one or more effect criteria. The sub-characteristics of the teacher behaviour variable were largely to do with maintaining order in class. Not surprisingly these characteristics correlated in particular with the criterion good behaviour. (Only one of the seven sub-characteristics correlated significantly and positively with examination results.)

For the punishment and reward category there was a divergent pattern of significant and insignificant rank correlations. The general thrust, however, was that positive reward was more effective than punishment.

The category pupil friendliness of the school also revealed a divergent pattern of rank correlations. A few sub-characteristics, such as school trips and pupil opinion on freedom to use the school building for a variety of activities, correlated positively with examination results. The same applied to the variable pupils' specific responsibilities. Thus the proportion of pupils who had been a class representative correlated highly positively with examination results.

Staff stability appeared to have a significant positive relationship with good behaviour, but not with the other effect criteria. Stability within a pupil's circle of friends only related highly positively with the number of pupils who had come into contact with the law. For the staff organization category it appeared that clear leadership in decision-making and participation in decision-making related positively to examination results.

From the school characteristics that correlated positively with one of the five effect criteria a general process score was designed per school by summing the rank numbers. This general process score showed rank correlations of 0.92 with good behaviour, 0.76 with examination results, 0.65 with attendance and 0.68 with delinquency. From these rather high rank correlations the researchers concluded that school characteristics strengthen and complement one another and that one can speak of schools with a generally positive atmosphere or climate and schools with a generally negative atmosphere.

The various environmental factors did not appear to be related to the effect criteria. The different characteristics of the composition of the intake group (particularly the variable academic balance) did display a significant relation with the effect criteria. The composition characteristics revealed only a weak link with the general process score.

Besides these more specific results, a general analysis was carried out in which all the main categories of variables were introduced at the same time. This was done using log-linear analyses and multiple regression analysis. From the former analyses it emerged that schools have a significant effect even after parents' jobs and verbal reasoning skills are taken into account. A similar conclusion followed after first taking the composition of the intake factors into account.

From the regression analysis it emerged that earlier achievement in verbal reasoning explained 26 per cent of the variance in examination results, parents' occupations 1 per cent, the composition of the intake factors 3.45 per cent and the overall process score 1.6 per cent.

Practical Implications

The researchers drew the following conclusions from the above-mentioned findings, noting that in the interpretation subjective aspects necessarily play an important role:

1 The secondary schools studied differed greatly in pupil behaviour and educational achievement.
2 These differences were not explained away by differences in intake; important net school differences remained.
3 The differences between schools in effectiveness remained relatively stable over a period of four or five years.

4 In general schools scored about the same for each of the effect criteria (that is to say, schools that had a good average achievement also had fewer pupils with behavioural problems).
5 The differences between schools could not be attributed to the physical and administrative characteristics of a school.
6 The differences between schools in outcome criteria were systematically related to process characteristics that can be manipulated by the staff of a school.
7 Differences between schools in achievement and other outcome criteria were also determined by the composition of the school population at the intake. Examination results were better in schools with a large proportion of pupils of at least average intelligence.
8 The effect of the composition at the intake was clearest with regard to the delinquency criterion and least clear with regard to the 'good behaviour' criterion.
9 The relationship between the overall process score and the effect criteria was much stronger than the link with the individual process indicators. This indicates a cumulative effect of the process indicators and shows that it is possibly useful to think in terms of a combination of values, attitudes and behavioural forms that are characteristic for a particular school.
10 The entire pattern of findings points to a causal link between the various variables categories, whereby it is particularly significant that manipulative process characteristics apparently matter.

On research-technical grounds there is cause to exercise some caution with regard to the interpretation of the findings reported above. First, the small number of schools should be pointed out. This is all the more relevant because it is at school level that the most important analyses took place. Second, an initial theory or concept is lacking: why were these specific school characteristics chosen; what is the possible background to certain correlations turning out high while others are low?

The analysis techniques applied come across as being somewhat crude. Why categorize continuous variables so as to be able to carry out analysis of variance? Why not spend more time on scale and instrument design so that working with rank correlations could have been avoided? At the same time, why not analyse school characteristics linked to outcome variables, using the primary data (either the pupils' scores or the aggregated scores at school level)? By reducing the information to rank ordering of schools all the information on the size of the differences between schools is thrown out. One could say that the data of this study lend themselves well to a secondary analysis using more advanced techniques.

Because of the number of individual rank correlations it is difficult to decipher what is now finally the balance of significant and insignificant correlations. From what is presented one has an impression of really substantial school effects. The blow comes on inspection of Rutter et al.'s Table 9.4 (p. 171), in which the effects are reproduced in more standard measurements (percentage of variance explained). The collective process characteristics explain only 1.6 per cent of the total explained variance. As well as this it must be taken into account that when constructing the composite variable process characteristics, Rutter et al. included only variables that correlated highly with the criteria. This implies chance capitalization, whereby the effects of process characteristics on achievement are almost certainly overestimated (see Goldstein, 1980, p. 24).

CHARACTERISTICS OF EFFECTIVE SCHOOLS

Background

Schweitzer (1984) cites as the main background to this study a response to the criticism levelled at effective schools research by a number of commentators (for example, Ralph and Fennessey, 1983). He aimed to show that school characteristics that emerged in earlier effective schools research as predictors of relatively high achievement could, in fact, explain differences between schools.

Research Questions

School characteristics that had emerged from earlier effective schools studies were:

- strong educational leadership from the school head;
- emphasis on acquiring basic skills (the three Rs);
- a safe and orderly climate;
- high expectations of pupils' achievement;
- frequent evaluation of pupils' progress by the headteacher and staff.

The hypothesis tested in this study was that these factors account for a significant amount of variance in average achievement between schools.

Design, Methods and Techniques of the Study

The study was carried out among a sample of sixteen inner-city primary schools of an American city. The school population consisted of almost 100 per cent black teachers, while an average 90 per cent of pupils from all sixteen schools came from the lower socio-economic strata (90.4 per cent of pupils were eligible for free school lunches).

Data on the five school characteristics were collected by means of a questionnaire with 49 items of the Likert type. This questionnaire was taken by the school heads and 456 teachers. For each school a score was determined per school characteristic by determining the average score for each item and then aggregating these averages. The reliability (internal consistency) of the scales was reasonable – coefficient alpha varied from 0.69 to 0.95. By determination of the correlations among the five scales within the groups (heads and teachers) and between the groups at each one of the schools, it was established that the correlations between the scores of the two groups were higher for each individual scale than the correlations between the scores for the various scales. This lent some support to the discriminant and convergent validity of the scales. In other words, what was measured turned out to be quite independent of the group that completed the questionnaire, and likewise the various scales measured separate, independent characteristics. Achievement data in the study were collected by using existing test results: the scores for the California Achievement Test, taken by all classes of the schools. Average scores per class were aggregated in order to reach a school achievement score. These were then correlated with the average scores of the scales by which the school characteristics were measured.

In order to present a clearer picture of the content given to the five effectiveness-promoting school characteristics in this study, an example of the items for each factor is given. For educational leadership the accent was on a school head's instructions to staff and in particular on his or her evaluation activities aimed at giving form and content to what is taught and how it is taught. For example, 'The principal frequently communicates to individual teachers their responsibility in relation to student achievement' and 'The principal reviews and interprets test results with and for the faculty.' Emphasis on achievement in basic skills includes items like 'The students in your school are told what objectives they are expected to learn' and 'Teachers in your building will do anything necessary to get all students to read and do maths well.' The items that formed safe and orderly climate are literally concerned with the safety of a school, the smartness of the building, the respect for authority of the pupils and a favourable atmosphere in which to learn. For the expectations category heads and staff had to give numerical estimates of pupils' school careers; for example, 'What percent of the students in school do you expect to complete high school?' The category frequent evaluation comprised items that referred exclusively to the use of tests and testing, like 'Criterion-referenced tests are used to assess basic skills throughout the school.'

Results

The results of this study are reproduced in Table A1.1. On the basis of these results Schweitzer concluded that the five effective schools characteristics are indeed significantly linked with the mean educational achievement of schools.

Table A1.1 *Correlations of the five school characteristics with school achievement*

Characteristic	Teachers	School heads
Educational leadership	0.58	0.09
Emphasis on achievement	0.79	0.44
Safe and orderly climate	0.50	0.28
High expectations	0.79	0.71
Frequent evaluation	0.68	0.21

From Schweitzer (1984).

Implications of the Data

Schweitzer's study shows that school effectiveness research becomes a lot simpler when it takes place among a group of schools that are homogeneous with regard to pupil intake. Nevertheless, within the very simplicity of the study lies its weakness.

First, it is doubtful whether the schools are really so homogeneous; socio-economic status of the pupils, for instance, was determined somewhat crudely (free school lunches). Second, the manner of collecting data – written questionnaires – capitalizes on the opinions of staff and headteachers and does not take into account the possible social desire in the replies. Third, the data analysis method employed (correlations) does not take into account the possibility of the various 'predictors' not being entirely independent, so that it is difficult to estimate the exact value of the influence of the individual characteristics.

On the other hand, the relatively high correlations between the school characteristics and average learning achievement cannot just be dismissed, even if there would be an interaction with differences in intake characteristics between the schools.

SCHOOL MATTERS

Research Questions

The central questions that were intended to be answered by Mortimore *et al.* (1988) were:

- Are some schools or classes more effective than others when controlled for variance in pupil intake?

- Are some schools or classes more effective for certain groups of pupils?
- If some schools or classes are more effective than others, what factors could account for this?

The study was commissioned by the Inner London Education Authority (ILEA). The study was carried out among a sample of 50 schools from the 600 primary schools that were under the control of ILEA. Effective schools research carried out since the late 1970s in the USA and UK was used as a reference point (Brookover *et al.*, 1979; Rutter *et al.*, 1979). The main author was a member of the research team that under Rutter's supervision published the report *Fifteen Thousand Hours*, discussed above.

The study also had a practical aim: it resulted in recommendations for educational authorities at national and regional level, teacher training colleges, heads, teachers and parents. The design of the study had a few distinctive features:

- not only cognitive but also non-cognitive effect criteria were taken into account;
- the study was longitudinal: effectiveness was expressed not only in terms of attainment reached at a certain point, but also in terms of individual pupil progress;
- use was made of direct observation within schools and classes, so that besides data collected by means of tests and questionnaires much descriptive material was drawn together on processes that had taken place at the schools.

It should also be mentioned that for this study use was made of newly developed techniques for multi-level data analysis. This means that the study can be regarded as the most extensive and advanced school effectiveness study reported this far.

Study Methods and Techniques

In the study data were collected on intake characteristics of pupils, cognitive achievement and non-cognitive outcomes of the education system, school characteristics, characteristics of education at class level and environmental characteristics of the school. In particular the following variables were measured:

1. Intake characteristics of pupils.
   (a) Background characteristics of pupils, family characteristics, socio-economic status, language, country of origin.
   (b) Early achievement in reading, arithmetic and visual and spatial skills (measured at the start of junior school).
   (c) Teachers' assessment of pupils' behaviour at the beginning of junior school.
2. Cognitive learning achievement.
   (a) Standardized tests in reading and arithmetic (the Edinburgh Reading Test (ERT) and the National Foundation for Educational Research Basic Mathematics Test (BMT)).
   (b) Individual tests in practical mathematics.
   (c) Annual measures of creative writing.
   (d) Measures for verbal expression skills of pupils (among a random sample of pupils).
   Note: these effect measures were taken at various times in the pupils' school careers between the first and third years of junior school.
3. Non-cognitive outcomes of the education system.
   (a) Class-teachers' assessment of pupils' behaviour.
   (b) Pupils periodically reporting on attitudes towards certain aspects of their school and education.

(c) Measures of how the pupils believed teachers and fellow pupils perceived them (at the end of the third year).

(d) Measures of pupils' self-image.

4 School characteristics and schooling at class level.

(a) Interviews with headteachers and deputy heads on school organization and school policy, including views on leadership, education philosophy, qualifications and experience of heads, grouping of pupils, assignment of teachers to classes, involvement of teachers in the decision-making process and the division of duties among staff.

(b) Didactic strategies, determined by structured, direct observation using existing observation timetables and qualitative data, such as observers' descriptions.

5 Characteristics of the environment and certain characteristics of the school determined by the environment.

(a) Views of parents on their children's learning and their own role in this.

(b) Descriptive characteristics of the school. Of importance was whether the school was combined with an infant school or was a private or state school.

The data were collected by researchers and assistant researchers, identified as field officers.

In analysis of the data the following calculations were carried out:

- careful attention was given to monitoring the differences in intake characteristics of the pupil populations of the individual schools;
- the influence of each background characteristic on results, like age, social class and so on, was separately established;
- effects were expressed in terms of attained scores in the third year of junior school as well as in terms of the pupils' progress from grade 1 to grade 3;
- use was made of modern techniques for analysing multi-level data.

Results

In the first place the study produced an enormous amount of descriptive information on the schools, varying from data on the school building to aspects of policy and the education philosophy of the school, school management and curriculum (achieved not only on paper but also in practice). These research data will not be summarized here. The general conclusion of this part of the study is that striking differences between schools were found (for example, in intake and state of buildings), but more general trends were also established: the observation, for instance, that in almost all schools tests were used and that for all aspects of the curriculum there was more communication between teacher and individual pupil than between teacher and the class as a whole.

Second, test and assessment data collected from pupils were used to determine pupils' progress and differences between sub-groups of pupils, and to compare teachers' expectations of pupils' achievement with actual achievement. The initial measures revealed differences between the pupils in favourable and unfavourable background characteristics as well as in learning achievement. The scores of the initial measures of cognitive skills (in the first year of junior school) correlated highly, in general, with the measures at the end of the third year (the highest correlation was for reading (0.80) and the lowest for practical arithmetic (0.57). The correlations between cognitive achievement (in the third year) and non-cognitive outcomes were also examined. Here it was discovered that there was only a slight link ($r \approx 0.40$) between cognitive performance and pupils' 'good' behaviour.

When sub-groups of pupils were compared for their achievement in subsequent years, besides the more standard categories like socio-economic status, sex and race, differences in the age of children at the beginning of junior school were looked at. Children born in the autumn can be as much as eleven months older when they arrive at school than children born in the summer. From the results of the study it clearly emerged that older children were at an advantage, both with regard to cognitive skills and in having fewer problems at school. It is also striking that older pupils in the class received more attention from the teacher, while in fact it is the younger children who need the extra attention. The differences in achievement between older and younger pupils remained stable throughout the period of the study, meaning that the younger children never caught up with the older ones.

For socio-economic status it appeared – as revealed in other studies – that the children of 'white-collar' workers had an advantage concerning cognitive achievement, that they had fewer behavioural problems and that teachers had positive expectations of them. The results of the study also revealed important differences between boys and girls in that the girls achieved more and were less often regarded as problem pupils. In groups divided into country of origin, significant differences in achievement were found, pupils of non-British origin performing less well on average. In addition, it was established that the problems of certain minorities increased as their school careers progressed.

With regard to the link between teachers' expectations of pupils and their actual achievement, it was discovered that teachers in general have an accurate impression of their pupils. It was noted, however, as mentioned earlier, that teachers have insufficient regard for the problems of younger pupils.

The third and last category of research results has direct bearing on the central questions of school effectiveness. It was examined whether a pupil attending a particular school affects his or her achievement level and progress after background variables have been taken into account. The elementary question here is whether or not the school matters. The factors that could explain any possible differences between schools were also investigated. The results of the study of school factors are reproduced in Table A1.2. In the first column the effect criterion is given. The second gives the percentage of variance in achievement at the end of the third year that can be explained by the school factor, after being corrected for intake difference between schools. In the third column is the percentage variance in progress made between the first and third years that can be explained by the school factor. (Progress is determined with covariance analysis, using the attainment of the first year as covariable.)

Table A1.2 *School effects in terms of cognitive and non-cognitive effect criteria*

Effect criterion	Percentage explained attainment	Percentage explained progress
Reading	9	24
Arithmetic	11	23
Writing	13	20
Verbal reasoning	27	–
Behaviour	10	–
Attendance	5.6	–
Pupils' self-image	8.4	–
Attitude towards education	7.5–12.2*	–

After Mortimore *et al.* (1988).

*Attitudes were determined according to various school subjects. The lowest and the highest percentage explained variance for reading and arithmetic, respectively, are stated.

For each effect criterion Mortimore *et al.* recorded the differences between the mean scores of the most effective and the least effective school in score points of the criterion variables. These differences are considerable: for instance, 25 points on a scale of 100 points for progress in reading. Because the differences are not indicated in standard deviations with regard to the mean, it is difficult to compare the findings with results measured in other studies. Moreover, with this manner of determining effects, which comes down to comparing extremes, one must take capitalization on coincidental fluctuations into account. It was also examined how far schools that are effective in one criterion are also effective in another and whether there are schools that score high for practically all the effect criteria. It appeared that schools that make good progress in arithmetic do the same for reading and that at these schools pupils have a more positive image of themselves. In general, however, effectiveness in cognitive skills does not go hand-in-hand with effectiveness in non-cognitive skills.

With these results the researchers considered that their basic question – Do schools matter? – was clearly answered in the affirmative.

From further differentiation of the effectiveness of schools for certain sub-groups of pupils (according to sex, socio-economic status and race) it appeared that schools were just as effective for each of these groups. In other words, an effective school is beneficial for all groups of pupils whether they come from a more privileged or a disadvantaged background. From a study of school and class characteristics that could explain why one school is more effective than another, twelve factors emerged, which are listed and briefly explained.

1 Purposeful leadership of the staff by the headteacher. This sort of leadership is characterized by a clear involvement by the head with the curriculum and what takes place in the classroom, without there being talk of 'poking their nose everywhere and wanting to be in charge of everything'. An emphasis on teachers maintaining records on pupils was one of the important expressions of this sort of 'remote' educational leadership. It is remarkable that schools where heads placed emphasis on acquiring basic skills were not the most effective.

2 Involvement of the deputy head. In schools where deputy heads played a clear educational role results were relatively high. This implies that a certain degree of delegation of authority from head to deputy is beneficial.

3 Involvement of teachers. Participation of staff in the educational policy of the school also works positively. In the successful schools teachers were actively involved in school curriculum planning.

4 Consistency among teachers. Pupils benefit from continuity in teaching staff and from all teachers following common guidelines.

5 Structured sessions. In effective classes the work is clearly arranged and organized by the teachers. Handling the learning material within a structured framework is beneficial for pupils, providing sufficient space within a pre-structured framework for pupils to work relatively independently.

6 Intellectually challenging teaching. Where teachers asked pupils stimulating questions relevant to creativity and higher reasoning skills, results were better. Other aspects of this factor are confidence in pupils' self-motivation and an enthusiastic attitude by the teacher.

7 Work-centred environment. When teachers spent more time on the content of work (as opposed to communicating on all sorts of routine matters and maintaining order) results were on average better. In these classes a quiet, work-directed atmosphere prevailed.

8 Sharp focus within sessions. It appeared to be more beneficial to centre learning material on a clear core theme than to allow pupils to work in groups on several themes. Where the latter was the case classes were noisier and the teachers had

less time to discuss the actual content. This focused subject matter does not mean that a certain differentiation in what is offered works unfavourably – quite the contrary.

9 Maximum communication between teachers and pupils. It appeared important that children had a lot of direct contact with their teachers. In practice this means that traditional teaching, where the teacher addresses the whole group, works better than being very busy with individual pupils. In cases of extreme individual-oriented contact there was less time for direct contact with the teacher.

10 Record keeping. Both for competent educational administration by the head and for competent teaching by staff, maintaining records on pupils appeared to be important.

11 Parental involvement. Parental involvement with school policy, curriculum and what takes place in the classroom appeared to go hand-in-hand with better results.

12 A positive climate. A positive climate is mainly characterized by the giving of frequent positive feedback to pupils. Other aspects that were regarded as important were the teacher's interest in the 'whole' pupil – interest in what happens to the child outside school hours – and good cooperation among teachers.

The authors rightly conclude that many of these factors have also emerged in other school effectiveness studies. An exception is the fact that a strong emphasis on basic skills is not linked to better results, while factors 8 (limited focus) and 2 (the significance of the deputy head) are relatively new.

To sum up, we can say that an 'effective school' according to the study of Mortimore *et al.* is characterized by: educational leadership at a distance, in which maintaining records on pupils' progress is an important resource; a positive and enthusiastic atmosphere backed up by the involvement of the head and parents; and structured and well-regulated teaching.

Interpretation of the Results and Implications for Educational Practice

This study has many strong points:

- there was an intensive collection of data;
- a broad spectrum of effective criteria was used;
- a longitudinal study was used so that effects on progress could be expressed;
- great care was given to the data analysis.

The researchers have also given much thought to the implications of their study data for the educational field. For this a separate chapter was reserved in their final report, where the practical implications for various targeted groups are set out.

Central government should be mindful that local education authorities do not stint on the costs of running school buildings. In addition, the government should provide facilities for smaller classes in the lower grades of primary school.

Teacher-training institutes should take into account the essential factors generated by this study, particularly with regard to what is within the reach of teachers (structured lessons, intellectually stimulating teaching, a task-oriented environment, a sharp focus with regard to subject matter presented during lessons, optimum communication, maintaining records, parental involvement, the use of positive feedback and praising of pupils).

The local education authorities should be able to do something with the finding that voluntary schools do better than state ones by, for instance, trying to provide the latter with the leeway voluntary schools have. Moreover, the LEAs could make infant classes smaller by making the top classes bigger if necessary. The optimal school size that emerged from the study, i.e. two parallel classes for each age group, could be used by the LEAs as guideline. The LEAs could also contribute to proper maintenance of school buildings, and to stability among staff, providing support for newly appointed school heads, for the youngest children in each age group and for increased parental involvement.

Teachers' unions should see the study findings, the researchers hope, as an incentive to focus more on the content of education (besides matters of terms and conditions) and in particular to do their utmost to achieve smaller classes and react positively to the design of tools for measuring pupils' progress.

School heads should be concerned with the study findings that relate to educational leadership, class size, involvement of the head and deputy head in school policy, consistency among teachers in the way the curriculum is interpreted, parental involvement, maintaining records on progress and creating a positive school climate.

Teachers should be more aware of the significance of having expectations of pupils' achievement and can also reflect on the core elements of the study related to the way subject matter is taught, such as structured lessons, intellectually challenging teaching, a task-oriented environment, a sharply focused subject matter during lessons and optimum communication between teachers and pupils during lessons (taking into account the balance between whole-class teaching and individual instruction).

Appendix 2

Dutch School Effectiveness Research

RESEARCH PROJECTS THAT HAVE SOME BEARING ON SCHOOL EFFECTIVENESS STUDIES

The Evaluation of Compensatory Programmes

In the 1970s various large-scale compensatory education programmes were launched, such as the Amsterdam Innovation Project, the Internal Differentiation Project (GEON) in Utrecht and the Education and Social Environment Project (OSM) in Rotterdam. At the same time a nationwide education incentive policy was undertaken. This was also aimed at providing extra education facilities for the educationally disadvantaged. An overview of these projects and the evaluation studies of them is given in Scheerens (1987). The evaluation study that is most relevant to the subject of school and instructional effectiveness is the one for the OSM project. For certain components of the programme of this large-scale innovation project learning principles were used that correspond with the characteristics of effective instruction discussed earlier. For example, part of the programme followed the principles of mastery learning. From the results of the evaluation of these improvement programmes presented so far, however, only a slight effect on learning achievement has been established (Slavenburg, 1986).

Other Studies

The other studies discussed in this section are not considered to be 'real' effectiveness studies because they fulfil one or two, but not all three, of the following criteria:

- effects defined as learning achievement or attained educational level;
- school effectiveness literature comprises an important source of inspiration for the study;
- the school factor or individual school characteristics are independent variables.

A study that is often included in Dutch school effectiveness research is that of Van der Wolf (1984), who made a study of thirteen Amsterdam schools. School drop-out rate was the central dependent variable in this survey. The thirteen schools were divided into (a) achievement-oriented schools, (b) cognitive-oriented pupil-centred schools and (c) affective-oriented pupil-centred schools. The achievement-oriented schools revealed the lowest drop-out rate and the affective-oriented pupil-centred schools the highest. Kreft (1984) makes critical comments on the validity of this study.

Stoel (1980) studied the relation between school size and the way pupils experience school. From the study it appeared that school size explains 5 per cent of the variance in the experience of a school.

In Kreft's PhD thesis (1987) she reports on a comparative evaluation between comprehensives on the one hand and specific secondary school types on the other. It appeared, among other things, that mean achievement (measured in terms of secondary education achievement) at schools for pre-university and higher levels of secondary training was higher than the mean achievement at comprehensives. However, the study produced no data concerning the causes. The question of whether the differences should be seen as selection effects or as a result of differences in school climate was asked, but not answered.

Within the context of evaluating the government's policy aimed at reducing the number of pupils from ordinary schools admitted to special education, Vinjé (1988) investigated which school characteristics could explain the differences in mean achievement in reading and spelling. The school characteristic with the most influence was the so-called school score, which gives an idea of the mean socio-economic status of pupils at a school. In the study no school or instruction characteristics were included that had an affinity with the known variables from school effectiveness research.

Van der Werf (1988) investigated the effects of the use of school curricula in primary schools on teaching behaviour and learning achievement. Teaching behaviour was operationalized as adaptive instruction and encouraging cooperative learning. Learning achievement was measured using the standardized achievement test (the CITO test) taken in the final year of primary school. The use of the school curriculum appeared to relate positively to teaching behaviour, but for teaching behaviour as characterized above a negative relationship with learning achievement was shown. Thus neither a direct nor an indirect effect (via specific teaching behaviour) of the use of school curricula could be demonstrated.

Apart from Van der Wolf's conclusion on achievement-oriented schools, the outcomes of these studies have little in common with the most important results of mainstream school effectiveness research.

DUTCH SCHOOL EFFECTIVENESS STUDIES

The core data of Dutch school effectiveness studies that were investigated are summed up in Table 4.4. From this it can be seen that ten studies were related to primary schools, five were carried out in secondary schools and one took place in both a primary and a secondary school. For most of these sixteen studies a fairly brief summary is given here. A few studies (Meijnen, 1984; van Marwijk Kooij-von Baumhauer, 1984; Vermeulen, 1987) are discussed in more detail.

The general research question posed by Meijnen (1984) was: which family and school characteristics explain academic achievement at the end of junior school? More specific research questions were also formulated:

- Are there differences between schools that are relevant for differences in pupils' academic achievement in general and for the educational achievement of manual workers' children in particular?
- Which family background characteristics affect academic achievement in junior schools?
- Which school and family characteristics reinforce or neutralize one another?
- Is progress in academic achievement in the lower school identical to that in the upper school? Are the same school characteristics relevant to both phases?

The survey was carried out among a random sample of 24 primary schools in the city of Groningen. The schedule for data gathering was as follows:

- in January of the first year of junior school, intelligence, school progress, socio-economic status and family background characteristics were measured;
- at the end of the third year, intelligence and school progress were measured again and characteristics of the lower school were recorded;
- at the end of the sixth year (top class), intelligence and school progress were measured a third time, school characteristics of the upper school were recorded and a new family background study was carried out.

Between these times data were gathered on transfers to special education, resitting classes and advice given by the school head on the choice of secondary school type. Understandably, with repeated measurement of individual pupils there was the problem of drop-outs. The first year began with 728 pupils, of whom there were 472 in the third year and only 367 in the sixth. In the third year the sample was augmented to 703, from whom 514 still remained in the sixth year.

Intelligence was measured using three age-commensurate versions of the PMA. Using these tests, scores were determined on three aspects of intelligence: general, verbal and spatial. In the first year school progress was determined by the teacher's assessments for language and number. In the third year the Groningen school progress test (GST 3–4) was administered and in the sixth year the Groningen selection test; both relate to language and number.

The family study in the first year was undertaken by interviewing mothers and asking fathers to complete a short written questionnaire. In the sixth year the mothers also completed a short questionnaire. A description of school characteristics in the lower school was achieved by interviews with teachers of the first three classes. In the upper school, school characteristics were recorded by means of a written questionnaire completed by the teachers of the top three classes. To determine the socio-economic status of pupils an index was designed based on the occupations and levels of education of parents.

In both the lower and upper school characteristics were divided into curriculum characteristics, the functioning of teaching staff and structural characteristics. Under curriculum characteristics the basic rationale was to contrast a cluster of characteristics classified collectively as 'pupil-centred' with a cluster of characteristics classified as 'subject matter related'. The curriculum was viewed on the one hand as a sum total of concepts (the ideological level) and on the other as a sum total of practical measures (the practical teaching side). Previously compiled characteristics at ideological and practical level were presented to teachers and this empirical material was then used to see whether the subject matter related or the pupil-centred type of curriculum emerged, and whether characteristics of both types consistently emerged at ideological and practical level.

Necessary adjustments were applied to the categories of data collected before the analyses were carried out. Data from school progress tests were standardized in the same way as for intelligence tests (with a mean of 100 and a standard deviation of 15) to determine the difference in scores between intelligence and school progress. Positive values of school progress score minus IQ score were regarded as overachievement (achievement above one's own level) and negative values as underachievement.

A preparatory processing of the school characteristics scores was undertaken to check whether the subject matter/pupil-centred dimension could be traced in the empirical material. This appeared to be the case at curriculum ideology level, but not with regard to practical teaching characteristics. Even a coherence between patterns of response to ideological and practical characteristics was missing. Because a clean division of school characteristics could not be made, it was necessary to revert to relating separately each school characteristic to the effect criteria (intellectual development and school progress). At the same time a typology of school characteristics was designed on the basis of a cluster analysis. In the lower school five school types were distinguished and in the upper school four.

The five school types of lower school were:

1   The standard school type. These schools scored in the average category for most of the characteristics: eleven out of 24 schools fell into this group;
2   The intellectually innovative type. These schools were characterized by a strictly traditional organization, a weak pupil-centred approach towards developing pupils' self-reliance and scant emphasis on learning goals related to the social sciences. Much emphasis was placed in these schools on problem-solving approaches to core subjects. The timetable was used in a supple manner. Five schools fell into this category.

3 The pupil-centred type. This school type fulfilled all the 'progressive' characteristics that were seen as pupil-centred in the study. Only one school fell into this category.

4 The formal subject matter oriented type. This school type came closest to the *a priori* views on formal subject matter orientated schools. Six schools fell into this category.

5 The educationally innovative type. One school had a pupil-centred curriculum, but did not break down the concept of a grade.

The four types that were distinguished in the upper school, again on the basis of cluster analysis, were:

1 The formal subject matter oriented type. See the description above. Thirteen schools fell into this category.

2 The educationally innovative type. Distinguished by being average in most school characteristics, but pupil-centred with regard to interaction and stimulation of motivation (four schools).

3 The culturally integrated type. Characterized by being traditional in a subject matter oriented emphasis and frequent testing for results and 'progressive' in active encouragement of independent learning and devotion of time to achieving learning objectives in the social sciences. Also characteristic is the high score for the component 'integration of school and out-of-school knowledge' (four schools).

4 The pupil-centred type. See the description above (three schools).

In order to answer the main research questions, the techniques used for analysing the data were product-moment correlation coefficients, t tests and analyses of variance.

With regard to the results of Meijnen's study, only outcomes related to the effects of school and school characteristics on intelligence and school progress will be considered here. The investigation includes the percentage of the total variance in IQ and learning achievement (reading and number) that can be ascribed to differences between schools. In the lower school this was 7 per cent of the dependent IQ variable. In the upper school 9 per cent of the total variance in IQ was determined by the school factor, with 7 per cent for reading and 23 per cent for arithmetic. Thus it appears that schools exercise more influence on arithmetic achievement than on language achievement.

The correlation analysis between each of the various school characteristics and the IQ and school progress data revealed only very tenuous relationships in both the lower and the upper schools (exceptions were significant correlations of about 0.15 between the number of staff changes and the experience of teachers on the one hand and a few dependent variables on the other).

In the lower school no significant difference was found in means among the five school types for the entire pupil population. When only the means of working-class children were looked at, the intellectually innovative type (strictly formal and much emphasis on problem-solving) appeared to do clearly better on verbal IQ than the other school types. The same applied to the upper school. In so far as one could in fact discern some significant differences these were found among the sub-group of working-class children. Here, too, the differences in verbal IQ were greater than for other IQ sorts. The most striking result was that development in verbal reasoning in educationally innovative and culturally integrated schools appeared to be negative, while working-class children showed most progress on this score in formal subject matter oriented schools.

In the lower schools of the intellectual innovative type overachievement was observed for arithmetic, particularly among working-class children. This was an even more striking result because IQ was also increased by this school type. Underachievement was recorded for pupil-centred and educationally innovative school types. In the formal subject matter oriented upper schools a slight drop for both language and number was recorded. Among educationally innovative and culturally integrated types slight progress was recorded. Here it should be taken into account that for both school types IQ had dropped in the same period. In pupil-centred schools a noteworthy drop (9 points) in language achievement was recorded among working-class children.

Various interpretations can be given to the outcomes of this study. The researcher himself reaches the conclusion that idealistic learning types, like formal subject matter oriented or pupil-centred schooling, are no favourable breeding grounds for reducing environmentally determined school achievement. Instead a mix of type, with a heavy emphasis on working with learning objectives on the one hand, and being aware as much as possible of the specific social and cultural characteristics of working-class children on the other, is recommended.

In the press, Meijnen's study was largely construed as reaffirming the importance of old-fashioned, formal teaching for working-class children. Soutendijk (1986, p.58), after re-analysing Meijen's relevant research results, concluded that in fact it would be correct to assume that 'old-fashioned traditional primary teaching' is harmful for working-class children and that 'democratically reforming primary education still appears to offer the best learning and development opportunities for educationally disadvantaged groups'.

The central problem in interpreting Meijnen's study is the fact that from combining the many 'independent' variables with the several dependent variables hardly any convincing consistent patterns emerge. On top of that, the number of study components (24 schools for determining the effectiveness of school types) is small in relation to the number of variables. Moreover, because of the composite nature of the school types one has quite a free interpretive hand in determining which characteristics are of overriding importance in characterizing a certain type.

Meijnen's study illustrates how difficult it is to reach unambiguous research results on school effectiveness – even with a study like this, with strong features, such as a longitudinal design, taking into account IQ development as well as school progress, and a theoretical framework for selecting school characteristics. In fact the data lend themselves well to a re-analysis using multi-level analysis techniques recently made available, especially as these enable the differences among schools in the relations between socio-economic status, intelligence and school progress to be estimated more accurately.

The study of van Marwijk Kooij-von Baumhauer (1984) is a hybrid of a comparative case study and a quantitative study. For a comparative case study the number of cases (25) is high. While quantitative analyses were carried out (largely correlation calculations) and the variables were likewise quantitatively defined, there appear to be no generalized findings attached to the results: at least, 'no generalised pronouncements based on the inductive statistics' (p. 161). Thus the author avoids stating significance levels and reliability intervals for the correlation coefficients. However, she does conceive it to be plausible on 'grounds regarding content' that the relationships found also apply to other school communities. These grounds regarding content are that 'there is a clear similarity with the findings of others' and that 'the results ... correspond with theoretical premises' (p. 161).

The study was set up on the basis of the following questions:

- Why do some schools succeed more than others in helping their pupils achieve well in school?
- Are there schools that help pupils achieve well and cater for their social development too, and why does one school succeed better at this than another?
- Can schools help pupils to achieve well, cater for their social development and

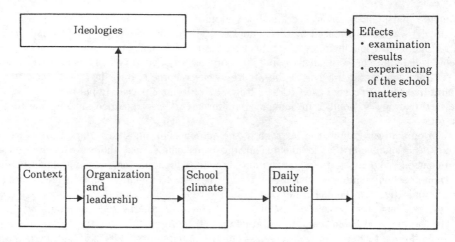

Figure A2.1 Variables used by van Marwijk-Kooij-von Baumhauer (1984)

let teachers and pupils experience school with pleasure and their work as meaningful, without making heavy demands on them?

The categories of variables chosen for this study are reproduced in Figure A2.1.

The effects of this study are measured as examination results (results of nationwide written examinations), specified by means of four variables:

- average grade for English and mathematics for pre-university (VWO), higher general (HAVO) and intermediate general (MAVO) secondary streams in 1979–80;
- average grade for English and mathematics per school in 1979–80 minus average grade in 1975–77;
- average percentage pass rate in 1979–80;
- average number of extra years pupils required to complete different categories of secondary education over and above the standard 10, 11 and 12 years, respectively;
- the ways in which pupils, teachers and school principal experience the school measured by means of a scale along the lines of 'this is a boring school', 'this is a good school', etc. (eight variables).

The school climate is defined as 'various aspects of teacher and pupil attitudes towards the school'. These include teachers' opinions of pupils' self-reliance, attitudes towards colleagues and the way they function, and pupils' opinions on the 'strictness' of the school. Within this category 24 variables were specified. The category organization and policy is split into a number of descriptive characteristics of the organization and opinions about it from teachers and pupils. Descriptive organization characteristics include how often school management meets, how often heads of departments meet, observed contact between principal and staff, and the way information is disseminated among teachers and pupils (20 variables). Examples of opinions on the organization are the degree to which teachers feel jointly responsible and clarity regarding the ideas of the principal, as judged by the teachers (fourteen variables). Context characteristics include the size of the school, denomination, level of urbanization and pass rate in previous years (1975–77). In total eighteen variables were specified within this category.

The data were gathered by interview (fifteen teachers, three deputy principals and 30 pupils per school), direct observations and archive consultation (school administration).

From the 125 combined VWO/HAVO/MAVO comprehensives in 1975 in the Netherlands, 25 were selected for the study. When schools that deviated too much from the mean regarding factors like composition of staff (age, sex), teacher–pupil ratio, and private general secondary schools, schools with a particular philosophy and experimental comprehensives were excluded, there remained schools with 'relatively many pupils from the lower socio-economic band' and an 'average' teaching staff (p. 180). The remaining schools were classified according to size, level of urbanization and denomination.

The deputy principals, fifteen teachers and 30 pupils were interviewed for each school. According to a specific classification scheme the teachers were divided across age groups and subjects. The processing of the data comprised the construction of cross tables and calculation of several thousand product-moment correlation coefficients. The data were also reduced by means of factor analysis. The question arises of how to draw conclusions from 1260 correlation coefficients that relate to the association between effect measures on the one hand and the other categories of variables on the other.

The following school characteristics show a correlation of at least 0.40 with the effect measures (pass rate and mean grades for English and mathematics);

- denomination;
- city pupils;
- average grades for English and maths in previous years;
- success rate in previous years;
- teachers' assessments of pupils' diligence;
- average number of pupils removed from lessons.

Two of these variables correspond with earlier achievement: one can possibly be interpreted as an indicator of an orderly school climate (pupils removed from lessons), while the assessment of pupils' diligence corresponds with confidence in pupils' achievement.

The effect of the denomination factor also appears in other research (Van der Hoeven-van Doornum and Jungbluth, 1987; Blok and Eiting, 1988b). The variable 'city pupils' can be regarded as an indicator of the less favourable starting point of a school's pupil population. The researcher chose other criteria for interpreting the link between school characteristics and effect variables. In the chapter dealing with this, differences in mean scores for English and Dutch between 1979–80 and 1975–77 were examined as well as correlations. In this way progress or decline can be recorded. Rather a lot of attention was given to the finding that schools that have regular meetings of department heads make better progress than schools that do not (a mean progress of 0.22 for the former versus 0.04 for the latter on a ten-point school-grade scale). The researcher refers to this as 'considerable' progress and sees this outcome as reaffirming the school organization models of Marx (1975). She concludes with the following recommendations:

- the departmental meeting is the most favourable organizational provision for schools that have to deal increasingly with pupils who, owing to their background, are unfamiliar with general academic secondary education;
- only candidates who have a proven record of inspiring and stimulating other teachers should be considered for the appointment of school principal;
- drab or indifferent schools should give attention to establishing which aspects of the school are liked and disliked by teachers and staff;
- state schools should have a governing structure in which the school is locally supported and also administered by a directly interested body in the area;
- it would be useful if the Association of Pre-university and General Secondary Education Teachers (NGL) gave more attention to matters of educational philosophy, in order to help members create a clearer identity for their school;

● schools should be given the opportunity to split when their size becomes unmanageable or is considered unacceptable.

Stroes (1985) gives a critical assessment of this study. Among other things, he points to the danger of spurious correlations and to the risks of drawing causal conclusions on the basis of correlations.

Stoel's (1986) study was designed as a follow-up project to the author's investigation of the relation between school size and pupils' well-being in secondary education (Stoel, 1980). The operational question of this study is: which school characteristics (from a large batch) are significantly linked with a number of outcome criteria (like the pass rate per school)? The study was carried out by a random sample of 132 general intermediate secondary schools (MAVO) and 123 lower vocational schools (LBO). (This sample originated as a result of approaches to 4000 schools; the response rate was 64 per cent).

The variables in the study comprised school characteristics on the one hand and behavioural characteristics of teachers and pupils on the other. Although this terminology has been carefully avoided in the study report because of the correlative nature of the research, the school characteristics are more in the nature of independent variables while the behavioural characteristics are more in the nature of dependent ones.

Within the school characteristics category the following groups of variables were distinguished:

● contextual and structural characteristics, including the degree of urbanization of the school's location; the average formal education level of parents, etc.;
● characteristics of the composition of teaching staff, age, full-time/part-time, etc.;
● organizational and policy characteristics of the school, including degree of planning, the number of staff meetings, the degree of outside contacts, etc.;
● instruction characteristics within the classroom, including the degree of individual teaching, pupil feedback and theoretical teaching;

In the educational outcomes category three groups of variables were distinguished:

● school achievement indicators: the pass rate for a particular school year, the rate of pupils resitting examinations, the rate of pupils reaching the final school-leaving examination class but not taking the examinations, the rate of pupils resitting the first, second or third year and the rate of pupils going on to other types of higher education;
● pupil satisfaction indicators, drop-out and absence data;
● teacher satisfaction indicators, the number of days on sick leave, etc.

The data were gathered using written questionnaires.

The results of Stoel's study are not summarized here. Knuver replicated the study among a new random sample of 67 LBO and 43 MAVO schools in 1988, only the school characteristics that correlated significantly with achievement in both studies are mentioned. These are: regular giving of homework (positive relationship, +); percentage of teachers who taught more than 20 hours a week (−); total number of students (−); degree of urbanization where school is located (+); number of part-time staff (+); frequency of staff meetings (−); and individual instruction (−).

Given the fact that only correlations have been calculated, no statements are possible on the direction of the effects. For instance, Stoel indicates that school characteristics like individualization can be interpreted as a school's reactive policy when confronted with disappointing results.

Vermeulen (1987) did a replication of Schweitzer's study, described in Appendix 1. The study was carried out in seventeen primary schools in Rotterdam (schools officially receiving special assistance owing to the many pupils with particular educational needs). A translated version of Schweitzer's procedure was used to measure the five school characteristics he investigated and data from the CITO test (a standardized achievement test taken in the last year of primary school) acted as outcome criteria.

The schools were comparable to those used in Schweitzer's study in that they were largely attended by the educationally disadvantaged. The Rotterdam schools, on the other hand, were less homogeneous regarding the ethnic composition of the pupil population. This appeared to have little effect on the link between school characteristics and learning achievement established in the study.

The scales used to measure the five school characteristics appeared in general to have a noticeably lower internal consistency (reliability) than in Schweitzer's study. Only three scales – educational leadership, safe and orderly environment and positive expectations of pupils' achievements – appeared to be sufficiently reliable when teachers were the respondents; when school heads were the respondents, only safe and orderly environment was sufficiently reliable. The consistency between the scores of teachers and heads on the school characteristics scales was considerably less than in Schweitzer's study (only with safe and orderly environment was a significant relationship found between teacher and school-head scores).

Analysis of variance was used to investigate the extent to which schools differed one from another on the five school characteristics. For three of the five (leadership, environment and expectations) there appeared to be significant differences. In mean achievement test scores the schools differed almost significantly ($P = 0.006$) from each other. In view of the recorded variance in school characteristics it was concluded that it would be useful to investigate further whether the differences in school characteristics were related to achievement.

The most important outcomes of this replication study comprise the product-moment correlation coefficients for the relation between each of the five school characteristics and learning achievement. These correlations are summarized in Table A2.1, which also gives those found by Schweitzer.

Table A2.1 *Correlations between five school characteristics and learning achievement (CITO scores) from Vermeulen's replication study*

	Teachers		School heads	
Educational leadership	0.05	(0.58)	−0.56*	(0.09)
Emphasis on basic skills	0.12	(0.79)	−0.19	(0.44)
Orderly and safe environment	0.34	(0.59)	0.21	(0.28)
High expectations	0.21	(0.79)	−0.45*	(0.71)
Frequent evaluations	0.23	(0.68)	0.13	(0.21)

Values in parentheses are the correlations from Schweitzer (1984).

The same comments on methods and technique can be applied to Vermeulen's study as to Schweitzer's. The intriguing question when comparing the results of both studies is how such great differences can be explained. Vermeulen assumes that they arise from the unsuitability of the instrument to measure school characteristics. He also refers to a more fundamental problem. Certain effectiveness criteria, like educational leadership and frequent assessment, share few similarities with the Dutch education system (especially the primary school category), so that questions on this evoked resistance among teachers.

Van der Hoeven-van Doornum and Jungbluth's publication (1987) is part of a long-term study of determinants of school effectiveness in primary education. One effect measure, attained education level, is used in the study, based on the secondary education category, which is chosen by every primary school leaver. The school characteristics data were collected by a written questionnaire for school heads. From the list of questions scales were designed for the factors staff consensus, school leadership, inclination towards educational reform and pressure for achievement. The reliability of some of these scales was lower than the standard norms, which could possibly explain the outcome that these variables appeared hardly to affect the school level attained (1 per cent explained variance).

Bosker and Hofman (1987) used the cohort junior school pupils in Groningen from Meijnen's (1984) study for theirs. School characteristics investigated in the study were transparency of the school policy, type of curriculum (with regard to flexibility and degree of evaluation), unambiguous regulations, parental involvement, achievement bias of teaching staff, autonomy of teachers, pupil guidance, teachers' experience and school size. The dependent variables were language and number achievement, head's advice regarding secondary school type and educational achievement at twelve years of age. In addition, some control variables at pupil level were included in the study, such as social class and intelligence. A study was made of 72 schools. Two school characteristics, achievement orientation and teachers' experience, apparently explained 53 per cent of the between-schools variance in arithmetic. The between-schools variance in arithmetic was 28 per cent of the total variance. For language these percentages were 82 per cent (explained between-schools variance) and 8 per cent (explained total variance).

Van der Grift (1987) studied the relationship between sub-scales taken from his written questionnaire for school heads and the mean learning achievement for two different achievement tests: the final one taken at the end of primary school and the entrance test for the sixth year. Where significant correlations could be found, with one exception they were negative.

Tesser's (1986) study fits in with the tradition of studying (in)equalities in education. It was based on data from a Central Bureau of Statistics (CBS) cohort study of 1977–8. The level of attainment after five years in secondary school comprised the effect variable. A part of the study looked at the extent to which certain school characteristics could explain the education level attained. The characteristics used in the study were classified under the heading school climate. School characteristics were established using questionnaires completed by the management of the schools concerned. Tesser regarded the results of this part of his study as disappointing. Although a few significant correlations were found between certain school characteristics and attained education level, these were not consistently encountered in the different secondary education categories.

Roeleveld's study (1987) was aimed at the question of whether schools differ when pupils' background characteristics are controlled for. His conclusion was that the net between-schools variance for the secondary education category ranged from 7 (lower technical secondary schooling) to 13 per cent (higher general and pre-university secondary schooling). Blok and Eiting (1988a) also studied the degree to which schools differ, but in primary schools and using language skills as effect criteria. They found a mean between-schools variance of 0.125.

De Jong's (1988) study was carried out in 58 junior schools and some 50 secondary schools in Rotterdam. His conclusion was that certain aspects of the school climate can significantly affect learning achievement. In the primary schools, more homework, giving high priority to intellectual achievement and an average level of child-centred education were the most important factors. In secondary education – the study covered the first two years – a strong involvement in the learning process and the amount of homework set appeared to be the most important factors.

Brandsma and Knuver (1989) published an article giving interim results of a long-term study on school effectiveness in primary schools. In this publication only achievement in arithmetic was studied. As in Bosker and Hofman (1987), variance component analysis was used with the help of the VARCL program, a recently developed technique for analysing multi-level data. Although in an early analysis (Brandsma and Knuver, 1988) the authors found a few interpretable effects that were consistent with the school effectiveness literature, in the findings reported here these appeared to have been explained away by other variables (Brandsma and Knuver, 1989). From the study it appeared that after controlling for gender, socio-economic status and intelligence the between-schools variance was 12.4 per cent of the total variance. The most meaningful school characteristics of the study together explained 37 per cent of the between-schools variance and 4.6 per cent of the total variance.

Blok and Eiting (1988b) studied the effects of a number of school characteristics on attained language skills in the top class of 107 junior schools. They distinguished various categories of independent variables, the first of which can best be identified as contextual variables (denomination, number of ethnic minorities, number of pupils whose parents were educated to lower technical school (LBO) level and teacher's experience). A few variables were also used to represent school policy (number of pupils resitting classes, class size) and the type of education given (whether the school benefits from special assistance policies, how much homework, extent of catering for differing educational needs). From the analysis of covariance structures they carried out, it emerged that the exogenous variables – denomination, teachers' experience, number of ethnic minorities (negative link), number of pupils whose parents had had a limited education (negative link) and number of pupils resitting classes – significantly affected the dependent variable (language skills attained). Amount of homework and differentiation did not show any significant relationship with the dependent variables.

Van der Werf and Tesser (1989), in an introductory study made in connection with evaluation of the government's educational priorities policy, investigated the effect of a number of school and instruction characteristics on the advice heads gave on the most suitable type of secondary education for each of their pupils to follow. The study took place in 184 primary schools and the school characteristics measured were educational leadership, central registration of pupils' results, an orderly school climate, high expectations of pupils' achievement, an emphasis on basic skills and the setting of high attainment demands. Instruction characteristics for which data were gathered were the amount of effective teaching time, the degree of structure in lessons, class discipline, working with minimum competency objectives, amount of homework, emphasis on basic skills, frequent evaluation, well-chosen learning materials and clear objectives.

Data were analysed by means of a random coefficient variance component model using the VARCL program. The results indicate that the net proportion of between-schools variance (that part of the total variance after adjustment for pupils' background characteristics) was only 3.4 per cent. The only school and instruction characteristics that contributed significantly to explaining this between-schools variance were high expectations, high attainment demands and structured teaching.

Hoeben (1989) studied the effect of implementing educational reforms in primary education and the effect of certain school organization and instruction characteristics already known from literature on school effectiveness, such as estimated level of subject matter mastery, amount of instruction, how often pupils' progress is evaluated and educational leadership. The study was carried out in 219 primary schools. The organization and instruction characteristics together explained 7 per cent of the total variance. The estimated level of subject matter mastery and the degree of pupil evaluation had a modest effect on learning achievement. Educational leadership appeared to correlate quite highly with frequency of evaluation, but had no direct effect on pupils' achievement.

Scheerens *et al.* (1989) carried out a secondary analysis of data from the second mathematics project of the International Association for the Evaluation of Educational Achievement (IEA). This included data on 1960 schools and 70,192 pupils in seventeen countries. The dependent variable in the study was a mathematics test taken in the second year of secondary school. From the total range of variables, those at school and class level that from school effectiveness literature had been demonstrated to be relevant were chosen.

The study was intended to see how far between-class and between-school variances are similar or different between countries, and to determine to what degree individual effectiveness predictors display a consistent relationship with the dependent variable across the various countries. From a comparative study of class and school variance components a great diversity of patterns emerged: in most cases the between-class variance in a country was larger than the between-schools variance. The independent variables that had a significant and – generalized across countries – consistent relationship with mathematics achievement were pupils' high expectations of their own school career, teachers' high expectations of pupils' achievement and opportunity to learn.

References

Achilles, C. M. and Lintz, M. N. (1986). 'Evaluation of an "effective schools" intervention'. AERA paper. San Francisco.

Ainscow, M. and Hopkins, D. (1991). 'Seeing school improvement whole: the design of the IQEA project. A discussion paper'. Cambridge: Cambridge Institute of Education, May 1991.

Aitkin, M. and Longford, N. (1986). 'Statistical modelling issues in school effectiveness studies'. *Journal of the Royal Statistical Association*, **149**, 1–43.

Aldridge, B. G. (1983). 'A mathematical model for mastery learning'. *Journal of Research in Science Teaching*, **20**, 1–17.

Alexander, K. L. and Eckland, B. K. (1980). 'The "explorations in quality of opportunity" sample of 1955 high school sophomores'. In A. C. Kerhoff (ed.), *Research in Sociology of Education and Socialization*. Vol. I: *Longitudinal Perspectives on Educational Attainment*. Greenwich, Conn.: JAI Press.

Anderson, C. S. (1982). 'The search for school climate: a review of the research'. *Review of Educational Research*, **52**, 368–420.

Averch, H. A., Carroll, S. J., Donaldson, T. S., Kiesling, H. J. and Pincus, J. (1974). *How Effective Is Schooling? A Critical Review of Research*. A Rand educational policy study. Englewood Cliffs, NJ: Educational Technology Publications.

Bangert, R. L., Kulik, J. A. and Kulik, C. C. (1983). 'Individualized systems of instruction in secondary schools'. *Review of Educational Research*, **53**, 143–58.

Bennis, W. G., Benne, K. D. and Chin, R. (1969). *The Planning of Change*. London: Holt, Rinehart & Winston.

Bereiter, C. and Kurland, M. (1982). 'A constructive look at follow through results'. *Interchange*, **12**, 1–22.

Berliner, D.C. (1985). 'Effective classroom teaching: the necessary but not sufficient condition for developing exemplary schools'. In G. R. Austin and H. Garber (eds), *Research on Exemplary Schools*, pp. 127–54. Orlando, Fla: Academic Press.

Block, J. H. and Burns, R. B. (1970). 'Mastery learning'. *Review of Research in Education*, **4**, 3–49.

Blok, H. and Eiting, M. H. (1988a). 'De grootte van schooleffecten: hoe verschillend presteren leerlingen van verschillende scholen?' (The size of school effects: between-school achievement differences). *Tijdschrift voor Onderwijsresearch*, **13**, 16–30.

Blok, H. and Eiting, M. H. (1988b). 'Openbare en bijzondere lagere scholen vergeleken op de taalvaardigheid van hun zesdeklassers' (Private and public schools compared in language achievement). *Mens en Maatschappij*, **63**, 260–76.

Bloom, B. S. (1968). *Learning for Mastery*. Washington, DC: ERIC.

Bloom, B. S. (1976) *Human Characteristics and School Learning*. New York: McGraw-Hill.

Boorsma, P. B. (1984). 'Doelmatigheidsprikkels en hoger onderwijsbeleid' (Efficiency stimulants and higher education policy). Diësrede. Universiteit Twente.

Boorsma, P. B. and Nijzink, J. P. (1984). *Doelmatigheidsprikkels en hoger onderwijsbeleid* (Dimensions of school quality). Enschede: Technische Hogeschool Twente.

Borger, J. B., Ching-Lung Lo, Sung-Sam-Oh and Walberg, H. J. (1984). 'Effective schools: a quantitative synthesis of constructs'. *Journal of Classroom Interaction*, **20**, 12–17.

Bosker, R. J. (1991) 'De consistentie van schooleffecten in het basisonderwijs' (The consistency of school effects in primary education). *Tijdschrift voor Onderwijsresearch*, **16**(4), 206–18.

Bosker, R. J. and Harskamp, E. G. (1990). 'Een experiment met schoolinterne determinanten van de leerprestaties van leerlingen in het voortgezet onderwijs' (An experiment with school-internal determinants of achievement in secondary education). In *Programma voor Fundamenteel Strategisch Onderzoek*. Enschede: OCTO; Groningen: RION.

Bosker, R. J. and Hofman, W. H. A. (1987). 'Dimensies van schoolkwaliteit: de algemene en milieuspecifieke invloed van scholen op de prestaties en het keuzegedrag van leerlingen' (Dimensions of school quality). In J. Scheerens and W. G. R. Stoel (eds), *Effectiviteit van Onderwijsorganisaties* (Effectiveness of school organizations). Lisse: Swets & Zeitlinger.

Bosker, R. J. and Scheerens, J. (1989). 'Criterion choice, effect size and stability: three fundamental problems in school effectiveness research'. In B. P. M. Creemers and B. Reynolds (eds), *School Effectiveness and School Improvement*. Lisse: Swets & Zeitlinger.

Bossert, S. T. (1988). 'School effects'. In N. J. Boyan (ed.), *Handbook of Research on Educational Administration*. New York: Longman.

Boyd, W. L. and Crowson, R. L. (1985). 'The changing conception and practice of public school administration'. *Review of Research in Education*, **9**, 311–73.

Brandsma, H. P. and Knuver, A. W. M. (1988) 'Organisatorische verschillen tussen basisscholen en hun effect op leerlingprestaties' (Organizational differences between primary schools and their effects on achievement). *Tijdschrift voor Onderwijsresearch*, **13**, 201–12.

Brandsma, H. P. and Knuver, A. W. M. (1989). 'De invloed van school- en klaskenmarken op rekenprestaties in het basisonderwijs' (The influence of school and class characteristics on pupils' achievement in arithmetic). In J. Scheerens and J. C. Verhoeven (eds), *Schoolorganisatie, Beleid en Onderwijskwaliteit*. Lisse: Swets & Zeitlinger.

Breton, A. and Wintrobe, R. (1982). *The Logic of Bureaucratic Conduct*. Cambridge: Cambridge University Press.

Bridge, R. G., Judd, C. M. and Moock, P. R. (1979). *The Determinants of Educational Outcomes: The Impact of Families, Peers, Teachers and Schools*. Cambridge, Mass.: Ballinger.

Brimer, A., Madaus, G. F., Chapman, B., Kellaghan, T. and Woodrof, R. (1976). *Differences in School Achievement*. Slough: NFER-Nelson.

Brookover, W., Beady, C., Flood, P., Schweitzer, J. and Wisenbaker, J. (1979). *School Social Systems and Student Achievement: Schools Can Make a Difference*. New York: Praeger.

Brophy, J. and Good, Th. L. (1986). 'Teacher behaviour and student achievement'. In M. C. Wittrock (ed.), *Handbook of Research on Teaching*, pp. 328–75. New York: Macmillan.

Bruner, J. S. (1966). *Toward a Theory of Instruction.* Cambridge, Mass.: Belknap Press of Harvard University.

Buchanan, J. M. and Tullock, G. (1965). *The Calculus of Consent: Logical Foundations of Constitutional Democracy.* Ann Arbor: University of Michigan Press.

Cameron, K. S. and Whetten, D. A. (eds) (1983). *Organizational Effectiveness: A Comparison of Multiple Models.* New York: Academic Press.

Cameron, K. S. and Whetten, D. A. (1985). 'Administrative effectiveness in higher education'. *The Review of Higher Education,* **9,** 35–49.

Carroll, J. B. (1963). 'A model of school learning'. *Teachers College Record,* **64,** 722–33.

Carroll, J. B. (1989). 'The Carroll Model, a 25-year retrospective and prospective view'. *Educational Researcher,* **18,** 26–31.

Chan, T. C. (1979). *The Impact of School Building on Pupil Achievement.* Greenville, SC: Office of School Facilities Planning.

Clauset, K. H. and Gaynor, A. K. (1982). 'A systems perspective on effective schools'. *Educational Leadership,* **40**(3), 54–9.

Cohen, J. (1977). *Statistical Power Analysis for the Behavioral Sciences.* New York: Academic Press.

Cohen, M. (1982). 'Effective schools: accumulating research findings'. *American Education,* January–February, 13–16.

Cohen, M. D., March, J. G. and Olsen, J. P. (1972). 'A garbage can model of organizational choice'. *Administrative Science Quarterly,* 17, 1–25.

Coleman, J. S., Campbell, E., Hobson, C., McPartland, J., Mood, A., Weinfeld, F. and York, R. (1966). *Equality of Educational Opportunity.* Washington, DC: US Government Printing Office.

Coleman, J. S., Hoffer, T. and Kilgore, S. (1981). *Public and Private Schools.* Chicago: National Opinion Research Center, University of Chicago.

Collins, A. and Stevens, A. (1982). 'Goals and strategies of inquiry teachers'. In R. Glaser (ed.), *Advances in Instructional Psychology,* vol. II. Hillsdale, NJ: Lawrence Erlbaum Associates.

Corcoran, Th. B. (1985). 'Effective secondary schools'. In A. M. J. Kyle (ed.), *Reaching for Excellence: An Effective Schools Sourcebook.* Washington, DC: US Government Printing Office.

Corte, E. De and Lowyck, J. (1983). 'Heroriëntatie in het onderzoek van het onderwijzen' (Research on teaching reconsidered). *Tijdschrift voor Onderwijsresearch,* **8**(6), 242–61.

Creemers, B. P. M. (1991). *Effectieve Instructie: Een Empirische Bijdrage aan de Verbetering van het Onderwijs in de Klas* (Effective instruction: an empirical contribution to the improvement of classroom teaching). The Hague: SVO Balansreeks.

Creemers, B. P. M. and Reynolds, D. (1989). 'The future development of school effectiveness and school improvement'. In B. P. M. Creemers and D. Reynolds (eds), *School Effectiveness and School Improvement,* pp. 379–83. Lisse: Swets & Zeitlinger.

Davies, J. K. (1972). 'Style and effectiveness in education and training: a model for organizing, teaching and learning'. *Instructional Science,* **2.**

Doddema-Winsemius, H. and Hofstee, W. K. B. (1987). 'Enkele controversiële onderwijsdoelstellingen in de context van evaluatie' (Some controversial educational objectives in the context of evaluation). *Pedagogische Studiën*, **64**, 192–200.

Dougherty, K. (1981). 'After the fall: research on school effects since the Coleman Report'. *Harvard Educational Review*, **51**, 301–8.

Downs, A. (1957). *An Economic Theory of Democracy*. New York: Harper & Row.

Doyle, W. (1985). 'Effective secondary classroom practices'. In M. J. Kyle (ed.), *Reaching for Excellence: An Effective Schools Sourcebook*. Washington, DC: US Government Printing Office.

Dronkers, J. (1978). 'Manipuleerbare variabelen in de schoolloopbaan: een toepassing van het Wisconsin-model op het Nederlandse primaire and secundaire onderwijs' (Variables that can be manipulated in school careers: an application of the Wisconsin model in Dutch primary and secondary education). In J. L. Peschar and W. Ultee (eds), *Sociale Stratificatie*. Boeknummer *Mens en Maatschappij*. Deventer: Van Loghum Slaterus.

Edmonds, R. R. (1979). *A Discussion of the Literature and Issues Related to Effective Schooling*. Cambridge, Mass.: Center for Urban Studies. Harvard Graduate School of Education.

Erbring, L. and Young, A. A. (1979). 'Individual and social structure: contextual effects as endogenous feedback'. *Sociological Methods and Research*, **7**(4), 396–430.

Essink, L. J. B. and Visscher, A. J. (1987). 'The design and impact of management information systems in educational organizations'. *Journal of Information Resources Management*, **1**, 23–51.

Etzioni, A. (1964). *Modern Organizations*. Englewood Cliffs, NJ: Prentice-Hall.

Evertson, C. M., Anderson, C. S. and Brophy, J. (1978). 'Process–outcome relationships in the Texas Junior High School Study: compendium': AERA paper. Toronto.

Faerman, S. R. and Quinn, R. E. (1985). 'Effectiveness: the perspective from organization theory'. *Review of Higher Education*, **9**, 83–100.

Firestone, W. A. and Herriott, R. E. (1982). 'Prescriptions for effective elementary schools don't fit secondary schools'. *Educational Leadership*, **40**, 51–3.

Firestone, W. A. and Wilson, B. L. (1987). 'Management and organizational outcomes: the effects of approach and environment in schools'. AERA paper. Washington, DC.

Fischer, F. (1980). *Politics, Values and Public Choice*. Boulder, Colo.: Westview Press.

Fraser, B. J., Walberg, H. J., Welch, W. W. and Hattie, J. A. (1987). *Syntheses of Educational Productivity Research*. Special issue of the *International Journal of Educational Research*, **11**(2).

Fullan, M. G. (1991). *The New Meaning of Educational Change*. London: Cassell; New York: Teachers College Press.

Fuller, B., Wood, K., Rapoport, T. and Dornbusch, S. M. (1982). 'The organizational context of individual efficacy'. *Review of Educational Research*, **51**(1), 7–30.

Gage, N. (1965). 'Desirable behaviors of teachers'. *Urban Education*, **1**, 85–95.

Glaser, B. G. and Strauss, A. L. (1967). *The Discovery of Grounded Theory: Strategies for Qualitative Research.* Chicago: Aldine.

Glasman, N. S. and Biniaminov, J. (1981). 'Input–output analyses of schools'. *Review of Educational Research,* **51**(4), 509–39.

Goldman, N. A. (1961). 'Sociopsychological study of school vandalism'. *Crime and Delinquency,* **7**, 221–30.

Goldstein, H. (1980). 'The statistical procedures'. In B. Tizard, *Fifteen Thousand Hours: A Discussion.* London: University of London, Institute of Education.

Good, Th. L. and Brophy, J. (1986). 'School effects'. In M. C. Wittrock (ed.), *Handbook of Research on Teaching,* pp. 328–75. New York: Macmillan.

Goodlad, J. I. (1984). *A Study of Schooling in the United States.* Reprinted from *Phi Dalta Kappan Tech. Report Series 1,* **61**, 3–6 (1979–80).

Gooren, W. A. J. (1989). 'Kwetsbare en weerbare scholen en het welbevinden van de leraar'. In J. Scheerens and J. C. Verhoeven (eds), *Schoolorganisatie, Beleid en Onderwijskwaliteit.* Lisse: Swets & Zeitlinger.

Gray, J., McPherson, A. F. and Raffe, D. (1983). *Reconstructions of Secondary Education: Theory, Myth and Practice since the War.* London: Routledge & Kegan Paul.

Grift, W. van der (1987). 'Zelfpercepties van onderwijskundig leiderschap en gemiddelde leerlingprestaties' (Self-perceptions of educational leadership and average achievement). In J. Scheerens and W. G. R. Stoel (eds), *Effectiviteit van Onderwijsorganisaties* (Effectiveness of school organizations). Lisse: Swets & Zeitlinger.

Groot, A. D. de (1986). 'Is de kwaliteit van het onderwijs te beoordelen?' (Can one appraise the quality of education?). In A. D. de Groot (ed.), *Begrip van Evalueren.* The Hague: VUGA.

Hallinger, P. and Murphy, J. (1986). 'The social context of effective schools'. *American Journal of Education,* **94**, 328–55.

Hallinger, Ph. and Murphy, J. (1987). 'Social context effects on school effects'. AERA paper. Washington, DC.

Hanson, M. (1981). *Educational Administration and Organizational Behavior.* Boston: Allyn & Bacon.

Hanushek, E. A. (1979). 'Conceptual and empirical issues in the estimation of educational production functions'. *Journal of Human Resources,* **14**, 351–88.

Hanushek, E. A. (1986). 'The economics of schooling: production and efficiency in public schools'. *Journal of Economic Literature,* **24**, 1141–77.

Hargreaves, D. H. and Hopkins, D. (1991). *The Empowered School.* London: Cassell.

Hargreaves, D. H., Hopkins, D., Least, M., Conolly, J. and Robinson, P. (1989). *Planning for School Development: Advice to Governors, Head Teachers and Teachers.* London: Department of Education and Science.

Hauser, R. M., Sewell, W. H. and Alwin, D. F. (1976). 'High school effects on achievement'. In W. H. Sewell, R. M. Hauser and D. L. Featherman (eds), *Schooling and Achievement in American Society.* New York: Academic Press.

Haywood, H. C. (1982). 'Compensatory education'. *Peabody Journal of Education*, **59**, 272–301.

Hoeben, W. Th. J. G. (1989). 'Educational innovation or school effectiveness: a dilemma?' In B. P. M. Creemers and B. Reynolds (eds), *School Effectiveness and School Improvement*. Lisse: Swets & Zeitlinger.

Hoeven-van Doornum, A. A. van der and Jungbluth, P. (1987). 'De bijdrage van schoolkenmerken aan schooleffectiviteit' (The relevance of school characteristics for school effectiveness). In J. Scheerens and W. G. R. Stoel (eds), *Effectiviteit van Onderwijsorganisaties*. Lisse: Swets & Zeitlinger.

Hofstee, W. K. B. (1982). 'Evaluatie: een methodologische analyse' (Evaluation: a methodological analysis). *Tijdschrift voor Onderwijsresearch*, **7**(5), 193–202.

Hofstee, W. K. B. (1991). 'Independent educational assessment: a social-psychometric perspective'. In P. Vedder (ed.), *Measuring the Quality of Education*. Lisse: Swets & Zeitlinger.

Hopkins, D. (ed.) (1987). *Improving the Quality of Schooling: Lessons from the OECD International School Improvement Project*. London: Falmer Press.

Hopkins, D. (1988). *Doing School Based Review: Instruments and Guidelines*. Leuven/ Amersfoort: ACCO.

Hopkins, D. (1989). 'Whole school evaluation'. In *Evaluation for School Development*, pp. 116– 33. Milton Keynes: Open University Press.

Hopkins, D. (1990). *Planning for School Improvement*. Cambridge: Cambridge Institute of Education.

Hoy, W. K. and Ferguson, J. (1985). 'A theoretical framework and exploration of organizational effectiveness of schools'. *Educational Administration Quarterly*, **21**, 117–34.

Jencks, C., Smith, M. S., Ackland, H., Bane, M. J., Cohen, D., Grintlis, H., Heynes, B. and Michelson, S. (1972). *Inequality*. New York: Basic Books.

Jencks, C. *et al.* (1979). *Who Gets Ahead? The Determinants of Economic Success in America*. New York: Basic Books.

Jesson, D. and Gray, J. (1991) 'Slant on slopes: using multilevel models to investigate differential school effectiveness and its impact on pupils' examination results'. *School Effectiveness and School Improvement*, **2**, 230–47.

Johnston, K. L. and Aldridge, B. G. (1985). 'Examining a mathematical model of mastery learning in a classroom setting'. *Journal of Research in Science Teaching*, **22**(6), 543–54.

Jong, M. de (1988). 'Educational climate and achievement in Dutch schools'. Paper presented at the International Conference for Effective Schools, London.

Joyce, B. R. (1991). 'The doors to school improvement'. *Educational Leadership*, May, 59–62.

Karweit, N. and Slavin, R. E. (1982). 'Time on task: issues of timing, sampling and definition'. *Journal of Educational Psychology*, **74**, 844–51.

Kerr, S. (1977). 'Substitutes for leadership: some implications for organizational design'. *Organizational and Administrative Sciences*, **8**, 135–46.

Kickert, W. J. M. (1979). *Organization of Decision-Making: A Systems-Theoretical Approach*. Amsterdam: North-Holland Publishing Company.

Klerk, L. F. W. de (1985). 'ATI-onderzoek en differentiatie: een reactie' (ATI research and differentiation). *Pedagogische Studiën*, **62**, 372–5.

Kreft, G. G. (1984). 'Enige aantekeningen bij een empirisch onderzoek in het lager onderwijs te Amsterdam' (Some comments concerning an empirical study in primary education in the city of Amsterdam). *Tijdschrift voor Onderwijsresearch*, **10**, 189–94.

Kreft, G. G. (1987). 'Models and methods for the measurement of school effects'. Doctoral thesis, University of Amsterdam.

Krogt, F. J. van der and Oosting, J. (1988). *De Relaties tussen MBO-scholen en hun Omgeving: Een Onderzoek naar de Externe Contacten en het Arbeidsmarktbeleid van MTO- en MEAO-scholen* (Relationships between vocational schools and their environment). Enschede: Universiteit Twente, Faculteit der Toegepaste Onderwijskunde.

Kulik, C. L. C. and Kulik, J. A. (1982). 'Effects of ability grouping on secondary school students: a meta-analysis of research findings'. *American Educational Research Journal*, **19**, 415–28.

Kyle, M. J. (ed.) (1985). *Reaching for Excellence: An Effective Schools Sourcebook*. Washington, DC: US Government Printing Office.

Laarhoven, P. van and de Vries, A. M. (1987). 'Effecten van de interklassikale groeperingsvorm in het voortgezet onderwijs: resultaten van een literatuurstudie' (Effects of heterogeneous grouping in secondary schools). In J. Scheerens and W. G. R. Stoel (eds), *Effectiviteit van Onderwijsorganisaties* (Effectiveness of school organizations). Lisse: Swets & Zeitlinger.

Lakomski, G. (1991). *Beyond Paradigms: Coherentism and Holism in Educational Research*. Special issue of the *International Journal of Educational Research*, **15**(6).

Lazar, I., Darlington, R. B., Murray, H. W. and Snipper, A. S. (1982). 'Lasting effects of early education: a report from the Consortium for Longitudinal Studies'. *Monograph of the Society for Research in Child Development*, **47**, nos 2–3.

Leune, J. M. G. (1987). 'Besluitvorming en machtsverhoudingen in het Nederlandse onderwijs-bestel' (Decision-making and the balance of power in Dutch education). In J. A. van Kemenade, N. A. J. Lagerweij, J. M. G. Leune and J. M. M. Ritzen (eds), *Onderwijs, Bestel en Beleid deel 2* (Education, system and policy part 2). Groningen: Wolters-Noordhoff.

Levin, H. H. (1988). 'Cost-effectiveness and educational policy'. *Educational Evaluation and Policy Analysis*, **10**, 51–69.

Levine, D. K. and Lezotte, L. W. (1990). *Unusually Effective Schools: A Review and Analysis of Research and Practice*. Madison, Wis.: National Center for Effective Schools Research and Development.

Liebenstein, H. (1978). 'On the basic proposition of x-efficiency theory'. *American Economic Review Proceedings*, **68**, 328–34.

Linden, W. J. van der (1987). 'Het zwalkende niveau van ons onderwijs' (The wavering level of our educational achievement). Diësrede. Universiteit Twente.

Linden, W. J. van der (1989). 'Een pleidooi voor het leren voor de toets' (A plea for teaching for the test). In J. Scheerens and W. Th. J. G. Hoeben (eds), *Evaluatie: Om de Kwaliteit van het Onderwijs* (Evaluation: for the quality of education). Lisse: Swets & Zeitlinger.

Lockheed, M. E. (1988). 'The measurement of educational efficiency and effectiveness'. AERA paper. New Orleans.

Lortie, D. C. (1973). 'Observations on teaching as work'. In R. M. W. Travers (ed.), *Second Handbook of Research on Teaching*. Chicago: Rand McNally.

Lotto, L. S. (1982). 'Revisiting the role of organizational effectiveness in educational evaluation'. AERA paper. New York.

McCormack-Larkin, M. (1985). 'Ingredients of a successful school effectiveness project'. *Educational Leadership*, March, 31–7.

Mackenzie, D. E. (1983). 'Research for school improvement: an appraisal of some recent trends'. *Educational Researcher*, **12**(4), 5–17.

Madaus, G. F., Kellaghan, Th., Rakow, E. A. and King, D. J. (1979). 'The sensitivity of measures of school effectiveness'. *Harvard Educational Review*, **49**, 207–30.

Mann, D. (1981). 'Education policy analysis and the rent-a-troika business'. Washington, DC: ERIC. Paper presented at AERA, Los Angeles.

March, J. G. (1978). 'American public school administration: a short analysis'. *School Review*, **86**, 217–50.

Marwijk Kooij-von Baumhauer, L. van (1984). *Scholen Verschillen: Een Verkennend Vergelijkend Onderzoek naar het Intern Functioneren van Vijfentwintig Scholengemeenschappen VWO-HAVO-MAVO* (Schools differ: an exploratory study into the functioning of 25 comprehensive schools). Groningen: Wolters-Noordhoff.

Marx, E. C. H. (1975). *De Organisatie van Scholengemeenschappen in Onderwijskundige Optiek* (The organization of comprehensive schools from an educational perspective). Groningen: H. D. Tjeenk Willink.

Masuch, M. and Verhorst, R. (1987). 'Over schadelijke organisaties' (About bad organizations). *Sociologische Gids*, **34**.

Masuch, M., La Potin, P. J. and Verhorst, R. (1989). 'Drowning in a sea of chewing gum: makework among members of bureaucratic organizations'. *Amsterdams Sociologisch Tijdschrift*, **15**, 652–72.

Medley, D. and Mitzel, H. (1963). 'Measuring classroom behavior by systematic observation'. In N. L. Gage (ed.), *Handbook of Research on Teaching*. Chicago: Rand McNally.

Meijnen, G. W. (1984). 'Van zes tot twaalf: een longitudinaal onderzoek naar de milieu- en schooleffecten van loopbanen in het lager onderwijs' (From six to twelve: a longitudinal study into school careers in primary education). Harlingen: Flevodruk b. v.; SVO-reeks.

Michaelsen, J. B. (1977). 'Revision, bureaucracy, and school reform'. *School Review*, **85**, 229–46.

Mierlo, J. G. A. van (1984). 'De economische theorie van het politieke proces en de representatieve democratie' (The economic theory of the political process and representative democracy). *Maandschrift Economie*, **48**, 256–85.

Miles, M. B., Farrar, E. and Neufeld, E. (1983) *Review of Effective School Programs*. Vol. 2: *The Extent of Effective School Programs*. Cambridge, Mass.: Huron Institute (unpublished).

Miller, S. K., Cohen, S. R. and Sayre, K. A. (1985). 'Significant achievement gains using the effective schools model'. *Educational Leadership*, March, 28–43.

Ministry of Education and Science (of the Netherlands) (1988). *De School op Weg naar 2000: Een Besturingsfilosofie voor de Negentiger Jaren* (The school in the year 2000: a government strategy for the nineties).

Mintzberg, H. (1979). *The Structuring of Organizations*. Englewood Cliffs, NJ: Prentice-Hall.

Moonen, J. C. M. M. (1990). 'Computers veranderen de wereld, doch veranderen ze ook het onderwijs?' (Computers change the world, but will they also change education?). Enschede: Universiteit Twente, oratie.

Morgan, G. (1986). *Images of Organization*. Beverly Hills, Calif.: Sage.

Mortimore, P., Sammons, P., Stoll, L., Lewis, D. and Ecob, R. (1988). *School Matters: The Junior Years*. Wells: Open Books.

Mosteller, F. and D. D. Moynihan (eds) (1972). *On Equality of Educational Opportunity*. New York: Random House.

Mullin, S. P. and Summers, A. A. (1983). 'Is more better? The effectiveness of spending on compensatory education'. *Phi Delta Kappan*, **64**, 339–47.

Murmane, R. J. (1981). 'Interpreting the evidence on school effectiveness'. *Teachers College Record*, **83**, 19–35.

Neufeld, E., Farrar, E. and Miles, M. B. (1983). *A Review of Effective Schools Research: The Message for Secondary Schools*. Huron Institute, Cambridge, Mass.: National Commission on Excellence in Education.

Niskanen, W. A. (1971). *Bureaucracy and Representative Government*. Chicago: Aldine-Atherton.

Nuttall, D. L., Goldstein, H., Prosser, R. and Rasbash, J. (1989). 'Differential school effectiveness'. In B. P. M. Creemers and J. Scheerens (eds), *Developments in School Effectiveness Research*. Special issue of the *International Journal of Educational Research*, **13**(7).

Oakes, J. (1989). 'What educational indicators?: the case for assessing school context'. *Educational Evaluation and Policy Analysis*, **11**, 181–99.

Odden, A. and Dougherty, U. (1982). *State Programs of School Improvement: A 50-state Survey*. Denver, Colo.: Education Commission of the States.

Odi, A. (1982). 'The process of theory development'. *Journal of Research and Development in Education*, **15**(2), 53–8.

Parkerson, J. A., Lomax, R. G., Schiller, D. P. and Walberg, H. J. (1984). 'Exploring causal models of educational achievement'. *Journal of Educational Psychology*, **76**, 638–46.

Pelgrum, W. J. (1990). *Educational Assessment: Monitoring, Evaluation and the Curriculum*. De Lier: Academisch Boeken Centrum.

Pfeffer, J. and Salancik, G. R. (1978). *The External Control of Organizations: A Resource Dependence Perspective*. New York: Harper & Row.

Pogrow, S. (1983). *Education in the Computer Age: Issues of Policy, Practice and Reform*. Beverly Hills, Calif.: Sage.

Purkey, S. C. (1984). 'School improvement: an analysis of an urban school district effective schools project'. AERA paper. New Orleans.

Purkey, S. C. and Smith, M. S. (1983). 'Effective schools: a review'. *Elementary School Journal*, **83**, 427–52.

Purkey, S. C. and Smith, M. S. (1985). 'Educational policy and school effectiveness'. In G. R. Austin and H. Garber (eds), *Research on Exemplary Schools*. Orlando, Fla: Academic Press.

Ralph, J. H. and Fennessey, J. (1983). 'Science or reform: some questions about the effective schools model'. *Phi Delta Kappan*, 689–95.

Reynolds, D. (1985) (ed.). *Studying School Effectiveness*. Lewes: Falmer Press.

Reynolds, D. (1989). 'Parents and the left: rethinking the relationship'. In F. Macleod (ed.), *Parents and Schools: The Contemporary Challenge*, pp. 165–81. Lewes: Falmer Press.

Reynolds, D. and Reid, D. (1985). 'The second stage: towards a reconceptualization of theory and methodology in school effectiveness research'. In D. Reynolds (ed.), *Studying School Effectiveness*. Lewes: Falmer Press.

Reynolds, D., Philips, D. and Davie, R. (1989). 'An effective school improvement programme based on school effectiveness research'. In B. P. M. Creemers and J. Scheerens (eds), *Developments in School Effectiveness Research*. Special issue of the *International Journal of Educational Research*, **13**(7).

Roeleveld, J. (1987). 'Verschillen in resultaten tussen Nederlandse scholen voor voortgezet onderwijs' (Achievement differences between secondary schools in the Netherlands). In J. Scheerens and W. G. R. Stoel (eds), *Effectiviteit van Onderwijsorganisaties* (Effectiveness of school organizations). Lisse: Swets & Zeitlinger.

Rosenshine, B. V. (1983). 'Teaching functions in instructional programs'. *Elementary School Journal*, **3**, 335–51.

Rosenshine, B. and Furst, N. (1973). 'The use of direct observations to study teaching'. In R. M. Travers (ed.), *Second Handbook of Research on Teaching*. Chicago: Rand McNally.

Rosenthal, R. and Rubin, D. B. (1982). 'A simple, general purpose display of magnitude of experimental effect'. *Journal of Educational Psychology*, **74**, 166–9.

Rutter, M. (1983). 'School effects on pupil progress: research findings and policy implications'. *Child Development*, **54**(1), 1–29.

Rutter, M., Maughan, B., Mortimore, P., Ouston, J. and Smith, A. (1979). *Fifteen Thousand Hours: Secondary Schools and their Effects on Children*. Cambridge, Mass.: Harvard University Press.

Scheerens, J. (1987). *Enhancing Educational Opportunities for Disadvantaged Learners*. Amsterdam: North-Holland Publishing Company.

Scheerens, J. (1989). 'Onderzoek naar schoolorganisatorische effectiviteit en de contingentie-benadering' (School effectiveness research and contingency theory). In J. Scheerens and J. C. Verhoeven (eds), *Schoolorganisatie, Beleid en Onderwijskwaliteit*. Lisse: Swets & Zeitlinger.

Scheerens, J. (1990). 'School effectiveness and the development of process indicators of school functioning'. *School Effectiveness and School Improvement*, pp. 61–80. Lisse: Swets & Zeitlinger.

Scheerens, J. (1991). 'Foundational and fundamental studies in school effectiveness: a research agenda'. Unpublished paper commissioned by the Institute for Educational Research (SVO) in the Netherlands.

Scheerens, J. (1992). 'Issues in educational productivity in Western European countries'. *Advances in Educational Productivity*, **2**, 41–66.

Scheerens, J. and Creemers, B. P. M. (1989). 'Conceptualizing school effectiveness'. In *Developments in School Effectiveness Research.* Special issue of the *International Journal of Educational Research*, **13**(7).

Scheerens, J. and Hopkins, D. (1992). 'Inventarisatie en diagnose' (Inventorization and diagnosis). In J. Scheerens, P. C. C. Stijnen and A. van Wieringen (eds), *Transformatie van Schoolorganisaties* (Transformation of school organizations). Heerlen: Dutch Open University, in press.

Scheerens, J. and Stoel, W. G. R. (1987). *Effectiviteit van Onderwijsorganisaties* (Effectiveness of school organizations). Lisse: Swets & Zeitlinger.

Scheerens, J., Vermeulen, C. J. A. J. and Pelgrum, W. J. (1989). 'Generalizability of school and instructional effectiveness indicators across nations'. In B. P. M. Creemers and J. Scheerens (eds), *Developments in School Effectiveness Research.* Special issue of the *International Journal of Educational Research*, **13**(7).

Schmuck, R. A. and Miles, P. A. (1971). *Group Processes in the Classroom.* Dubuque, Iowa: W. C. Brown.

Schweitzer, J. H. (1984). 'Characteristics of effective schools'. AERA paper. New Orleans.

Simon, H. A. (1964). *Administrative Behavior.* New York: Macmillan.

Simons, P. R. J. (1989). 'Leren leren: naar een nieuwe didactische aanpak' (Learning to learn: towards a new didactic approach). In P. R. J. Simons and J. G. G. Zuylen (eds), *Handboek Huiswerkdidactiek en Geïntegreerd Studievaardigheidsonderwijs* (Handbook for homework didactics and learning how to learn). Heerlen: Meso Consult.

Slavenburg, J. H. (1986). *Onderwijsstimulering en gezinsaktivering* (Compensatory education and family activation programs). The Hague and Rotterdam: serie Berichten summatieve evaluatie project Onderwijs en Sociaal Milieu.

Snow, R. E. (1973). 'Theory construction for research on teaching'. In R. M. W. Travers (ed.), *Handbook of Research on Teaching.* Chicago: Rand McNally.

Soutendijk, S. (1986). 'Striptease van een valse boodschap. Of hoe onderzoek aantoont dat democratisch onderwijs beter is' (Striptease of a false message. Or, how research indicates that democratic education is better). *Vernieuwing van Opvoeding*, **45**(7).

Spade, J. Z., Vanfossen, B. E. and Jones, E. D. (1985). 'Effective schools: characteristics of schools which predict mathematics and science performance'. AERA paper. Chicago.

Stallings, J. (1985). 'Effective elementary classroom practices'. In M. J. Kyle (ed.), *Reaching for Excellence: An Effective Schools Sourcebook*. Washington, DC: US Government Printing Office.

Stallings, J. and Mohlman, G. (1981). *School Policy, Leadership, Style, Teacher Change and Student Behavior in Eight Schools*. Final report to the National Institute of Education. Washington, DC.

Stebbins, L. B., St. Pierre, R. G., Proper, E. C., Anderson, R. R. and Cerva, T. R. (1977). *Education as Experimentation: A Planned Variation Model*. Vol. IV-A: *An Evaluation of Follow Through*. Cambridge, Mass.: Abt Associates Inc.

Stoel, W. G. R. (1980). *De Relatie tussen de Grootte van Scholen voor Voortgezet Onderwijs en het Welbevinden van de Leerlingen. Deel I en II* (The relationship between school size and attitudes toward schooling of pupils in secondary education. Part I and II). Groningen: RION.

Stoel, W. G. R. (1986). *Schoolkenmerken en het Gedrag van Leerlingen en Docenten in het Voortgezet Onderwijs* (School characteristics and teacher and student behaviour in secondary education). Groningen: RION.

Stoll, L. (1991). 'School effectiveness in action: supporting growth in schools and classrooms'. In M. Ainscow (ed.), *Effective Schools for All*. London: David Fulton Publishers.

Stringfield, S. and Teddlie, C. (1990). 'School improvement efforts: qualitative and quantitative data from four naturally occurring experiments in phases III and IV of the Louisiana School Effectiveness Study'. *School Effectiveness and School Improvement*, **1**, 139–66.

Stroes, D. P. (ed.) (1985). 'Verslag studiebijeenkomst over de dissertatie "Scholen verschillen" van L. van Marwijk Kooij-von Baumhauer' (Report on the discussion session about the doctoral thesis 'Schools differ' by L. van Marwijk Kooij-von Baumhauer). SISWO publication 306. Amsterdam.

Sweeney, J. (1982). 'Research synthesis on effective school leadership'. *Educational Leadership*, **39**, 346–52.

Teddlie, C. and Stringfield, S. (1984). 'The Louisiana School Effectiveness Study'. AERA paper. New Orleans.

Teddlie, C., Stringfield, S. and Wimpelberg, R. (1987). 'Contextual differences in effective schooling in Louisiana'. AERA paper. Washington.

Tesser, P. (1986). *Sociale Herkomst en Schoolloopbanen in het Voortgezet Onderwijs* (Social background and school careers in secondary education). Nijmegen: ITS.

Thompson, J. D. (1967). *Organizations in Action*. New York: McGraw-Hill.

Thorndike, R. L. (1973). *Reading Comprehension Education in Fifteen Countries*. Stockholm: Almqvist & Wiksell.

Toft Everson, S., Scollay, S. J. and Vizbara-Kessler, B. (1984). 'Application of the research on instructionally effective schools and classrooms: a study of an effective schools project impact at district, school, teacher and student level'. AERA paper. New Orleans.

Tyler, R. (1950). *Basic Principles of Curriculum and Instruction*. Chicago: University of Chicago Press.

Vedder, P. H. (1985). *Cooperative Learning: A Study on Processes and Effects of Cooperation between Primary School Children*. The Hague: SVO.

Vermeulen, C. J. A. J. (1987). 'De effectiviteit van onderwijs bij 17 Rotterdamse stimulerings-scholen' (The effectiveness of 17 Rotterdam specially supported schools). *Pedagogische Studiën*, **64**, 49–58.

Vinjé, M. (1988). *Evaluatie van Twee Jaar Zorgverbredingsbeleid: Resultaten van het Landelijk Onderzoek Leesvaardigheid in 1987* (Evaluation of reading achievement in primary education). Arnhem: CITO.

Voogt, J. C. (1989). 'Scholen doorgelicht: een studie over schooldiagnose' (School diagnosis). Dissertation, Rijksuniversiteit Utrecht.

Vos, H. de (1989). 'A rational-choice explanation of composition effects in educational research'. *Rationality and Society*, **1**(2), 220–39.

Walberg, H. J. (1984). 'Improving the productivity of American schools'. *Educational Leadership*, **41**, 19–27.

Weber, G. (1971). 'Inner-city children can be taught to read: four successful schools'. Washington, DC: Council for Basic Education.

Weeda, W. C. (1986). 'Effectiviteitsonderzoek van scholen' (Effectiveness research of schools). In J. C. van der Wolf and J. J. Hox (eds), *Kwaliteit van het Onderwijs in het Geding* (About education quality). Publicaties van het Amsterdams Pedologische Centrum, nr. 2. Lisse: Swets & Zeitlinger.

Weick, K. (1976). 'Educational organizations as loosely coupled systems'. *Administrative Science Quarterly*, **21**, 1–19.

Weiss, C. H. and Bucuvalas, M. J. (1980). 'Truth tests and utility tests: decision-makers' frames of reference for social science research'. *American Sociological Review*, **45**, 303–13.

Werf, G. van der and Tesser, P. (1989). 'The effects of educational priorities on children from lower income families and ethnic minorities'. In B. P. M. Creemers and B. Reynolds (eds), *School Effectiveness and School Improvement*. Lisse: Swets & Zeitlinger.

Werf, M. P. C. van der (1988). *Het Schoolwerkplan in het Basisonderwijs* (School development plans in primary education). Lisse: Swets & Zeitlinger.

Willems, J. and van Hout Wolters, B. (1989). 'Metacognitieve vaardigheden met betrekking tot zelfstandig leren' (Meta-cognitive skills). In P. R. J. Simons and J. G. G. Zuylen (eds), *Handboek Huiswerkdidactiek en Geïntegreerd Studievaardigheidsonderwijs*. Heerlen: Meso Consult.

Windham, D. M. (1988). *Effectiveness Indicators in the Economic Analysis of Educational Activities*. Special issue of the *International Journal of Educational Research*, **12**(6).

Wolf, C. van der (1984). *Schooluitval: Een Empirisch Onderzoek naar de Samenhang tussen Schoolinterne Factoren en Schooluitval in het Regulier Onderwijs* (School drop-out). Lisse: Swets & Zeitlinger.

Wolf, R. G. (1977). *Achievement in America*. New York: Teachers College Press.

Name Index

Subject Index